Teaching

Sharleen L. Kato, EdD
Professor and Family and Consumer Sciences Department Director
Seattle Pacific University
Seattle, Washington

Publisher
The Goodheart-Willcox Company, Inc.
Tinley Park, Illinois
www.g-w.com

Library of Congress Catalog Card Number 2009051718
ISBN 978-1-60525-291-9

4 5 6 7 8 9 – 10 – 15 14 13 12

Library of Congress Cataloging-in-Publication Data

Kato, Sharleen L.

  Teaching / Sharleen L. Kato.

      p. cm.

  Includes index.

  ISBN 978-1-60525-291-9

  1. Teaching--Vocational guidance--United States--Juvenile literature. I. Title.

  LB1775.2.K37 2010

  371.1'0023--dc22   2009051718

INTRODUCTION

This book has a simple title—*Teaching*. Teaching implies action. This is a book about how and why you should take action to become a teacher—not just any teacher, but a well-prepared, committed, engaging, skilled, effective, and creative teacher.

The book is also about educators who came before you, their motivations, and their accomplishments. These historical accounts will help you understand the business of education. You will also learn about how schools are funded, who is in charge, and how schools impact society.

You will explore the world of education today and what makes a teacher effective. For example, how can classrooms promote active learning? How can technology enhance and promote learning? This book will teach you about students and how they change physically, intellectually, emotionally, and socially as they grow and mature.

Will you learn how to teach? Yes. In this book you will learn how to design an instructional plan, choose teaching strategies, and measure whether learning has taken place. You will learn to ask questions of experienced teachers, those teachers who motivate and inspire you to learn more. You will observe teachers who know how to manage classrooms and create an effective learning environment for their students.

Will you be a teacher when you finish this book? No. Becoming a teacher requires much more preparation. Becoming an excellent teacher requires experience and the lifelong desire to keep learning. However, this book will inspire you to explore the teaching profession. Remember, *teaching* requires action. Begin to take action toward your teaching career today.

About the Author

Sharleen L. Kato, EdD, loves teaching as well as learning. She is a Professor at Seattle Pacific University where she encourages students to become creative and successful. She has taught undergraduate students for over 20 years. She currently serves as the Family and Consumer Sciences Department Director. She holds a Doctorate in Education, a Master's in Human Ecology, and an undergraduate degree in Home Economics. Dr. Kato has served on the Bellevue Christian Schools Education Committee and Board of Directors, the Health and Wellness Advisory Committee for Seattle Public Schools, and education committees and task forces for Washington State Public Schools. Dr. Kato has published many articles and presented papers in the education field. She is passionate about inspiring others to take on the challenge of becoming effective teachers.

Reviewers

The author and Goodheart-Willcox Publisher would like to thank
the following professionals who provided valuable input:

Susan Abramson
Family and Consumer Sciences Teacher
Oceanside High School
Oceanside, New York

Mary Ann Adams
Educational Consultant
Des Moines, Iowa

Angelina Bencomo
Former Family and
Consumer Sciences Teacher
Canutillo High School
Canutillo, Texas

Irma T. Bode
Family and Consumer Sciences Teacher
Wakefield High School
Raleigh, North Carolina

Nancy Burkhart
Family and Consumer Sciences Teacher
Burke High School
Omaha, Nebraska

Carolyn Mack
Family and Consumer Sciences
Department Chair
Hinsdale Central High School
Hinsdale, Illinois

Richard Nicholson
Industrial and Technology Education
Consultant
San Gabriel, California

Ann Pogue
Family and Consumer Sciences Teacher
South Grand Prairie High School
Grand Prairie, Texas

Mary Rash
Teacher Academy Instructor
CAT-Brandywine
Coatesville, Pennsylvania

Susan A. Reichelt, PhD
Family and Consumer Sciences Education
Chocowinity, North Carolina

Adriana Mares Rodriquez
Instructor
Richland College
Dallas, Texas

Richard K. Simmons, EdD
Education Professor
College of DuPage
Glen Ellyn, Illinois

Denice K. Stanforth, CFCS
Teacher
Hillsborough High School
Tampa, Florida

Patti Stanley
Teacher
Yosemite ROP Educational Center
Modesto, California

Kerry O'Connor Swistro
Family and Consumer Sciences Teacher
Bulkeley High School
Hartford, Connecticut

Brooke Weekes
Family and Consumer Sciences
Department Chair/Teacher
Carmel High School
Carmel, Indiana

BRIEF CONTENTS

CONTENTS

Chapter 7
The Modern History of Education in America   148

Chapter 8
Schools and Society   168

Contents

Unit 4   The Teacher

UNIT 1: YOU: THE TEACHER OF TOMORROW

1 Teaching as a Profession

2 Becoming a Teacher

1 TEACHING AS A PROFESSION

Key Terms

extracurricular activities

curriculum

school-based curriculum

nonsectarian

paraprofessional

self-contained classrooms

abstract thinking

concrete thinking

collaborative learning

postsecondary education

technical schools

corporate trainers

Objectives

After studying this chapter, you will be able to

- **give examples** of how the qualities of effective teachers apply in actual classroom situations.

- **analyze** challenges related to teaching and how teachers meet them.

- **identify** the educational requirements for teachers at various levels.

- **summarize** career opportunities for teachers outside schools.

- **describe** employment opportunities and trends in teaching.

- **identify** the factors that impact school employment opportunities.

- **analyze** teacher salary and benefits.

Katie laid the stack of student papers on her desk and sat down. (She had only been a middle school English teacher for six months.) It was a beautiful spring afternoon. The windows were open, letting in the fresh breeze. Katie felt a sense of satisfaction. As usual, she was spending a few minutes of reflection on her day before leaving school, noting what had gone well and what changes she might make in the future. Today had been a successful day. The students stayed reasonably focused, and there were no major concerns for that particular school day. She even had time to have a couple of one-on-one conversations with students about some of their personal matters. As she regrouped, her thoughts turned toward her speaking engagement tonight at her high school. Just four years earlier she had graduated, having completed a teaching academy program.

Katie's task this evening was to speak to students about the field of education. She wondered how she could possibly convey to her audience just how much she had learned during this short time. She wanted to share an honest account of what it was like to be a teacher, including both the positive and negative experiences. As her thoughts went back to when she first decided to be a teacher, the words she would say this afternoon took shape in the following way:

In high school, I was quite confident about my decision to go to college and major in education. I wanted to be a middle school teacher and work with children in those awkward, frustrating preteen years of self-discovery.

I applied to the university's teacher education program and was accepted. Even though my goal was to teach middle school, my certification would be to teach all subjects from kindergarten to grade 9. Consequently, I worked with children of various ages as part of my teacher education training. I also had to choose two areas of specialization. I chose English and social studies. I really enjoyed the classes, as well as observing and working with children.

When it came time to complete my student teaching, I was placed at a middle school in the city. The first day I walked in, I realized that this was a whole new world. Although it hadn't been that long since I was in middle school, very little seemed familiar to me. This urban school was very different from the suburban one that I had attended.

My feelings must have been obvious. When my supervising teacher asked me what I thought of my first day, I told her that everything seemed chaotic. I said that I didn't feel that I would be able to relate effectively to students with such diverse backgrounds. She asked me what had led me to teaching and what my career goals were. I told her of my dream of teaching young teens. Fortunately, she was very understanding. She reminded me that all preteens are basically similar, and that I was focusing too much on exterior differences. She assured me that this would be a challenge, but that it was one she was sure that I could meet. She reminded me just how much these students needed enthusiastic teachers who cared about them. She predicted that I would learn from them, as well as about them. It was at that moment I decided to prove that I could be an inspiring teacher.

Before I started teaching, I thought anyone could be a good teacher. I was going to touch young lives and be everyone's favorite teacher. Students would come to me and share their secrets. I would prepare and deliver meaningful lessons that would change lives. In the summers, I would travel the world. No one told me what teaching was really going to be like. These are the things I never knew.

I never knew that I would spend infinite evenings planning lessons that would be met by rolling eyes, groans, and complete apathy. I never knew that in the rare case that a new lesson went off brilliantly, the fire alarm would sound and the rest of the class time would be lost forever. I never knew how many homework assignments could be "lost." I didn't realize that I would often feel more stress over giving a failing grade to a student than the student receiving it. I didn't know that students wouldn't always give me the respect I thought all teachers deserved (even though I was known for my silly teacher impersonations when I was in middle school).

I now know the exhilaration of creating a lesson that leaves students buzzing as they leave the room. I know how it feels to work in an atmosphere with other intelligent and like-minded staff who pull together and help one another. Back then, I didn't know how appreciative I would be when a holiday card was laid on my desk or when a "thank you" escaped a smiling face. I didn't know how I would learn to laugh at myself. I now know that I laugh when I trip over an electrical cord in front of 30 13-year-olds.

No one told me that I would be haunted at night by a conversation with one of my many students who have traumatic home lives. Take Eli for example. His mother overcame a drug addiction, but couldn't find a job that paid enough for basic expenses. She and Eli ended up living on the streets. I didn't find out about Eli's situation right away. It became apparent over time. I know I can't solve all my students' problems, but I have seen that listening to and encouraging them are gifts I can give. During breaks, I find myself wondering how "my kids" are doing.

Most of all, I did not know that I would feel so needed. I have discovered that teaching happens in one-on-one relationships. Often, I'm teaching my students that they are capable and able to learn. I try to convey why reading, writing, and communication skills are so important by making my lessons connect with their lives.

My life is so varied. No two days are the same. No two students are the same. My days are filled with planning lessons, grading assignments, following through on discipline issues, and keeping up on individual student needs. As a first-year teacher, I am creating every learning activity from scratch. Sometimes I'm so busy living each day that I forget why I became a teacher—because I care deeply about cultivating minds and spirits. There aren't many people who get to witness these profound changes in people on a daily basis.

Suddenly Katie realized that an hour had passed. As she got into her car, she paused and sighed. She thought about how full her life was. All things considered, teaching was a lifestyle and a career choice that was right for her.

Why are you interested in teaching? Is it a love for children? Do you want others to love learning as you do? Perhaps a favorite teacher inspired you or had a significant impact on your life. Maybe you want to make a difference in the world.

Teaching is an exciting profession. It requires patience and persistence. It requires an appreciation for diversity and individuality. What makes teaching truly different from many other professions is the potential long-term effect that you can have on the lives of others, 1-1.

Although being a student may have drawn you to teaching, being on the "other side of the desk" may be a far different reality than your expectations. You may wonder if you are up to the challenge. Can you manage a classroom full of students? Should you pursue a job with higher pay? Does the responsibility of the position concern you? This class can help you to assess if teaching is right for you. You will learn about some aspects of teaching that you may not have considered. You will also have opportunities to try some of the tasks associated with teaching. You will observe teachers and students. You may also take part in activities with children of various ages. With more knowledge, experience, and insight into your own goals and aptitudes, you will be better able to make a career decision.

1-1
A teacher can impact the lives of students for many years to come.

What Are the Qualities of an Effective Teacher?

Think about the teachers you have had throughout your education. Which were your favorites? Which ones taught you the most? What was it about these teachers that made them successful? Most likely, your favorite teachers were not all alike. Effective teachers come in many forms. They may be outgoing and dramatic, demanding and firm, soft-spoken and reflective, or introverted and quiet. Their approaches to life can differ greatly, too.

Although teachers may vary, effective teaching requires a common set of qualities. Effective teachers are able to motivate, inspire, and influence their students. They communicate well with both students and adults. They are able to convey their own enthusiasm for learning. In addition, effective teachers need to be well organized to deal with the planning, record keeping, and many administrative tasks that go along with the job. While there are many other key skills, these are some of the most basic.

Effective teachers have many personal qualities in common, as well. A brief list might include:

- caring

- commitment

- courtesy

- honesty

- kindness

- patience

- responsibility

- tolerance

This list of personal characteristics is important in all teaching situations. Can you think of other qualities to add to the list? Successful teachers respect their students, love learning, have high expectations for themselves and their students, and are adaptable.

What Happens in a Teacher's Typical Day?

Most of a teacher's day is spent designing and presenting classroom learning experiences. This is where creativity and knowledge of students' learning styles and abilities is necessary. As time permits and depending on class size, teachers may also work with students individually.

Teachers are responsible for assessing the learning of students. This involves grading assignments and evaluating student participation in class activities. These evaluations are summarized on report cards and at meetings with parents or guardians.

In addition to classroom activities, teachers coordinate with other specialists, which may include counselors, reading specialists, and speech therapists. They may supervise **extracurricular activities** (those before or after school) and other duties, as well.

Determining What to Teach

Do teachers teach whatever they want? No. **Curriculum** must be decided before teaching begins. Curriculum is the term used to describe what is taught in a school. (*Curricula* is the plural form.) It includes all the courses taught and what is taught in each course, as well as how the courses are sequenced. See 1-2.

Who determines the curriculum? That depends. There are usually a number of influences. Each subject area has national curriculum

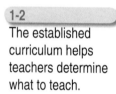

1-2
The established curriculum helps teachers determine what to teach.

standards developed by related national education organizations and state departments of education. While use of these is voluntary, they have significant influence. In addition, some states set curriculum standards for courses taught in the state. This helps make certain that students are ready to advance to the next level of courses, even if they move to another school. **School-based curriculum** is another alternative. Teachers are involved in making decisions about what is taught in their classrooms and schools. According to advocates of school-based curriculum, local teachers can best design curriculum to meet the needs of students.

The Rewards of Teaching

Many experienced teachers will tell you that teaching is inspiring, challenging, and as unique as each student. Every student presents an opportunity to the teacher. Since each has his or her own learning style and personality, the teacher's challenge is to determine how to best help each individual maximize learning.

Teaching is a career that does make a difference in the world, even though you might not feel it on a daily basis. Because learning takes time, seeing the effects of your efforts requires patience. Still, there are everyday victories. You help a young child deal successfully with conflict on the playground. A struggling student passes a tough test. A reluctant reader chooses three books from the library.

As a teacher, you will see your students change. You will see them grow physically. You will see them make strides emotionally and socially. You will also see them learn, day by day.

Most teachers agree that seeing students develop new knowledge, skills, and confidence can be the most rewarding part of teaching. You will have the satisfaction of knowing that you played a significant role in that process.

The Challenges of Teaching

Is teaching always rewarding? Of course not. Every job has its challenges, and teaching is no exception.

Teachers work hard. They typically spend long hours outside of school preparing lessons and grading students' work. During vacations, they are often thinking ahead and planning. Updating their knowledge and skills takes additional time. Most teachers attend workshops or conferences. Many take classes toward a more advanced degree.

The conditions under which teachers work are not always ideal. Classes can be large and workloads heavy. Many school buildings are old. School districts vary in their ability to provide teachers with up-to-date textbooks, educational technology, and other learning aids.

Schools also reflect the problems of society. Poverty, alcohol and other drug abuse, and similar problems affect students. That can make teaching emotionally draining. Teachers must sometimes cope with disrespect, unruly behavior, and even violence in schools.

These and other problems are receiving careful analysis. The goal is to make schools safe and positive for both teachers and students. Effective teachers find strategies to help them deal with the problems they encounter.

Where Do Teachers Work?

You may think it is obvious that teachers work in schools. However, they may work for a variety of employers, and some are self-employed. Both full-time and part-time teaching work is available. The following sections explore the nature of work in schools and some of the other settings in which teaching takes place.

Teaching in Schools

Since children are required to attend school, that is where most teachers work. Within that category, however, there is great variation. Schools range from preschools to colleges and universities. To add to the mix, some schools are small and some are large. Schools can be in rural areas, suburbs, or major urban areas. Most schools are *public*, funded by tax dollars, but there are also many *private* schools. Some of these are sponsored by religious organizations, while others are **nonsectarian** (not based on or affiliated with any religion). The purpose of all schools, however, is the same—to promote learning.

Schools are generally divided by grade levels. Chart 1-3 shows the most common designations. However, variations are fairly common.

1-3

These are common school designations. (Some ages and grade levels may vary among school districts.)

Common School Designations		
Level	**Grades**	**Typical Student Ages**
Preschool		2–4
Prekindergarten		4–5
Elementary	Kindergarten—grades 4, 5, or 6	5–11
Middle school	Grades 5 or 6–8	10–13
Junior high	Grades 7–8 or 9	12–14
High school	Grades 9 or 10–12	14–18

Preschool and Prekindergarten Programs

Increasing numbers of children are enrolled in educational programs prior to kindergarten. Child care programs focus primarily on providing a safe, caring environment. Preschool and prekindergarten programs have a stronger educational focus than in the past. Preschool programs are generally for children ages two to four. Prekindergarten programs, where available, are for children who will be in kindergarten the following year, usually four-year-olds. (Prekindergarten programs are often referred to as Pre-K.)

Play is the main occupation of young children. It is also how they learn. They listen to and tell stories. They pretend to be shoppers, pilots, and dogs. They build sandcastles and block towers, 1-4. They express themselves in paintings and songs.

Preschool and Pre-K teachers plan activities that build on children's curiosity and interest in play. These are based on a thorough understanding of child development and experience with children. The activities help children develop the many skills they will need for kindergarten and beyond. Children in these programs also spend time in unstructured play, choosing their own play activities.

1-4
If you enjoy working with young children, you might want to consider teaching in a preschool or prekindergarten program.

Requirements for leading preschool and Pre-K programs vary. Many require that teachers have at least an associate's degree in early childhood development and education, which generally requires two years of study and practice. Some, especially those linked to elementary schools, require a bachelor's degree from a four-year college or university. Some states require certification by a nationally recognized authority, such as the Child Development Associate (CDA) designation from the National Association for the Education of Young Children. See Chart 1-5 for a description of the various academic degrees. Paraprofessional positions are also available for those with less education or experience. A **paraprofessional** works under the supervision of a more highly educated professional.

Elementary Schools

What do you remember about elementary school? Who were your best friends? Which grade did you enjoy most? Do any favorite teachers, field trips, or class projects come to mind? Did you lose your lunch money, miss

1-5

Teaching positions require various levels of education.

Understanding Academic Degrees			
The specific degree granted (such as BA vs. BS) depends on the student's area of study, program requirements, and the tradition of the institution granting the degree. Many other degrees exist. Note that an ABS (Associate of Baccalaureate Studies) degree is granted by community colleges to students who complete a program of study equivalent to the first two years of a four-year bachelor's degree. These students normally transfer to a four-year college or university as a junior.			
Degree	**Institution Offering Degree**	**Years to Achieve**	**Typical Degrees**
Associate's	Community college	2	AA, Associate of Arts AS, Associate of Science ABS, Associate of Baccalaureate Studies
Bachelor's	University or four-year college	4	BA, Bachelor of Arts BS, Bachelor of Science
Master's	University or four-year college	1–2	MA, Master of Arts MS, Master of Science MEd, Master of Education
Doctorate	Some universities	3 or more	PhD, Doctor of Philosophy EdD, Doctor of Education

the bus, encounter a bully, or struggle to learn long division? Elementary school is a time of great exploration, language development, social development, and the introduction of scientific and mathematical concepts.

Think about the tremendous developmental changes that occur between kindergarten and fifth grade. The physical, intellectual, social, and emotional differences between a child in kindergarten and an 11-year-old are enormous. In this time span, small children grow into preteens. They learn to read, compute, and tackle more complex information. They make friends and figure out how to handle disagreements. They deal with feelings and develop a sense of who they are. In these early years, students often have classroom experiences that affect their success or failure in school, work, and even their personal lives.

Most elementary school teachers teach in **self-contained classrooms**. That means the same teacher and group of students remain in one classroom for most of the day, with one teacher teaching most or all subjects. Elementary school classrooms are typically active and visually stimulating. Teachers use a variety of teaching methods. Lessons may incorporate games, music, art activities, computer programs, and visuals, as well as textbooks and teacher presentations. Most traditional elementary schools employ teachers who specialize in one grade level, although some school systems are structured so teachers instruct across several grades.

Middle Schools and Junior Highs

Most schools have older preteens and young teens on their own school campus or area. They recognize that students in these age groups have different needs. Middle schools usually include grades 6, 7, and 8, although some have grade 5 as well. Schools with a junior high system include students in grades 7 and 8 or 7, 8, and 9. Even if these students remain physically within the same building with younger grades, their teaching and learning experiences change.

There are good reasons for these levels. Brain development at this stage encourages thinking at a higher level. Students think faster and more creatively. They can identify multiple solutions to problems. They also become able to think abstractly. **Abstract thinking** is about ideas and concepts, such as justice or love, rather than only what is actually experienced—the **concrete thinking** of younger students. Students who think abstractly are interested in why things are as they are. Abstract thinkers can also connect how they feel to what they are thinking.

These changes in thinking and learning make the role of middle school and junior high teachers different from that of an elementary school teacher. Because older students study topics more in depth, most teachers specialize in teaching one or two areas, such as social studies or science or math. That means that students have several teachers during the day—moving them toward the system they will have in high school. Learning is often less structured, incorporating more projects and activities. Students can be lively and creative. Because learning social skills is so important in this stage of life, students often work in groups and solve problems together. This is known as **collaborative learning**.

Middle school and junior high students are expected to become more responsible for their own learning and conduct. Information and tasks are more complex. Students are encouraged to learn to structure their time and make plans, then organize and carry out the plans. Teachers should help them systematically build these and other skills and habits needed for high school.

High Schools

High school brings new subject areas. General math gives way to algebra, geometry, and trigonometry. Topics are studied in much more depth. Students like you have five to seven different classes (and teachers) each day.

Students are also expected to take primary responsibility for their learning. It is not unusual to have homework in every subject every night, along with long-term projects. Students are expected to ask for help if they do not understand concepts. More assignments require complex thinking skills, and students routinely practice solving problems by gathering and evaluating information.

High school teachers typically specialize in one subject or a group of related subjects. In small schools, however, teachers may have a more diverse teaching schedule. More content depth is needed to teach high school courses. Teachers must have at least a bachelor's degree from a four-year college or university and be certified to teach in their state. Training for high school teachers is more focused on the subject areas they have chosen.

Even with curriculum guidelines, teachers usually still have some flexibility in what and how they teach. Teachers determine how much to emphasize various topics and how to best present them. Which topics will they assign for papers? Can a concept be learned most effectively through a teacher presentation, group discussion, lab experience, or combination of these and other techniques? These are among the many aspects managed by individual teachers, 1-6.

High school teachers usually have additional responsibilities besides teaching. They may monitor study halls, serve as advisors for school organizations, tutor, coach sports, and chaperone events. (Some responsibilities are considered part of their regular teaching duties, but they may receive extra pay for others.) Many teachers are willing to help students outside class with issues, such as choosing colleges or careers or dealing with personal concerns.

1-6
This high school geography teacher guides students working on a map project.

Teaching Specialists

In addition to regular classroom teachers, most schools also rely on teachers who play special roles. In elementary school, you may have had separate teachers for music or physical education. Perhaps in middle school, specialty teachers taught Spanish or Chinese once a week. Reading specialists typically work with students who have difficulty with that key skill. They are trained to identify specific reading problems and help students progress.

Special education teachers also fall into the category of teaching specialists. They work with students who have special learning needs. They use various techniques to help students learn. The needs, strengths, and weaknesses of each individual student are carefully considered, and a plan of action is developed. This is developed by a team of teachers and specialists (often a therapist and psychologist), in addition to the child's parents or guardians.

Many special education teachers work with students who have mild to moderate learning difficulties. These students typically spend most of their day in regular classrooms. Some special education teachers assist students with specific impairments in speech, hearing, sight, or language. Often they help regular classroom teachers adapt their teaching for these students. Others help children with emotional problems that impact learning.

A few special education teachers work with students with more severe developmental or learning disabilities. With these students, they work on both basic literacy skills and life skills. Life skills can include social skills, self-care skills, and job-related skills for high school students.

Career and technical education teachers instruct and train students to work in a wide variety of careers. They assist students in exploring career interests and connecting what is taught in the classroom with what will be encountered in the real world. They help students know what to expect when dealing with employers.

Career and technical education covers many career pathways. For example, in trade and industrial fields, it includes training as automotive technicians, carpenters, and electricians. Career preparation in family and consumer sciences may include early childhood education, food production, hospitality management, apparel, and interior design. Career and technical education teachers also prepare students to work in the health occupations field, in public safety and security, and other technical areas. Career and technical education teachers teach in middle schools, high schools, and two-year colleges.

Postsecondary Education Programs

There are many opportunities for teachers in **postsecondary education,** which takes place after high school. Technical schools, community colleges, and four-year colleges and universities are the most common options.

- *Technical schools.* **Technical schools** are designed to teach the specific skills needed to begin working in a trade. Most courses are directly related to those skills. Technical schools are sometimes recognized by other names, such as trade schools, vocational colleges, business schools, technical institutes, or fashion institutes. There are technical colleges for a wide range of occupations, including culinary arts, Web design, nursing, graphic design, fashion design, mechanical, and medical skills. Courses of study are focused and generally shorter than college programs.

  Although a college degree is often preferred, having related skills and experience is most important for teachers employed at technical schools: For example, to teach culinary arts, a teacher must have extensive knowledge and experience in the culinary field, often as a head chef.

- *Community colleges.* The purpose of community colleges is to focus on meeting the educational and training needs of the communities they serve. Most offer two-year associate's degrees. Many also offer programs that lead to certification in areas such as respiratory therapy or welding. Some students go to a community college for their first two years of a four-year degree program, then transfer to a four-year school. This requires close coordination between community colleges and the colleges and universities in their states to make sure courses will transfer. However, students usually save considerably on educational costs under this plan.

  Entrance to a community college is generally open to anyone with a high school diploma, although requirements vary. The student population tends to be quite diverse, with full-time and part-time students, recent high school graduates, adults, and even high school students taking classes for college credit. Adults may be going back for an education they never completed, improving skills for their present job, or studying for a new occupation.

  Currently, there are over 1000 community colleges in the United States. They serve almost half of the high school graduates each year. Because of the breadth of programs offered, many teaching positions exist. Most community colleges require a teacher to hold at least a master's degree (a two-year degree beyond the traditional four-year college degree). Because the student population is so varied, teachers must be prepared for working with students at various skill levels.

- *Four-year colleges and universities.* Colleges and universities are the traditional places for higher education. Although the terms are often used interchangeably (as in a "college education"), universities offer graduate degree programs. Colleges often offer degrees in one area. A university offers degrees in a variety of areas because it is actually composed of a collection of colleges.

  Students in colleges and universities complete general education courses plus classes specific to their area of specialization. *General education requirements* (sometimes called core courses) are meant to provide a broad background of knowledge. If you plan to become a high school social studies teacher, you would complete a variety of general education courses, social studies courses (such as American and world history, geography, political science, and government), courses in education, and a student teaching experience. This would lead to a bachelor's degree.

  College teachers specialize in one particular area and teach a limited number of different courses. A doctorate degree (usually called a PhD or EdD) is required for most professors, although most schools also have teachers with master's degrees. At this level, teachers are expected to conduct research in their field and do scholarly writing in addition to their teaching duties.

Teaching in Other Settings

Trained and skilled teachers do not always teach in the school system. Because education is key to so many aspects of society, teachers find their skills in demand in other places as well. Opportunities are quite varied. A few examples are described here.

Business and Industry

Many businesses and industries provide education to their employees. The teachers who provide this education are often called **corporate trainers**. The types of education they offer depend on company needs, 1-7. Some programs focus on technical work skills, but most seek to improve key personal skills such as motivation, effective communication, leadership, or team building. International companies may hire people to teach employees moving to other countries the languages they will need to know.

Large companies often employ corporate trainers as full-time employees. Others are self-employed or work for a company that specializes in providing corporate trainers on an as-needed basis.

1-7

A corporate trainer may be hired by a company to introduce a new computer program to its employees.

Businesses may employ teachers for many other purposes. For example, a teacher may be hired to teach about the history of destinations on a cruise ship voyage. Teachers provide classes or one-on-one instruction to children undergoing long-term treatment in hospitals. Whatever the challenge, basic teaching skills are simply adapted to fit the situation.

Adult Education

In a society where jobs require up-to-date knowledge and skills, the need for adult education is ongoing. Literacy programs, for example, may focus on teaching adults to gain and improve reading skills or learn the English language. For those who did not get a high school diploma, General Equivalency Diploma (GED) programs can provide the equivalent of a diploma. Other programs provide general or specific job skills, technical skills in areas such as computer training, or personal enrichment. Most professional degrees also require some level of continuing education in order to maintain or renew licenses.

Adult education teachers plan, deliver, and evaluate educational programs. Their roles are similar to elementary, middle school, high school, and college educators, but their audience is different. As other teachers do, they may use lecture, hands-on learning, computer programs, group work, and projects to teach course content. They must stay informed and current in their teaching. As in all teaching, personal interaction between students and the teacher is important at all levels.

Adult education programs are often government funded. Sometimes they are supported through private funds and/or companies that must make a profit. Community colleges and universities may also provide adult education programs, although these do not normally lead to a degree. Because the field is so varied, career opportunities range from teaching one course to full-time positions. Adult education teachers can also be found in job training centers, community centers, or any environment where training and education programs are needed.

Cooperative Extension Service

Cooperative Extension educators, or agents, are community teachers. They provide useful, practical and research-based information to individuals and communities. They also provide technical assistance to agricultural producers and small business owners.

It is common for cooperative extension educators to coordinate youth 4-H activities and to recruit, train, and develop community leaders. They are professional employees of state universities and are supported by the federal government. Their job duties are varied and include offering formal and informal educational outreach opportunities to community members.

1-8
A fitness instructor motivates people to reach fitness goals.

Sports and Fitness Programs

Most communities have opportunities for people of all ages to learn and play sports as well as to assist others in improving their physical fitness, 1-8. Sports and fitness programs depend on people such as coaches, athletic trainers, athletic directors, aerobics instructors, camp directors, and recreation specialists. Sports and fitness teachers must have knowledge and experience, although a college degree is not always required. These educators must be able to motivate others to learn and to accomplish goals. They may work as a coach or trainer in a private gym. Others may be self-employed as coaches and trainers.

Clubs, Community Organizations, and Religious Groups

Some teachers work for community organizations such as the Boys and Girls Clubs of America, summer camps, or park districts. Many organizations sponsor educational programs on topics of interest.

These may range from gardening and cooking to religious studies. For example, a community group might sponsor defensive driving classes. Many music teachers find employment with religious organizations, providing music for services or organizing and leading musical groups such as choirs.

Employment Opportunities and Trends

Will there be a need for teachers by the time you are ready to teach? Yes! There will always be a need for talented teachers. Education is the key to a successful society. Children need to be educated to be contributing members of society. Adults need to learn new skills and deepen their knowledge. In fact, it is predicted that over the next 10 years, the United States will need over two million new teachers in schools alone.

Why are more teachers needed? First, many current teachers will be reaching retirement age soon. Second, there is a national movement for educational reform. Many people believe that having more teachers who are well trained will help students get a better education.

What kinds of teachers will be needed? It depends. Some subject areas are in greater demand, including math and science. More teachers are needed who speak a language in addition to English. *Bilingual education* (teaching in two languages) is growing in many parts of the country. Teachers who have the skills to teach in two or more languages, as well as teachers of children with disabilities, will be greatly sought.

Teacher shortages already exist in some geographic areas, inner-city schools, and rural schools. In addition, population growth is expected to be greater in some states than others. Consequently, teachers who are able to relocate may have an advantage over those who are not.

If you want to teach, develop the knowledge, skills, and passion that will make you a great teacher. Teachers are always in demand.

Teacher Salaries and Benefits

Teacher salaries vary considerably. Location, amount of education, years of experience, and additional responsibilities are among the variables. Public school salaries tend to be higher than those of private schools, especially nonprofit private schools.

Schools usually pay teachers extra for some out-of-class activities, such as coaching and advising clubs and activities, such as student council. In addition, since most schools have more than two months of vacation in the summer, teachers often take part-time jobs to boost their income.

For teachers who complete additional education, there is often an increase in pay. A four-year college or university degree is required for school teachers. However, in order to encourage teachers to stay current in their field, many districts offer a higher salary for taking additional classes or obtaining a higher degree, such as a master's degree. Although public schools provide benefits that vary by district, most offer the following additional benefits:

- health insurance

- retirement savings plans

- leaves of absence, paid or unpaid

- various other benefits including travel expenses to attend meetings or reimbursement for the cost of additional education

Some public school districts, in an effort to attract top teaching candidates, offer additional incentives such as signing bonuses. A few offer home loan assistance and tax breaks for teachers living within the school district.

Public schools are funded by tax dollars. In good economic times, they often have extra money to spend. When the economy takes a downturn, their budgets tighten. Some programs and positions may be eliminated to compensate. Still, teaching is one of the most basic occupations, and flexible teachers can find many ways to use their skills.

Summary

Effective teachers have individual personalities and talents, but they share important skills and personal characteristics. They also have a desire to share their love of learning.

Teachers spend most of their time planning, presenting lessons, and evaluating learning. They often have additional responsibilities, such as supervising extracurricular activities.

Teaching can be a rewarding and fulfilling career. Teachers help their students acquire the knowledge and skills that prepare them to become valuable members of society. They see students learn, grow, and change.

Teaching is also challenging. Caring teachers put in long hours of work. Conditions are not always ideal, and many of society's problems affect students. This may make teaching more of a challenge.

The field of education offers many career opportunities. Traditional classroom teaching opportunities exist from the preschool through college levels. Many out-of-school career opportunities also exist for those interested in teaching.

Effective teachers will always be needed. With more teachers reaching retirement age, more openings for teachers will occur. Teaching opportunities are expected to vary by subject area and location.

Teaching salaries vary but generally increase with experience and additional education. Benefits often include health insurance, retirement plans, vacation time, and other incentives.

Review

1. How do school-based curriculum and state curriculum differ? What would supporters of each give as an advantage?

2. Why are the personal rewards of teaching often considered long-term?

3. Under what circumstances might a paraprofessional work in a prekindergarten classroom?

4. What are self-contained classrooms? At what level are they most common?

5. What is collaborative learning? At what level is it first used extensively?

6. What are the minimum educational requirements to be a teacher at each of the following levels: preschool, elementary school, high school, community college, university?

7. Why would having a bachelor's degree with teaching certification, even if not required, be an asset in teaching situations outside schools?

8. Identify at least four educational or societal trends that are likely to impact employment opportunities for teachers.

Reflect

1. The chapter identifies some of the personal qualities that effective teachers share. Choose four of these qualities. For each, give an example of a specific situation in which a teacher might need this quality.

2. Identify at least five additional personal qualities that you feel an effective teacher should have. Explain why each is important to teaching success.

3. Think about challenges related to teaching that concern you. Choose one. Research how teachers cope with this type of challenge. Write a report identifying the challenge you chose, summarizing your research findings, and telling what strategies you would use to try to meet the challenge.

4. Develop a list of differences between teaching elementary students and high school students. Consider categories such as *work environment*, *responsibilities*, *student abilities*, and others. Put the categories in one column of a three-column chart. Describe the differences in the remaining columns.

Act

1. Ask an adult to describe the characteristics of his or her favorite teacher. What grade did the teacher teach? What impact did the teacher have on the person? Write a summary of your conversation.

2. Access the United StatesDepartment of Labor Bureau of Statistics Web site at http://stats.bls.gov/oco. Choose career profiles for two types of teachers. For each, write a one-page summary in your own words on the career description, typical working conditions, job outlook, and expected earnings.

3. Calculate the potential savings from completing the first two years of a bachelor's degree at a community college. Check college catalogs or access college Web sites for information on schools in your state. Find the cost per semester hour or yearly tuition cost at each. Use 32 semester hours per year as your basis. Compare tuition costs for the following:

   • four years at a state university

   • four years at a private college or university

   • two years at each, community college and a state university

   • two years at each, community college and a private college or university

   Identify each school's name and location (city).

4. Research teacher shortages nationally or in your state. (Use key words such as *United States government*, *teacher shortage*, *education*, and your state's name.) You may choose to focus on the types of teachers in short supply, where the greatest shortages exist, or why there is a shortage of teachers of a particular type. Summarize your findings in a two- or three-page paper. Include information on the Web sites or other sources of information that you used as a basis for your report.

5. Use the Web to research average teacher salaries in four states. Choose your own state, one that is similar in population, and two that are very different. Make a chart showing how average salaries compare. Include the ranking of teacher salaries for each state. Identify the years of the surveyed information and its source. Then write a report identifying the factors that may influence differences in teachers' salaries.

2 BECOMING A TEACHER

Key Terms

teaching academies

teacher education programs

grants

job shadowing

service-learning

prerequisite course

proficiency test

student teaching

cooperating teacher

certified teacher

reciprocal agreements

teaching license

career goal

personal portfolio

artifacts

philosophy of teaching

articulate

Objectives

After studying this chapter, you will be able to

- **identify** the steps to becoming a teacher.
- **compare** ways of gaining experience with children while in high school.
- **research** the requirements for admission to a teacher education program.
- **develop** a personal career goal.
- **begin** developing a personal portfolio for teaching.
- **write** your own philosophy of teaching.

$$A_v = \frac{R_1 + R_f}{R_1}$$

$$\frac{10k\Omega + 100k\Omega}{10k\Omega} = 11$$

You are considering teaching as a career, but that may seem to be years into the future. In reality, you need to begin the process now. This chapter will help point you in the right direction. You will learn about the steps you need to take to reach your goal and what you can accomplish while you are still in high school.

What if you change your mind along the way? That is okay, too. Through your experiences, you may decide you still want to teach, but perhaps a different level or subject. That is a valuable insight. If you decide that teaching is not for you, you can explore another career path knowing more about your interests and abilities. Virtually everything you learn along the way will serve you well, regardless of the career you will eventually choose.

What Are the Steps to Becoming a Teacher?

What does it take to become a teacher? It depends. Specific teacher preparation standards vary by state and by the level of teaching. However, the same general steps are involved across the country.

The class you are taking will provide you with an excellent start. It will help guide you as you begin the process. You will explore the teaching profession, gain helpful experience, and begin to build the skills you will need to be a successful teacher.

Step 1: High School Preparation

High school is the best place to start the process toward a career in teaching. By setting your goals and working systematically toward them, you will have a real advantage over students who begin later. What you do now really does have a major impact on your future.

Maximize Your Educational Opportunities

As a student, you are in a school setting every day. You have years of experience as a student. More high schools are offering students the opportunity to explore careers in teaching through special career exploration classes or programs. Some of these programs are called **teaching academies**. They help high school students to explore the teaching profession through classes, observations, and hands-on experiences. You may be enrolled in such a class or program now.

Make the most of your high school educational experience. Choose challenging high school courses, and commit to doing as well in them as possible. Why is this so important? First, the knowledge you gain will serve as a solid basis for your college career. Every course will give you insight into a new subject area. In addition, a strong academic record will make you a better candidate for the college or university of your choice and admittance into a teaching program.

In subjects that come more easily for you, you may choose to help others learn the material. There is an old saying, "If you really want to know a subject well, try teaching it to someone else." When you have difficulty with a class or particular topic, ask for help. The experiences you gain mirror that of your future career.

Observe Your Teachers

Take the opportunity to observe your teachers, 2-1. It is your chance to see how a variety of teachers work. Notice how they interact with students. What are their particular teaching styles? How do they adapt material for different levels or interests? What are their class rules and procedures? How do individual teachers earn the respect of their students? Be sure to note your observations for future reference.

Utilize your own teachers as resources about teaching. Ask what led them to teaching and their specific career paths. What advice would they give to someone interested in the profession? Most will be happy to share their knowledge and experiences with you.

2-1
As a student, yourself, you have a great opportunity to observe teachers every day.

Explore College Programs

Begin now to gather information about colleges and universities that offer teacher training. These programs are called **teacher education programs** or *teacher preparation programs*. Many schools have such programs, but some are more highly regarded than others. Your high school guidance staff can be an excellent source of information. Ask your teachers for their recommendations. Search online to find possible schools and learn more about them. This will help you decide which schools interest you most and might be a good fit for you.

When you narrow your list of potential colleges and universities, visit their Web sites to learn about their entrance requirements and what courses you would take. Try to visit the colleges or universities at the top of your list during your junior year. Applications for admission should be sent to colleges in the fall of your senior year.

Guidance counselors also have a wealth of information. For example, if the cost of college is a concern, ask for information about financial aid. Scholarships are awarded on the basis of academic excellence or other criteria. Some **grants** are available, usually for those who show real economic need. Grant money does not need to be repaid. Student loans are usually available at low interest rates and can be repaid over a longer time period than normal loans. Your guidance counselor can help you figure out options for financial aid possibilities and other options for coping with educational expenses.

Gain Experience and Improve Your Skills

While in high school, gain as much experience working with children of various ages as you can. Why gain experience now? You have opportunities now that are different from those open to you later in life. Working with children can help you make a better decision about whether teaching in an elementary or secondary school is a good career choice for you. In addition, colleges and universities look favorably on applicants who have shown community involvement. There are many ways you can gain experience in teaching and working with children.

- *Job shadowing*. In many high school teaching programs, students have the opportunity to visit a classroom and job shadow a teacher. In **job shadowing**, you follow a person on the job for a few hours, a day, or even longer to experience what the person's career typically involves. This can give you valuable insight into the person's daily tasks, activities, and interactions with others. Seeing a professional in action will help you identify the skills you will need. You may also have the opportunity to discuss the experience with the person you are shadowing and ask questions.

Since job shadowing is only a short-term activity, you might try to shadow a variety of people in careers that interest you. You could, for example, spend time with teachers at different grade levels or perhaps a special education teacher and/or a reading specialist. Besides what you learn, each experience will bring you a new professional contact. Sometimes teachers and counselors arrange for job shadowing, but you can also make arrangements to do so yourself.

- *Volunteering.* Volunteering is an excellent way to actually interact with children. Much of the important work in communities is done by volunteers. Once you become aware of needs, you are likely to find many opportunities. You can learn more about children of different age levels. You might volunteer to help with an after-school program at an elementary school. You could become a tutor in a youth program. You could get involved in programs such as Cub Scouts or Brownies. You could help coach a sport. Summer camps, child care programs, Special Olympics, and community recreation programs all benefit from enthusiastic and committed volunteers. Short-term projects are also an option. You might help with an elementary school fundraiser, set up a school's art fair, or help a middle school group with a car wash. Volunteering can give you valuable leadership experience. In essence, teachers are those who lead others in learning.

  All volunteer experiences, even those that do not involve children, can help you improve the skills you will need for success in college and a career. You may assist with planning, carrying out, and evaluating activities. Volunteer activities typically require creativity and problem-solving skills. You will have opportunities to work with people of different backgrounds and ages. Dedication to your volunteer job, even if it is inconvenient, strengthens your sense of commitment. Every experience will teach you much and help you stretch and grow as a productive citizen.

  Volunteer work can also be a valuable addition to your résumé. In addition, some of the adults with whom you work may be willing to act as references, attesting to your character, commitment, and work.

- *Service-learning.* A special type of volunteer effort, called service-learning, links classroom learning with hands-on experience in order to meet community needs, 2-2. Service-learning projects require analyzing needs, learning related information, planning a way to help, following through, and evaluating the experience. For example, a child development class might look into the problem of injury and death rates among young children involved in vehicle accidents. Research might show that many child safety seats may be improperly installed, while others may have been recalled. The class might work with an agency such as the American Red Cross to organize a

2-2

By volunteering as a tutor in a service-learning project, you can gain valuable teaching experience to improve your skills, while helping others.

safety-check day. Parents of young children could bring their vehicles to school to have the child safety seats checked. In addition, the class might prepare a handout on child safety to give to parents who attend the safety check day. Both the parents and students would evaluate the experience. A service-learning project such as this enhances learning, fills a community need, and helps students see that they can make a difference. If your school does not have a service-learning program, talk to your teachers about establishing one.

- *Part-time work.* Part-time work is another way to gain experience with children while still in high school. Child care centers, recreation programs, and after-school care programs are just a few of the places that hire part-time or summer staff. Your interest in teaching, related classes you have taken, and any volunteer experiences would help make you a good candidate.

There are many opportunities for learning more about the field of education through actual experience with children. Take advantage of as many as possible to test your interests and boost your skills. Whom would you be interested in job shadowing? What volunteer opportunities exist in your community? Does your school have service-learning projects? Perhaps you can find a part-time or summer job related to your career goal. Whatever your choices, they will enhance your learning and your life.

Step 2: College Preparation and Teacher Training

To teach in kindergarten through high school, a bachelor's degree is required. This degree, sometimes called an *undergraduate degree*, is generally completed in four years. It is usually either a Bachelor of Arts (BA) or Bachelor of Science (BS), depending on your college major and the course requirements you have met.

Colleges and universities have individual requirements for admission to teacher education programs. Some require students to wait until their junior year of college to apply. By this time, students have completed most of their general education or core courses, and the teacher education program can better evaluate applicants. Entrance requirements often include personal interviews, prerequisite courses, a minimum grade point average, and proficiency tests. A **prerequisite course** is one that must be completed before entering a program or prior to taking a higher-level course. **Proficiency tests** measure skill and knowledge in a subject area. Teacher education candidates or majors may be required to pass proficiency tests in subjects such as reading, writing, and math. These skills will be integrated into every teacher's classes. Many programs ask applicants to list related experiences they have had working with children.

Elementary and secondary education students must complete course work related to education. Some courses provide background about education as a profession and how schools function. Others help students learn specific teaching strategies and classroom management techniques. Students focusing on elementary education also take courses to prepare them to teach all subject areas. Students preparing to teach for middle grades and high school, study one or two subject areas in much more depth, such as science or physical education.

Step 3: Classroom Experiences and Student Teaching

An important part of preparing to become a teacher is gaining necessary experience. As part of course requirements for teacher education students, most classes require working with children or teens. Students may observe, help a teacher, tutor students, teach a lesson, or be involved in some other capacity. There are real advantages to this practice. Teacher education students gain more experience, improve their skills, and see how they like various aspects of teaching.

Teacher education culminates in a **student teaching** experience. Students are placed in public or private school classrooms to immerse themselves in the practice of teaching. There, they have at least one **cooperating teacher**—a classroom teacher who supervises and mentors a student teacher. A professor at the college oversees the student teaching experience. All states require teacher education programs to include a student teaching experience.

Student teachers begin by observing in the classroom. By the end of their experience, which usually lasts one semester, they are often taking over for the teacher while under his or her supervision. This includes planning and teaching material, assigning work, evaluating and assessing learning, and interacting with parents and school personnel.

Step 4: Gaining Certification

Kindergarten through high school teachers must be certified in the state where they want to teach. A **certified teacher** is one who has met the state requirements for teacher preparation. Typically, this includes having a bachelor's degree or higher, successfully completing an approved teacher education program (including student teaching), and any other state requirements, 2-3. In many states, students can complete a bachelor's

2-3
Once you have successfully completed your student teaching, earned a bachelor's degree or higher, and met state requirements, you become a certified teacher.

degree and approved teacher education program within four years. However, some states require one or two years of education courses after completing a bachelor's degree.

A certified teacher receives a teaching license or teaching certificate. Through this official document, the state verifies for schools that the person is qualified to teach. A teaching license specifies the grade levels, and sometimes subject areas, for which a teacher is qualified. For example, teachers may be licensed to teach at the early childhood level, the elementary grades, the middle grades, or secondary school. A specific subject area, such as music, may be identified. Not all private schools require teachers to have a teaching license, but most do.

College and university teacher education programs are usually keyed to the licensing requirements of their state. What if you plan to teach in a state other than where you go to college? It is important to know the specific requirements of the state where you will be teaching as early as possible. You can work with your advisor to develop a plan. States usually have **reciprocal agreements** with some other states regarding teaching licenses or certifications. This means that they agree to honor teaching credentials issued in another state with which they have an agreement.

A **teaching license** is a formal document, issued by a state, verifying that a teacher is qualified to teach at specific grade levels or particular subject areas. Teaching licenses are issued for a specific time period. Then they must be renewed. States typically require teachers to document additional education or training to have their license renewed. Some require that teachers eventually obtain a master's degree, such as a Master of Education. This is a graduate degree and requires the equivalent of one or two years of full-time course work. Many teachers begin working on their master's degrees part-time shortly after they begin teaching.

If your goal is to teach at the college level, you may need to complete a master's degree to teach at the community college level. This degree is usually not in education, but in a particular subject area or specialization. To teach at a four-year college or university, a doctoral degree may be required. This, too, is usually in a specialized area.

Getting Started

Now that you have seen the big picture, where do you begin in your quest to be a teacher? Taking the class you are in is your best guide to exploring the teaching field. Observe what you see around you. Look for examples of effective teaching and learning. Take advantage of every opportunity for learning. Gain experience working with different age groups.

There are several other keys to beginning the path toward teaching: defining your career goal, creating a personal portfolio, and developing a philosophy of teaching. Together these will help you get started.

Set a Career Goal

Dreams rely on chance. Goals take concerted effort, 2-4. However, your life's dreams can become life's goals. How can you make your dream of becoming a teacher—and others—reality?

Think seriously about what subjects and age group you would like to teach. These are two important questions in understanding your desire to become a teacher. First, think about what you would like to teach. Do you have a passion for a particular subject? Some people love a single subject area such as biology or art. Others like to teach in all basic areas, including reading, writing, and math. Are you drawn to young children, those in middle grades, younger teens, older teens, or young adults?

When you know what you want to achieve, you are more likely to achieve it. Use your personal answers to the "what" and "who" questions as a basis for writing a career goal. A **career goal** is a clear, concise statement of what you want to become in life. Write down exactly what you want to accomplish in specific terms. Perhaps your goal is to be a third grade teacher. Maybe you want to teach in a rural school. How will you feel when you accomplish this goal? Although you may modify your goal later, having a career goal will help you move ahead.

Your career goal forms the base for identifying interrelated goals that will help you achieve it. For example, to become that third grade teacher, you might set the goal of being admitted to a particular university with an excellent teacher education program.

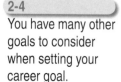

2-4
You have many other goals to consider when setting your career goal.

Think of the process like a tree. Your main career goal is the trunk. Your related goals, such as acceptance into the university of your choice, are the main branches. For each of those, you will identify the specific steps that will be needed to achieve them. These steps are like smaller branches off the main ones. You can identify even more specific ways to achieve those. In this way, you have a series of very specific goals to meet that will lead you to your main one. You have a path to follow.

Next, outline the steps you will take to complete each goal. If you want to get into a particular university with an excellent teacher education program, figure out what you need to do to get accepted and be able to attend. Perhaps you need to improve your grades, apply to the university early in your senior year, and develop a plan for paying for the cost of your education. Determine the specific things you will do to achieve each of these steps. For example, to improve your grades, you may commit to writing down each assignment, doing your homework as soon as you get home (with your cell phone off), and studying an extra hour each day. You will reevaluate your strategy at the end of each month and modify it if your grades are not improving. Consider possible roadblocks or challenges to meeting your goal. How can you deal with these?

Does it all seem overwhelming? It doesn't have to be. Begin your career planning today. Consider what can you do today, this week, this month, or this year to help you toward your goal. Perhaps you can begin by searching the Internet for information about college teacher preparation programs. Find a volunteer or paid work experience. Maybe you can have a conversation with one of your teachers about his or her career path. Now is a good time to set goals, enjoy your experiences, and be open to the changing world around you. See 2-5 for an example of one student's career plan. How will yours look?

Create a Portfolio

Professional portfolios are commonly used by artists, photographers, architects, designers, and writers as a way to showcase their abilities and work. In other words, they are used as an expanded, visual résumé. A written *résumé* simply lists a person's accomplishments, skills, and experience, but a *professional portfolio* adds visual evidence to support it.

Portfolios can be used by anyone, and they are becoming increasingly common in education. Now is the time to start developing a **personal portfolio** for teaching. A personal portfolio is an organized collection of materials and information that shows how personal knowledge, skills, and attitudes have developed over time. It can be adapted to serve as a professional portfolio when you are ready to enter your career field. Your teacher may make developing a portfolio a requirement for this course. Even if it is not required, you will find it very helpful.

2-5
This sample career plan can help you develop your own plan.

Sample Career Plan	
High School	Gain experience working with children and youth
	Job shadow
	Take a career exploration course
	Meet with guidance counselor and discuss interests
	Look for college teacher preparation program
	Apply to colleges
	Choose college program that best meets your needs
College	Meet with guidance counselor and enroll in courses
	Job shadow
	Gain additional experience working with children and youth
	Complete necessary coursework
	Complete student teaching
	Graduate
During last year or after college	Apply for certification
	Conduct job search

Your portfolio is a personal collection of materials and reflections that illustrate your learning, accomplishments, strengths, and best work. These examples show what you have learned over time.

Think of your portfolio as an opportunity to keep track of your learning. It can be used to display and record your developing skills and abilities. The pieces you include in your portfolio are sometimes called **artifacts**. These may include items such as projects or papers you prepare for class, examples from a related volunteer activity, and academic and other awards, just to name a few. As you add items to your portfolio, it will show how your knowledge, thinking, and skills are growing. Your portfolio also serves as a source of personal reflection, such as a visual journal.

Characteristics of Effective Portfolios

Effective portfolios share several common features. As you prepare and evaluate your own, keep the following in mind:

- Portfolios have a clear purpose. Remember that the purpose of your teaching portfolio is to record and highlight your experiences and abilities that will make you a good candidate for teaching. It is not simply a scrapbook about your life.

- Portfolios reflect your uniqueness. Your abilities and experiences are not the same as anyone else's. Because of this, your portfolio should be original. You may choose to include different artifacts than others in your class. You might, for example, include photographs, certificates, descriptions of your work with children, and evidence of your personal leadership experiences.

- Portfolios show your progress. Your portfolio is not just a random collection of things. Think carefully about what to include. Identify and date each item. For each, you also need to include a thoughtful statement about why the item is meaningful and what it demonstrates. These statements, along with the changing quality of your work, show how your thinking, understanding, and skills have evolved. For example, you might include the first lesson plan you develop for your teaching class, along with a paragraph about what you learned from the experience. Later, you may add other teaching materials that you have developed. The differences in their quality and your thoughts about them will show how you have progressed from your earlier efforts. Remember that portfolios evolve over time, but they should be current. You may remove some items (or store them elsewhere) as you add new ones and progress in your professional preparation.

- Portfolios reflect professionalism. An effective portfolio is well-organized, neat, and easy to understand. One of the most common methods of organizing a portfolio is to use a three-ring binder with tab dividers. Make the pages interesting. Even the paper you choose, the way you arrange items, and the lettering you use say something about you. Make sure that what you have written is accurate, clear to the reader, and grammatically correct. To be effective, a portfolio must be error-free. Proofread carefully several times. It is a good idea to ask at least two people to review your portfolio before you turn it in for a class or use it for another purpose.

What Should You Include in Your Portfolio?

Even though portfolios vary, there are several documents that often are part of a personal teaching portfolio. If you are preparing this as a class project, your teacher will give specific guidelines. The following are some items to include in a portfolio:

- basic information about yourself, including your name and year in school

- an essay focusing on your career goals and personal interests

- projects, assignments, or examples from experiences that display your skills

- journal entries about your experiences related to teaching

- a list of the courses you have taken in high school

- a list of community activities, including any community service

- information about any jobs you have had

- academic recognition, such as letters, certificates, or honors

- information on leadership positions you have held or demonstrated

- documentation of special skills, such as foreign language or exceptional computer skills

Throughout this book, you will find ideas for developing a portfolio. Look for the *Add to Your Portfolio* section at the end of each chapter. In addition, artifacts and reflections from many of the other activities may be good additions to your portfolio.

Using Your Portfolio

As you move through high school, your learning experiences multiply. It is easy to lose track of what you did and the importance of individual activities. A portfolio allows you to keep the important components of your career goals in an organized format. Recording how you changed, or grew, or what you learned from the experience each component represents shows meaningful reflection and documents the significance of each milestone.

If you are creating a portfolio as a part of a teaching course or academy program, your portfolio may be used as part of your final grade. You might use materials from your portfolio if you apply for a part-time job. Colleges and universities often use portfolios to assess students' levels of knowledge and experience when they apply to teacher preparation programs. Starting a portfolio in high school will assist you in building a solid professional foundation that can move with you through your college career.

Electronic Portfolios

Preparing your portfolio in an electronic format is an alternative to an actual physical one, 2-6. There are benefits to this option. With an electronic portfolio, information can be easily stored on a computer hard drive or storage device, transported, and accessed with minimal effort. With traditional portfolios, items included in the portfolio can be lost. Materials also take up a lot of space and must be stored in boxes, notebooks, binders, or files. By scanning or taking digital photos of objects, you can preserve their images. A portfolio in electronic form can be shared electronically. Electronic portfolios also serve to demonstrate the creator's computer skills. Just be sure the technology used is compatible and accessible to the viewer. However, some people prefer to be able to see and touch the actual items in a portfolio.

2-6
You can use an electronic portfolio to highlight your education, skills and teaching experience.

Develop Your Philosophy of Teaching

Teachers and student teachers are often asked about their philosophy of teaching. A **philosophy of teaching** is a personal statement about your thoughts, views, and values as they relate to teaching.

As a high school student interested in the teaching field, you already have ideas about the characteristics and qualities of good teaching. What do you think a classroom environment should be like? How should teachers and students relate to each other? Ideas and opinions such as these form your philosophy of teaching.

Why do you need a statement of your philosophy of teaching? The process of developing such a statement will help you think seriously about your current ideas and beliefs, 2-7. Your statement will give others insight into what is important to you. The courses you take and experiences you have are likely to have an impact on your thinking. You can update or rewrite your statement to reflect these changes. This, too, is a sign of growth. You can use your philosophy of teaching statement when you apply to a college teacher preparation program. Eventually, it may be used when you apply for your first teaching position.

The most difficult part about writing a philosophy of teaching is to **articulate** your thoughts, or put them into words. It is often made easier by starting with questions. Use the questions in 2-8 to start your thinking.

When writing your statement, use language that everyone will understand, rather than words you think will impress others. The format is up to you. You may decide to write in the form of a story, use relevant quotations, include visuals, or use a question/answer format. It is usually best

2-7
Developing your philosophy of teaching takes careful thought.

Developing Your Philosophy of Teaching

The following questions can help you in developing your personal philosophy of teaching. Think about each of them, and jot down your thoughts. Your philosophy statement may include some, but not necessarily all, of these points.

- Why do you want to teach?
- What characteristics make a teacher effective?
- How do students learn?
- What is an ideal classroom?
- What should the relationship between teacher and student be?
- What motivates students to learn?
- What should be the primary goal of a teacher?
- Who is the best teacher you have ever known? What made him or her so special?
- What is the most important role of a teacher?

2-8
Use these questions to guide you in developing your philosophy statement.

to use a first-person or "I" perspective. Keep your philosophy statement short. As a student, two or three paragraphs are sufficient.

Giving serious thought to your goals, career, and personal objectives will pay off in the long run. You will know what you want to put your time and effort in to achieving. You will know when you have reached your goals and objectives.

Summary

Teaching is a career that offers variety, challenge and rewards. Although specific teacher preparation standards vary by state, the same general steps are involved in becoming a teacher. You can start the process today.

High school is an excellent time to begin exploring the field of teaching. It is also a good time to gain experience working with children and people of all ages.

There are additional ways to begin your journey toward teaching. First, set a specific career goal. Second, begin developing a personal portfolio to keep track of your learning and to display and record your developing knowledge, skills, and abilities. You can use this as the basis for a professional portfolio later. Third, write a statement of your personal philosophy of teaching. This describes your beliefs and attitudes about teaching and learning.

Review

1. List four steps to becoming a teacher.
2. What are the advantages of taking challenging courses while still in high school?
3. What is job shadowing? Why is it recommended?
4. How are volunteering and service-learning similar? How are they different?
5. What are at least two ways working with children of different ages can be helpful while you are still in high school?
6. What is the role of a cooperating teacher during a student teaching experience?
7. What does it mean to be a certified teacher? Why is certification needed?
8. Explain why setting a career goal is important, even if you change it later.
9. What is the purpose of a personal portfolio?
10. What is a philosophy of teaching statement and what is its purpose?

Reflect

1. Review the criteria identified in the chapter that teacher education programs typically use to evaluate students applying to the program. Explain why each may indicate probable success in the program and as a teacher.
2. Observation is a key skill for those interested in becoming a teacher. You may observe teachers, children of various ages, and educational programs. Work in groups to identify what it takes to be a good observer. Consider how to prepare, what to do during the observation, and how to follow up afterward.
3. Many colleges and universities offer at least some of their courses online. What would be the advantages and disadvantages of taking teacher education courses online?
4. Analyze why it is important for each of the following groups that teachers are certified: states, schools, parents, students. Identify as many reasons as you can for each group. Write out your answers. As a class, compile students' individual answers to develop as complete a list as possible.

Act

1. Use the Internet or college catalogs to identify one college or university in your state that has a teacher education program. Find out when students may apply to the program. Choose one level of teaching (early childhood through high school) and research the types of classes that would be required, how many courses are required, and how long the student teaching experience lasts. Prepare a report of your findings. Your teacher may post the reports or make them available online to share information about what a variety of schools offer. Include the Web address for the school in your report.

2. Find out the requirement for teacher certification in your state. What education and training is required? How many years is the license valid? What, if any, requirements must be met to renew the license? What categories of licenses are issued (such as kindergarten through grade 6, etc.)?

3. Write a concise career goal based on your current interest in teaching. Be sure to include specific information on the type of position in which you are interested.

4. Using the questions in 2-8 as a guide, develop a philosophy of teaching statement of two or three paragraphs. Ask your teacher for feedback, then revise your statement.

Add to Your Portfolio

Purchase a large binder for use as a teaching portfolio. Using guidelines provided by your teacher or those in this chapter, organize the binder into sections. Think about what you would like to include to make it reflect your own uniqueness.

UNIT 2: THE LEARNER

3 UNDERSTANDING HUMAN DEVELOPMENT

Key Terms

growth

development

physical development

gross-motor skills

fine-motor skills

cognition

cognitive development

social-emotional development

sequence

developmental theories

behaviorism

classical conditioning

operant conditioning

Objectives

After studying this chapter, you will be able to

- **distinguish** between growth and development.
- **identify** the main types of human development.
- **develop** examples that illustrate principles of development.
- **define** a developmental theory.
- **apply** developmental theories to real-life situations.
- **analyze** how developmental theories impact teaching.

Stacy has invited five girls from her kindergarten class to her sixth birthday party. In the past, she always invited her cousin, Jake, to her birthday party, but now she only plays with girls at school. The girls play games Stacy's parents planned, and Stacy opens presents, including the newest fashion doll, a soccer ball, nail polish, and books.

On the same day, Becca is celebrating her thirteenth birthday. A couple of her girlfriends come for pizza and a sleepover. They stay up until the early morning hours laughing, listening to music, and talking. Their talk centers on boys, sports, and the upcoming dance at school. There are no games, and Becca's friends give her gift certificates.

A six-year-old is very different from a 13-year-old. Both are different from an infant or an adult. Why? Life is a process of growth and development. **Growth** refers to physical changes in size, such as gains in height and weight. Most growth occurs during the first 20 years of life. **Development** is related. It is the gradual increase in skills and abilities that occurs over a lifetime. While each person progresses in an individual way, the stages of development are similar for almost everyone. Babies learn to walk, talk, and feed themselves. Children learn to jump, tell a joke, and spell. Human development occurs throughout the lifespan.

Areas of Development

There are four main types of development. These are physical, cognitive (or intellectual), social, and emotional. Social and emotional development are intertwined, and they are often referred to together as social-emotional development. During each stage of life, a person's physical, cognitive, and social-emotional development can be identified.

Physical Development

The rapid physical growth of the first years of life is matched by amazing strides in physical development. **Physical development** is advances in physical abilities. A newborn cannot change position, but a two-year-old can run. Many individual developmental steps make this change possible. Random movements of the newborn's legs and arms add strength. The infant eventually becomes strong enough to roll over. Crawling follows. Next, the baby learns to stand upright and finally takes a few steps. It takes months of walking practice for steadiness and coordination to improve, then running is possible.

Many other aspects of physical development are happening at the same time. These are often referred to as *motor skills*, since they depend on increasing strength and coordination of muscles. **Gross-motor skills**, such as walking and throwing, depend on development of the large muscles, including those in the arms, legs, back, and shoulders. **Fine-motor skills**, such as picking up objects and eating with a spoon, depend on development of the small muscles, such as those in the hands and wrists, 3-1. Beyond infancy, physical development continues, but the skills and abilities become more complex.

Cognitive Development

Humans are able to think. Thinking takes many forms. You *know* your locker combination. You *sense* what is happening around you. You *memorize* facts for a test and try to recall them during a test. You *organize*

3-1
Physical development during the first years of life is dramatic.

your thoughts to write a paragraph. These and other processes involving thought and knowledge are called **cognition**. The way people change and improve in their ability to think and learn throughout life is called **cognitive development**, or *intellectual development*.

Like physical skills, cognitive abilities increase gradually. Consider your math skills as a first grader, an eighth grader, and now. Your skills have improved dramatically over that time span. As a result, the way you are taught math has changed, too. Your current teachers assume you have mastered the most basic concepts. As time progresses, they present more difficult concepts and expect you to do more independently by reading your textbook and solving homework problems.

With increasing understanding of how the brain develops and works, scientists are providing new insights into cognitive development. The development of connections between nerve cells in the brain is a key component to cognitive development at all stages of life. Brain connections grow and strengthen with new experiences and repetition of familiar ones. For example for an infant, the faces of parents and other primary caregivers become familiar because they are seen most often. After a few months, the sight of these people may be rewarded with a smile of recognition. Later, the names of those caregivers may be among the child's first spoken words.

Social-Emotional Development

Social-emotional development includes the areas of relationships and feelings. Individuals must learn social skills and how to care about others. They must develop both self-confidence and self-esteem. For example, learning self-control is an important skill for kindergarteners. Students learn to wait their turn, form a line, and listen while the teacher gives instructions.

At each stage of development, social and emotional challenges increase. New skills must be developed to deal with increasing independence of childhood, the more complex social situations of adolescence, establishing an identity, adult relationships, parenting, careers, retirement, and the other challenges of life. How well individuals meet those challenges depends on the skills they developed earlier in life and how well they are able to adapt them to new situations, 3-2.

Principles of Human Development

It is the nature of human beings to try to figure things out. Observations about human development go back to the beginning of recorded history.

3-2
As teens encounter new situations, they rely on social-emotional developmental skills.

The research continues, but the following include some of the basic principles that explain what is already known:

- Development is relatively orderly.
- Development is a gradual, continuous process.
- Development is interrelated.
- Development varies among individuals.

Development Is Relatively Orderly

Development occurs in a predictable and orderly manner—a **sequence** of steps that consistently follow one after another. Children learn sounds, then words. Eventually, they learn the letters of the alphabet and that these can be combined to represent words. Each of these steps must occur before children can read. Teachers use their knowledge of how development progresses to design effective learning strategies appropriate to the age of their students.

Development Is a Gradual, Continuous Process

Most developmental changes happen gradually and are apparent over time. A three-year-old may learn to ride a tricycle, while a six-year-old masters the more difficult skills needed to ride a bike. A teen refines these skills and uses them, along with additional knowledge and judgment, to learn to drive a car. An adult driver typically has fewer accidents than a teen because years of practice and experience have improved his or her skills.

Development Is Interrelated

Most development is not solely physical, cognitive, social, or emotional. Acquiring new skills typically requires gains in several of these areas. Think about what it takes to become a skilled basketball player. You need physical stamina, coordination, and endless practice to be able to hurl the ball precisely into the hoop from any angle on the court. It also takes cognitive development to learn plays and to figure out those of your opponents. You must be able to judge the potential success of a shot. Socially, teamwork is required as is the ability to "read" the intent of the player you are guarding. You will note the body language and expressions of other players. Emotionally, you must have confidence, decisiveness, and perseverance. It takes all of these aspects of development, and more, to play well.

Development Varies Among Individuals

Although development is orderly and predictable, each individual's progress is unique. That is because so many factors affect development. No two people—even twins raised together—have exactly the same experiences, 3-3. Each individual faces life-changing experiences and responds to them based on his or her personality, knowledge, and prior experiences. Everyone grows and changes at a different rate and on a slightly different time schedule.

Theories of Development

You are waiting in the checkout line at the store when a small girl in front of you starts screaming. Your natural reaction is likely to try to figure out what caused the outburst. Is the child in pain, or is this a temper tantrum? Did her dad just tell her that she had to put back the candy bar she picked up? The screaming continues. You listen for the father's response. Will he handle the situation well? Your opinions about why the situation occurred and how well the parent responded are based on your current knowledge and past experiences.

Researchers also analyze behavior and development to better understand how and why it occurs. They may have more knowledge and experience and use more scientific methods, but the process is much like your own. They observe people, perform experiments, and consider earlier research studies. Then, they formulate their own explanations about why people act and behave the way they do and how they change over time. These are called **developmental theories**.

3-3
Development varies among individuals—even identical twins are unique in their development.

Why should you, as a future teacher, learn about developmental theories? While these are theories, not proven facts, they can be very useful. They can help you better understand what students are capable of doing and why. Instead of relying only on your own limited personal experiences and observations, understanding developmental theories will give you a broader picture. This knowledge can make you a better teacher.

The developmental theories summarized in this chapter are just a brief overview of the many that exist. However, they are ones that have had a real influence on teachers and teaching. As you read about them, evaluate how their conclusions match your own life experiences, and think about their potential impact in the classroom.

Heredity Versus Environment

The most basic debate about influences on development is that of the relative importance of heredity versus environment. Consider two classmates sitting in class waiting for their turn to read aloud. Andre is shy and reserved. He is nervous about reading in front of the class. His classmate Bryson is bursting with energy and can hardly wait for his turn to read.

When Bryson's turn comes, he speaks loudly and confidently, even when he stumbles over words. Were Andre and Bryson born that way? Was Andre taught to be shy by his shy parents, or is it a natural part of who he is? If Andre was born with a tendency to be shy, would he have been more outgoing if raised in Bryson's family rather than his own?

This question has been debated over and over again. Is it *nature* (heredity) or *nurture* (environment)? In other words, are a person's personality traits, abilities, skills, and tastes a result of genetics (what they were born with) or a result of their environment (a person's surroundings and the people in it)? Most researchers today will answer "both." It is not a matter of which, but how large a part, each plays. How much did heredity affect Andre's shyness or Bryson's outgoing personality? How much did the people around them have an effect on them? Did their own experiences affect each child?

The challenge for researchers is that heredity and the environment interact in complex ways. The genes a person has at birth have far-reaching influence. They carry a person's biological inheritance that determines basics such as hair and eye color. Genes also impact intellectual potential and much more.

Genetic predisposition even influences the kind of environment a person seeks. For example, Bryson is sociable and outgoing. He enjoys being with people. He loves to be around friends so much that when none are around, he seeks one out. He makes friends quickly. In short, what children experience in any environment is a personal response between their own genetic makeup and the environment in which they develop. Shy adults tend to parent shy children. However, a shy child *can* become a more outgoing person.

No single gene determines a particular behavior. Behaviors, like all complex traits, involve multiple genes that are affected by a variety of environmental factors. Genes do influence human development, but they are just part of the story. Just because a person has the genetic makeup to have a trait, it does not necessarily mean that a particular trait will develop.

How does environment influence development? A person is shaped by his or her individual experiences. Social and emotional traits are affected by the environment, but physical traits and cognitive abilities are, too. For example, infants who are held and cared for develop more connections between brain cells. The same is true of children who grow up in a stimulating environment.

The term *environment* applies to many aspects of life. However, some influence development more than others. As you read about those listed here, think about how your life has been shaped by your experiences. Also consider the impact your own words and actions have on others.

- *Family.* Families often have the greatest effect on human development. It is in families that infants gain their first experiences with the world through the care and attention they receive. The bond between parent and child is the most basic. Most children learn how to interact with others within the family. Not surprisingly, research studies suggest that the quality of the home environment is especially important to children's development, and that these influences are very complex. Parents impact all aspects of development—physical, cognitive, social, and emotional. In addition, parents guide children's moral development.

Effective parenting techniques and providing a stimulating home environment are consistently associated with better outcomes for children. These qualities are not dependent on having an advanced education or a high income. Parents who lack effective parenting skills can learn them. Doing so is the best gift that they can give their children, 3-4.

Researchers continue to study how and why families affect various aspects of development. Sibling relationships, the impact of being an only child, birth order, and the emotional climate of the home are a few areas of study for researchers.

- *Peers.* Although families have the greatest social influence on children's early development, the impact of peers increases during later childhood and adolescence. The ability to make and maintain friendships as well as attaining, social power and status, acceptance, and belonging all affect social and emotional development. Peers offer equal status, a relationship that does not exist in child-adult relationships. Peer relationships remain important to development throughout life.

3-4
Parents impact all areas of their children's development.

- *Community.* Where a person lives also influences development. Behaviors that are modeled by others in neighborhoods and communities can impact the behavior and career expectations of its residents. Some researchers see a relationship between feelings of self-worth and how people perceive their environment and their feelings of self-worth. Some communities have more cultural opportunities than others. Schools are also part of communities. The culture of a school, the expectations conveyed to its students, and the abilities and attitudes of its teachers have an impact on students.

- *Media.* Teachers hear it all the time—students mimicking television characters, reciting lines from performances, or singing ad jingles. Media messages are everywhere, and they have been blamed for many negative social problems in our society. Researchers know that no two people experience the same media message in exactly the same way. How a person interprets a message and its effects depend on things unique to that person's life. These can include age, related experiences, values taught in the home, and media education. Media messages can be positive or negative influences. Their effect may not be immediately apparent. A child who watches a superhero fight may mimic the actions immediately while playing. Repeatedly viewing violent images over time can have long-term effects.

- *Health.* Health influences development in a number of ways. Some diseases and illnesses may interrupt the normal development of a person. For example, a mother who abuses alcohol or other drugs may have a child that will have a lifetime of developmental delays. A child with autism may have difficulty in forming close friendships, and may have limited or delayed speech. A child with a chronic illness may miss more days from school and have difficulty with schoolwork. The availability of health care can also influence development. When children receive regular checkups, developmental problems are likely to be detected and responded to promptly. This precaution often limits the impact of potential complications.

- *Nutrition and physical activity.* Everyone, especially children and teens, needs nutritious food and adequate exercise for normal physical growth, development, and functioning. Lack of proper nutrition affects cognitive development, therefore limiting learning and productivity. Poor nutrition and lack of exercise can also impact social and emotional development. For example, children and teens who are overweight are more likely to have poor self-esteem. Due to the fact they are overweight, they may be teased or find it difficult to develop social relationships.

Behaviorist Theories

One of the earliest theories in development is behaviorism. **Behaviorism** is a theory based on the belief that individuals' behavior is determined by forces in the environment that are beyond their control. According to behaviorists, how people behave (their thoughts, feelings, and actions) depends on what they have learned through experience, rather than genetics or free will. In the debate of heredity versus environment, behaviorists believe that environment wins.

According to behaviorists, infants come into the world as "blank screens." The behaviors people exhibit are a direct result of their experiences in life. If eight-year-old Tyler is a bully on the playground, it is assumed he learned that behavior.

Pavlov's Classical Conditioning

One of the earliest behavioral experiments was conducted by a Russian researcher named Pavlov. He noticed that a dog naturally salivated at the sight of food. Pavlov began to ring a bell each time he fed the dog. Eventually, if the bell was rung, the dog salivated, even if no food was given to the dog. This response is an example of **classical conditioning**—the theory that behaviors can be associated with responses.

Can classical conditioning occur without specific training? Behaviorists say it can. For example, a parent who is afraid of bugs may unknowingly pass that fear along to their child. Perhaps the parent takes a loud deep breath or communicates alarm at the sight of a bug. If that happens repeatedly, the child is likely to acquire the same fear. You have probably experienced classical conditioning in your own life. Do you have a favorite song that makes you feel happy when you hear it because it reminds you of a positive experience? All of our experiences, whether positive, negative, or neutral, can affect our emotions, attitudes, and behaviors.

Skinner's Operant Conditioning

When you have a pleasant experience, such as receiving a compliment, you internalize the experience as positive. B. F. Skinner was a researcher well known for identifying this basic principle. This principle is called operant conditioning. **Operant conditioning** is when people tend to repeat behaviors that have a positive result or are reinforced. If your teacher praises you for your history project, you may decide that you like history. If you repeatedly get high grades on tests and projects, you may decide that you are good at history.

Skinner found that to make new behaviors permanent, the reinforcements (positive experience) are to be removed gradually, and in unpredictable patterns. Sometimes the behavior is reinforced, but not at others. Even if you get an occasional lower grade in history, you still believe that you are good at the subject and try harder each time you are assigned a project. Your behavior has been changed. Behaviorists call this "learning."

It is easy to see why operant conditioning became so popular in American education. Providing continuous positive reinforcement when a new skill or behavior is learned, followed by gradual removal of the rein- forcement, is believed to result in a permanent behavioral change. Negative reinforcement, or punishment, can reduce unwanted behaviors.

You have probably observed the effects of behaviorism when working with children. Encouraging children's efforts, modeling positive behav- iors, and maintaining a positive attitude can have a very real effect on the behavior of children.

Bandura's Social Cognitive Theory

Is it really that simple? Imagine that you are babysitting several active young children. They are arguing over toys, whining, complaining, and hitting one another. Despite all your encouragement, modeling of appropriate behav- iors, and having a positive attitude, the children won't behave. If all it takes is simple positive reinforcement and punishment, why don't children learn and behave after positives are rewarded and negatives punished? If behaviorism really works, why does behaviorism fail to control behaviors in adults?

Albert Bandura argued that people are very different from Pavlov's dog. He stated that people are much more complex. He believed that people of all ages observe and imitate the behaviors of others, regardless of rewards and punishments involved. People are affected by rewards and punish- ments, but their reactions to them are filtered by their own perceptions, thoughts, and motivations. Bandura called this *social cognitive theory*.

Social cognitive theorists believe that a child who observes a kind act may imitate it. This kind act may be shared with a classmate. A teen may tackle a tough geometry problem by imitating a teacher. However, the same experiences will not have the same result on every person. Each person's response is based on personal reactions and how the individual processes information. A child who observes aggressive behavior may become a bully or a person who avoids conflict. It all depends on the individual.

Piaget's Cognitive Theory

While many researchers were celebrating behaviorism, some began looking for a theory that would better explain the differences in how people think throughout the stages of life. One of the most well known researchers in this area was Jean Piaget, a Swiss researcher.

Piaget's observations led him to identify four stages of cognitive devel- opment. His studies showed that at any stage of life, thinking skills of individuals are similar. At each new stage, individuals incorporate new experiences into what they know based on skills they have developed earlier in previous stages. Chart 3-5 summarizes Piaget's findings.

By carefully documenting the thinking skills of many people at various ages, Piaget improved the understanding of how cognitive skills develop over time. Young children base their thinking on what they know through their senses. Their experiences are limited. Therefore, when Shana, age three, thinks that the moon is following her, it is a logical conclusion. This type of thinking will change with her gaining further knowledge and experience.

Although many researchers have added to the understanding of how thinking occurs, Piaget's four stages of cognitive development remain important. His theory helps teachers understand how children learn and develop and explains why they need continuous exposure to experimentation, discovery, and first-hand experiences.

Vygotsky's Sociocultural Theory

Many researchers have challenged Piaget's theory, especially his belief that humans learn primarily through experimentation with objects. They point out the importance of human interaction as well as a person's social

Piaget's Stages of Cognitive Development		
Age	**Stage**	**Description**
Infancy (Birth to age 2)	Sensorimotor	Babies begin to learn about the world through their senses. At first, learning relies on reflexes but more purposeful movement later enhances learning.
Toddler (Ages 2 to 7)	Preoperational	Toddlers and young children communicate through language. They recognize symbols and learn concepts. Both hands-on experiences and imaginative play are keys to learning.
Early childhood (Ages 7 to 11)	Concrete operational	Children in this stage learn to think logically. They can make generalizations, understand cause and effect, group and classify items, and suggest solutions to problems.
Adolescence and adulthood (Age 12 and up)	Formal operational	Both logical and abstract thinking are mastered during this stage. This includes making predictions and considering "what if" questions.

3-5
Piaget identified four stages of cognitive development.

and cultural environment. Through the generations, older people pass knowledge on to younger people.

Lev Vygotsky, a Russian theorist, believed that children are social beings and develop their minds through interactions with parents, teachers, and other students. He believed that this social interaction is critical to cognitive development.

When Tasha's teacher shows her how to fold and cut out a paper heart, Tasha may later repeat her teacher's instructions to herself. Through this and many other interactions, Tasha will learn to be more skilled at problem solving.

Erikson's Psychosocial Theory

Erik Erikson was one of the most influential developmental researchers of the twentieth century. His focus was on the development of personality. According to Erikson's *psychosocial theory*, personality development occurs during eight stages of life. At each stage, people face, and must successfully resolve, a psychological or social conflict. If they do not, their unsuccessful resolution will affect future stages of their development. See Chart 3-6.

During the first stage, a baby must resolve the conflict of trusting or not trusting others. The baby's sense of trust is built on learning that crying consistently results in being fed and comforted. Developing this sense of trust as an infant allows the child to develop other trusting relationships in life. Of course, a child also must gradually learn to meet his or her own needs.

According to Erikson's psychosocial theory, other stages follow. In early childhood, for example, preschoolers learn to develop initiative by carrying out plans or taking advantage of others. For example, Claire, age three, wants her younger sister and neighbor to play school with her. She wants to be the teacher, and they are to be her students. They go along with her plan, but once she becomes bossy, they lose interest. It is important for Claire to take the initiative to carry out her plan to play school, but at the same time, she has to learn to make the game enjoyable for the other children.

During their elementary school years, children must master social and academic skills, such as making friends and learning to read. These are examples of skills that are important throughout life. Erikson calls this conflict "industry versus inferiority." Children who are unable to keep up with their peers feel inferior, or less important. This may hinder later development.

During the teen years, individuals must resolve the conflict of identity versus role confusion. Teens seek to figure out who they are as individuals. They are concerned about how others see them and they begin to decide what they want to do in life.

Erikson's theory did not stop with adolescence. He believed that development occurs throughout a person's life. People are always changing and developing. Even elderly adults must face conflicts as they try to assess their lives.

Erikson's Psychosocial Developmental Stages		
Stage/Age	**Task**	**Description**
Infancy (Birth to 1 year)	Trust versus mistrust	Babies learn about trust from their caregivers who meet their needs, including food, attention, physical contact, interaction, and safety. When needs are not met, they perceive the world as an unpredictable place.
Toddler (1 to 3 years)	Autonomy versus shame and doubt	Toddlers learn self-help skills, such as feeding, toileting, dressing, and undressing and, as a result, increase confidence. Toddlers who lack control or independence may experience shame and doubt. Some caregivers punish toddlers for not doing things "right" while they are still learning new skills. This can undermine confidence.
Early childhood (3 to 6 years)	Initiative versus guilt	Through discovery and exploration, young children learn about the world and their place in it. They learn what is real and what is imaginary. They learn to take initiative to claim their place in the world. Too much criticism and punishment can result in feelings of guilt and shame.
Middle childhood (6 to 12 years)	Industry versus inferiority	Children develop competency both at school and at home. They develop a sense of self and confidence from becoming competent in the outside world. If they or others consistently compare them negatively against others, feelings of inferiority can surface.
Adolescence (13 to 18 years or older)	Identity versus role confusion	Preteens and teens begin to understand and experiment with a number of different roles. A task during this stage is to integrate multiple roles such as sister, daughter, student, athlete, friend, and employee. If a central, or core, identity is not established, role confusion exists.
Young adulthood (18 to 40 years or older)	Intimacy versus isolation	During later adolescence and early adulthood, close relationships form. These relationships should involve sharing oneself emotionally. Success in this stage is based on success in earlier stages. Failure to establish intimacy results in emotional or psychological isolation.
Middle adulthood (40 to 65 years)	Generativity versus self-absorption	Adults in middle adulthood begin to place emphasis on assisting others and improving the next generation. This can be done in many ways, including parenting, teaching or training others, or passing on cultural values. Failure to do so leads to self-absorption.
Older adulthood (65 years and older)	Integrity versus despair	In the last stage of life, adults review their life and reflect on its meaning. If people are satisfied with their life, there is a sense of integrity. Without it, despair may emerge as the end of life approaches.

3-6

Erikson described personality development as occurring during eight stages of life.

Kohlberg's Theory of Moral Development

Should you steal medicine from a pharmacy if you really need it but do not have the money to pay for it? What if it is a matter of life and death? Lawrence Kohlberg asked a similar question to children, teens and adults as part of his work to better understand how people decide what is right and wrong. His research led him to identify three different levels of moral development. He believed that, beginning in childhood, everyone follows that same progression, although not all individuals attain the highest level. Each level involves different ways of thinking and solving moral problems.

He called the first level *preconventional morality*. Decisions about what is right or wrong depend on whether you will be punished or rewarded for your behavior. For example, very young children believe that stealing is wrong because they may be caught and punished. Moral decisions are viewed from a personal perspective.

The second level of moral development is *conventional morality*. Some older children, many teens, and some adults are in this stage. There is an understanding that society depends on people to observe basic rules of behavior. Moral decisions are motivated by society's laws and rules and how a person who disobeys might be perceived. People may set their own personal interests aside for the good of society as a whole.

Kohlberg's last level is *postconventional morality*. Some teens and most adults make moral decisions based on principles such as justice and individual conscience. They believe that there are universal moral laws related to human rights that are most important to follow. Decisions are motivated by integrity rather than personal interest or punishment.

Kohlberg believed that instead of being taught about specific "virtues," such as kindness and honesty, children and teens should move to the next level of moral development with the help of adults. He felt students should work together with teachers to agree on school rules and policies.

Since Kohlberg observed men and boys to develop his theory, some researchers believed his findings did not include the way women and girls make moral decisions. Carol Gilligan was one of these researchers. She believed that the idea of justice was typical of males, but less typical of females. She believed many women used the idea of caring for others as a motivating factor in making moral decisions.

Which Theory Is Correct?

Although there are many different, yet sometimes conflicting, ways to explain human development, each is valid to some extent. Some theories may be more sound than others. Sometimes the conflict between two theories leads to more valid insights. As a teacher, you can benefit from understanding several approaches to development and applying them to the classroom, 3-7.

3-7
By understanding different developmental theories, teachers can apply them to their own classroom situations.

Throughout your teaching career, more theories will emerge as knowledge about human development grows. This makes teaching and learning exciting. For example, in recent years scientists have been debating whether the specific characteristics or traits of people, such as mathematical problem-solving abilities, are inborn or learned. Gaining greater understanding of the way humans learn would help teachers develop more effective teaching strategies.

Summary

The study of human development provides insight to how people change from birth to old age. These include the progression seen in physical growth, intellectual or cognitive abilities, and social and emotional development. General principles of development have been identified that are helpful in understanding how people change throughout life.

In trying to understand the precise nature of human development, researchers observe, experiment, and study people. They form theories based on their findings. The developmental theories try to explain and predict behavior. These range from the basic debate over the impact of heredity versus environment to theories that seek to explain learning, personality, and moral development.

Theories are not facts, but they help people better understand human development. This is especially helpful for teachers whose work is to help their students develop as human beings, not just to teach them information.

Review

1. Explain the difference between growth and development.
2. Identify the major areas in which people develop over time and give an example of each.
3. What are four principles of human development?
4. Give an example of a sequence of development (physical, cognitive, or social-emotional), other than one used in this chapter.
5. What is a developmental theory?
6. Who described operant conditioning? Explain what operant conditioning is.
7. How would Bandura explain why two people respond to the same experiences differently? What is his theory called?
8. According to cognitive theory, why do young children think differently than teens?
9. Vygotsky believed that a child's learning is influenced by the people who interact with the child. Give an example of this type of learning.
10. Taking Erikson's theory into consideration, how might a child who has not successfully developed trust have a more difficult time starting kindergarten than a child who had developed trust?

Reflect

1. If development were not an orderly process, how would education be different?
2. Predict how believing that only heredity determines intelligence would impact the way a teacher relates to students. What if the teacher believed that intelligence was determined only by environment?
3. Some educational computer programs reward correct answers and negatively reinforce incorrect ones. What educational theory is this based on? What types of positive and negative rewards are typically used in these programs? How do you think they impact learners?
4. Imagine the following scene: *Six-year-old Caesar, his dad, and his baby sister are visiting the local park and swimming pool. Caesar's dad is pushing the baby's stroller. Caesar begins exploring, moving farther and farther away. His dad calls out "Caesar, come back here right now. Caesar, I mean it! Come here. Caesar, listen to me." Caesar keeps his distance and slowly moves farther away. He does not acknowledge his dad's instructions. His dad begins again, "Caesar, come here. I need to be able to see you. You have to stay with me." Caesar continues to explore.*

   How would a behaviorist view this situation? How might a social cognitive theorist, such as Bandura, interpret Caesar's behavior?

Act

1. Choose two members of a family who are biologically related. Make a list of at least five characteristics that they share. For example, they may share the same eye or hair color, skin tone, height or weight characteristics, personality traits, skills, interests, or abilities. List at least five characteristics that they do not share. Which of these shared or individually distinct traits do you believe are inherited? Which are learned or due to environment? Give reasons for your answers.

2. Find an original example of three of the four principles of development explained in the chapter. Write each on a separate piece of paper. In class, combine all of the examples of each principle to get a broader view of the many ways these principles apply to everyday life.

3. Observe someone you know, your age or younger, and identify the stage of Piaget's cognitive theory that person is in according to his or her age. Then give three to five specific examples of that person's cognitive development at that stage.

4. Choose one of the developmental theories in this chapter that interests you. Research one aspect of that theory that you think will help your classmates better understand it. Explain your findings to the class. You may use visuals to help with your explanation.

Add to Your Portfolio

Choose an age level that you may be interested in teaching. Develop at least four questions you might ask one of the theorists in this chapter that would help you better understand students of that age. Specify the theorist, and make certain your questions relate to that person's area of research.

4 MIDDLE CHILDHOOD: GROWTH AND DEVELOPMENT

Key Terms

developmental delay

visual-motor coordination

hand-eye coordination

dexterity

conservation

self-concept

seriation

classification

transitivity

executive strategies

Objectives

After studying this chapter, you will be able to

- **explain** the importance of readiness for learning for children entering kindergarten.

- **trace** the growth pattern of children during middle childhood.

- **analyze** the physical and cognitive skills required to master a task.

- **link** children's thinking skills at various ages to Piaget's stages of development.

- **develop** a list of the social skills children must learn.

- **explain** how the development of self-concept during this period is related to Erikson's psychosocial theory.

- **identify** the change in moral development that occurs about the end of this period.

Today, I am a kindergarten teacher, but I can still remember being a kindergarten student. Because of my circumstances, starting school left a lasting impression.

My parents came from China as young adults. They spoke only Chinese in our home when I was young. They socialized with other Chinese people, so, when I started kindergarten, I neither spoke nor understood English.

Of course, school was bewildering at first. I can remember standing back and watching the other children, trying to figure out what they were saying. Fortunately, children pick up new languages easily. My parents have told me I began to learn English words and phrases rather quickly. Each day when I came home, I would play school with my younger brother and sister, teaching them what I had learned.

I was fortunate to have a wonderful teacher. She spent extra time helping me with the language, but she did much more than that. She made me feel special instead of different. She incorporated learning about China into many lessons. She even invited my mother to come and share some of our Chinese customs and foods with my kindergarten class.

I never forgot that experience or my kindergarten teacher. Today, many schools have special classes for students who don't speak English. However, my own experience taught me that a creative and caring teacher can make a real difference in students' lives. I try to remember that every day with my own students. Each child needs acceptance and recognition. Acceptance and recognition do not just help them socially and emotionally. When children feel secure, they learn more, as well.

As Li Shao's story indicates, the first years of school are crucial for children. The degree to which children feel comfortable and successful impacts their achievement in school for the years ahead. Not every child has the background knowledge, high intelligence, and social skills for that to happen automatically. Teachers can make the difference. They set the tone in their own classroom. They evaluate each child's abilities and monitor progress, providing extra support and encouragement as needed. All of this takes knowledge and skill. Most essential is a thorough understanding of how children develop.

As you learned in Chapter 3, development follows predictable patterns. Researchers know much about children's typical physical, cognitive, and social-emotional development at each age, 4-1. Chart 1 summarizes the developmental stages described by Erikson and Piaget that were presented in Chapter 3. In this chapter, you will learn more about the development of children from ages five to 12. This spans the years from children starting school to the beginning of adolescence.

It is also important to remember that information about development is based on averages. Each child's development actually unfolds in an individual way, and slight variations are normal. However, significant deviation in any area of development needs to be evaluated. Some children

Erikson's and Piaget's Developmental Stages		
Stage/Age	**Erickson's Psychosocial Theory**	**Piaget's Cognitive Theory**
Infancy (birth to 1 year)	Trust versus mistrust	Sensorimotor
Toddler (1 to 3 years)	Autonomy versus shame and doubt	Preoperational
Early childhood (3 to 6 years)	Initiative versus guilt	
Middle childhood (6 to 12 years)	Industry versus inferiority	Concrete operational
Adolescence (13 to 18 years or older)	Ego identity versus ego diffusion	Formal operational
Young adulthood (18 to 40 years or older)	Intimacy versus isolation	
Middle adulthood (40 to 65 years)	Generativity versus self- absorption	
Older adulthood (65 years and older)	Integrity versus despair	

4-1
Erikson's and Piaget's developmental theories align to various ages and stages.

show a **developmental delay**, a noticeable lag in a particular aspect of development. It is important to identify and treat developmental delays as early as possible before the gap widens. Children who fall behind at this stage can often catch up fairly quickly, depending on the severity of the issue and if their problems are addressed. Children whose development is significantly above average in any area may also need evaluation and support. Teachers who see classrooms of children the same age every year are in a unique position to evaluate their development.

Remember that development is a logical, step-by-step process. Even if you eventually teach children who are younger or older than this age group, understanding how development progresses through adolescence is essential.

Beginning School

Most children start their formal schooling at age five as kindergarteners, 4-2. Each state sets age requirements for children starting school, usually identifying a date by which a child must turn five in order to enroll in kindergarten. Consequently, children within a single grade may be up to

Most kindergarteners are eager to begin school.

12 months apart in age. This may make little difference for older children, but gains in maturity and skill levels during a single year can be significant in kindergarten and first grade. Teachers may notice great differences between some of the youngest and oldest students in their classrooms.

As scientists have learned more about how children's brains develop, educators have applied those findings. Researchers have discovered that about half of a child's critical brain development takes place before a child enters kindergarten. The importance of the early years of life on influencing a child's intellectual abilities is clear. That has led to efforts to educate parents, children's first teachers, about ways to stimulate brain development from birth. It has also spotlighted the importance of making sure preschools and child care centers have high-quality programs that foster learning.

Initiatives such as these help children enter kindergarten prepared to learn. The first years of formal school are also crucial to brain development and to school success. Most schools offer readiness assessments or issue guidelines for kindergarten readiness. See those in 4-3. These help parents and educators make certain children come to kindergarten with the skills they need for learning.

Kindergarten Readiness Skills
Gross-Motor Skills
• Throws a ball overhand • Jumps forward • Skips • Walks on tiptoe • Rides a tricycle
Fine-Motor Skills
• Holds a crayon or marker correctly • Cuts with scissors • Copies a square and triangle • Completes a puzzle with 10 to 12 pieces
Self-Help Skills
• Dresses self without help • Eats independently • Uses the bathroom without help
Cognitive Skills
• Knows own full name • Speaks in complete sentences of five to six words • Counts to 10 • Knows most colors and some letters • Understands basic concepts such as in/out, front/back, on/off • Can tell a simple story • Sorts items by size, shape, and color • Engages in make-believe play
Social-Emotional Skills
• Plays with a small group of children • Expresses feelings • Developing self-control • Understands right and wrong • Follows directions and rules • Can work independently for a short time • Adapts to changes

4-3
Children who are equipped with these skills are usually ready for kindergarten and prepared to learn.

To maximize the opportunities uncovered by brain research, more children today are attending full-day kindergarten programs. In the past, most programs met for half a day or on alternate days. The effects of full-day schedules are still being studied. It appears that children in these programs develop learning skills that provide a smoother transition into first grade and beyond. Results also suggest long-term learning gains. Educational researchers will continue to evaluate children from both types of programs to determine how to best support young learners.

Children Ages Five to Seven

You only have to walk into a classroom of young children to be convinced about each child's individuality. Every student has a distinct personality and unique combination of interests, abilities, and experiences. Some children cannot sit still, while others are quiet. Some children are comfortable with change, while others are fearful of new experiences.

As a group, five- to seven-year-olds are talkative, imaginative, and great at exploration. They focus on the present rather than the future. They show their feelings through laughs, smiles, and tears. Adult approval is important to them. They are eager to learn. Children at this stage can be sensitive to the needs and feelings of others. In their friendships, they can be cooperative yet competitive.

Physical Growth and Development

Compared to the fast pace of growth from birth through age four, height and weight slows somewhat during the period from ages five to seven. On average, children grow two to three inches and gain four to five pounds per year. Height is primarily influenced by heredity. Weight is also dependent on nutrition and adequate exercise. During this time, children's bodies look longer and leaner. Boys and girls are similar in size.

The toothless smile of a first or second grader is one of the happiest smiles to be found, 4-4. Over a period of several years, each baby tooth falls out and is replaced by a larger permanent one. Additional permanent teeth are added as the child's jaw grows to its adult size.

Gross-Motor Skills

Children at this stage are generally eager to conquer new physical skills. Their gross-motor skills are better developed than their fine-motor skills. Successfully swinging across the bars at recess, throwing a ball, or making a swing fly as high as it will go makes them feel grown-up and independent.

4-4
As physical development continues, first and second graders experience the loss of baby teeth, which are replaced by permanent teeth.

Five- to seven-year-olds are full of energy. Not only can children jump, skip, and hop, but also they can also run fast, dodge objects, and change directions. They can jump over objects, climb trees, and roller skate. These activities build muscle strength and continue to improve balance and coordination. Unfortunately, children this age, lacking the judgment that comes with maturity and experience, also tend to be more fearless. Accidents can happen when they go beyond their abilities.

At this stage, children's visual-motor coordination improves. **Visual-motor coordination** involves matching body movements to coordinate with what is seen. Improvement allows children to learn to jump rope and to catch a small ball.

Fine-Motor Skills

As children practice fine-motor skill activities, their hand-eye coordination and dexterity improve. **Hand-eye coordination** consists of the ability to move the hands precisely in response to what the eyes see. It is a specific type of visual-motor coordination. **Dexterity** is the skillful use of the hands and fingers.

Many fine-motor skills require and build the ability to make precise movements. This is important in accomplishing new tasks, such as writing. Writing combines cognitive development with physical development. For example, printing the letter "D" requires recognizing its shape and understanding it consists of a straight vertical line with a connected curved line to its right. Then a child must be able to reproduce these lines with a pencil or crayon. Only after much practice does the process become automatic. Even then, some children continue to reverse similar letters, such as lowercase "b" and "d."

Consistent improvement in fine-motor skills is evident in many ways. Children draw recognizable objects that become increasingly detailed. They begin from writing individual letters in kindergarten to writing sentences in second grade. Cutting and coloring are mastered. They build elaborate structures. Fine-motor skills help them become more proficient at handheld electronic games as well.

Self-care skills also depend on fine-motor development. Children this age can dress independently, buttoning and zipping clothes and learning to tie their shoes. They handle forks and spoons skillfully and learn to cut most foods with a knife. Some difficult tasks may require the help of an adult.

Cognitive Development

Children at this stage are eager to learn. They are excited about starting school, and they want to do well. Curiosity and a desire for independence drive them. They simply want to understand the world and learn new skills. Succeeding at learning increases their feelings of competence. They believe that they can accomplish what they try to do.

Five- to seven-year-olds have limited attention spans. In school, this means lessons must be fairly concise. Children at this stage learn best through experience, rather than listening to explanations. For example, numbers are more real for kindergarteners when they count actual objects or pictures of them.

Thinking Skills

Between five and seven years of age, children become more logical thinkers. This paves the way for improvements in problem solving, planning, and decision making.

Jean Piaget's experiments highlight these changes in thinking. According to Piaget, five-year-olds are unable to solve logic problems involving conservation. **Conservation** refers to the fact that something can remain the same (its properties are conserved), even if it appears different. Children at this stage are only able to focus on how things appear. For example, a five-year-old believes that a tall, narrow bottle of milk contains more milk than a short, wide bottle, even when shown that the same amount of milk is poured into each. The greater height of the milk in the taller bottle makes it appear as if there is more milk. At about age seven, most children begin to consider multiple aspects of the bottle when solving the same problem. They may take both height and width into account. This is one of the signals of improved thinking skills that indicate a shift in Piaget's concrete operational stage.

The ability to plan is based on understanding a sequence of steps. At the beginning of this stage, most children can follow simple two-step directions. This builds to the understanding of multistep directions by the end of second grade. A first-grade teacher may instruct his students to "put your pencil down and place your paper on my desk." At the end of second grade, a teacher might add "and line up at the door" to that instruction. Children begin to base plans of their own on simple sequences.

Many five- to seven-year-olds love to tell jokes. As their cognitive skills become more sophisticated, they are able to mix words and logic. Humor has various aspects. It can be used positively as a form of self-expression. It can aid cognitive development. Sometimes children also use humor as a coping mechanism, especially when they are uncomfortable. For example, when a classmate is reprimanded, the child's classmates may laugh as a way of distancing themselves from the situation.

Although logical thinking improves during this stage, imagination is still vivid. Children use their creativity and imagination in their drawings and the stories that they create. Sometimes they still confuse fantasy and reality. They may believe that objects, such as a stuffed animal, have feelings.

The use of imagination plays another important role for children. It allows them to express their anxieties and conflicts. For example, acting out roles using action figures or dolls can help a child dramatize situations that are causing feelings, such as fear, sadness, or jealousy.

Language and Reading

Language is composed of symbols that communicate meaning. In earlier years, children make tremendous strides in verbal communication. It continues at this stage as they build language skills and learn to read and write.

Although reading should begin with being read to before starting school, formal reading instruction begins with the identification of alphabet letters, followed by the recognition of the sounds they make. Children learn letter combinations, and then they begin to read whole words. Whole words are combined into sentences and paragraphs. Before long, children are reading books.

Although some children learn to read before entering school, most begin the process during kindergarten and first grade. First and second graders typically make great strides in their reading ability. By the time they reach the end of their second grade year, many children are competent readers enjoying books with chapters.

It is important that children who have difficulty with reading at this stage receive extra help. Sometimes additional one-on-one instruction by the classroom teacher or a reading specialist is enough to help the child catch up with the class. Sometimes testing is needed to determine the specific cause of the problem and identify appropriate intervention strategies. Reading skills are central to future school success so problems cannot be ignored.

Social-Emotional Development

Erik Erikson described the task at this stage as industry versus inferiority. This is the need to develop feelings of competence by learning and mastering new skills. As they can do more for themselves, children's self-confidence grows. They like to feel grown up and often boast about their abilities. However, if often compared negatively to other children, their feelings of inferiority can surface. Parents and teachers play a vital role in providing the encouragement children need.

Peer Relationships

As children move into the world of school, peers play a more important role in their lives. They have "best" friends, but their choice of friends may change often. Sharing secrets, sticking up for each other, choosing partners, and playing together become prominent elements of their friendships, 4-5. New social skills enable them to form closer one-on-one and group relationships. Although boys and girls comfortably play together in

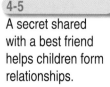

4-5
A secret shared with a best friend helps children form relationships.

preschool, girls usually play with girls and boys usually play with boys in early elementary school.

Family Relationships

What are family relationships like at this stage? In general, children want to please others, especially their parents and other adults. They respond well to established expectations and family rules. Tattling on others is a common way to attract adult attention. Given clear instructions, they are also very capable of completing simple household tasks.

Relationships with siblings vary from helpfulness to arguments, depending on their mood. Boys tend to have more physical fights than girls do.

Self-Concept

Self-concept is a person's own assessment of himself or herself. It is based on an evaluation of personal abilities, successes, failures, and comments from other people. Childhood is a critical time for developing self-concept. Those who see themselves in a positive way, see themselves as capable, worthwhile people and are likely to act in ways that enhance their abilities. Those who develop a negative self-concept often adopt self-defeating behaviors. Once a person's self-concept is established, it can change, but that is a difficult task to achieve.

Erikson's description of the conflict at the stage of industry versus inferiority is linked to self-concept. Children have a drive to learn new skills and become more independent. When adults help them succeed, their sense of competence gives them the self-confidence to keep meeting new challenges and mastering additional skills. They develop the positive self-concept they need to move forward. They are then able to believe in their abilities.

Moral Development

Moral development is most closely related to social-emotional development, although cognitive skills are also a factor. It focuses on decisions about right and wrong as well as how society expects people to interact.

Five- to seven-year-olds can tell the difference between right and wrong. Although their judgments are often based on potential rewards and punishments rather than on universal moral truths or family values, they start to care more about doing the "right" thing. (Review Kohlberg's theory in Chapter 3.) For example, six-year-olds may decide not to steal candy from a store because of fear of being caught. Because of their increased cognitive skills, they are also capable of making up stories to avoid punishment.

An understanding of rules and abiding by them is one aspect of moral development. Children at this stage are able to wait for their turn when playing in a group or on a team. They know how to share toys and often come up with rules for doing so. They do best when activities are based on cooperation, rather than competition. When competition is fierce, they may express anger and jealousy in physical ways. This is a sign that they are not emotionally ready to compete.

Children Ages Eight and Nine

Children ages eight and nine are usually in second through fourth grades. During this time, the newness of starting school is over and the preteen years have not yet begun. Children at this stage have increased skills, greater knowledge and better judgment, resulting in increased independence. Eight-year-olds tend to be more easygoing than children at the age of nine.

Physical Growth and Development

Physical growth among eight- and nine-year-olds shows more individual variation than at younger ages. The primary reason for this is the wide range of ages at which puberty begins. A few children show distinct signs as early as age eight or nine. For others, it may not happen until well into their teen years. Most children at this stage continue to experience steady growth. Girls tend to have slightly larger gains than boys.

Motor Skills

Children's strength increases during this period, allowing improvement in gross-motor skills. Better body control also helps children become more graceful. This makes it a good age for physical activities such as sports, dance, and gymnastics. Physical activities such as these help children build stamina and confidence.

Hand-eye coordination also continues to improve. Children become better at activities that rely on this skill. They can shoot basketballs with more accuracy and learn to play musical instruments, 4-6. They also enjoy electronic games requiring hand-eye coordination and quick reflexes.

Cognitive Development

Children in third and fourth grade face new challenges at school. Their learning becomes more complex. Although most are still eager learners, teachers note that more students have a downturn in interest and enthusiasm. If they fall behind in their studies, they have a more difficult time catching up later, since the pace of learning continues to increase.

4-6
Hand-eye coordination is important in learning to play a band instrument.

Thinking Skills

Improvements in key thinking skills help students cope with greater demands in the classroom. They are able to focus their attention for longer periods of time. Memory improves. This is important for a variety of tasks including remembering math facts, doing well on spelling tests, and retaining content from one lesson to the next.

Eight- and nine-year-olds are in Piaget's concrete operational period (ages 7-11). They continue to learn best through experience with actual objects. However, Piaget's experiments showed that children between the ages of 7 and 11 are learning to think in more complex ways. They are learning to solve problems mentally. Piaget noted development of these important skills during this period:

- **Seriation** is the ability to place objects in order by a characteristic, such as smallest to largest.

- **Classification** is the ability to sort items by one or more characteristics they have in common. Children at this stage are able to identify objects with two or more characteristics, such as separating out all of the small green balls from a group of balls of mixed colors and sizes.

- Conservation (discussed earlier in this chapter) is the ability to understand that a simple change in the shape of an object does not change its amount. (Water poured into a container of a different shape is still the same amount; a ball of clay that is flattened retains the same amount of clay.)

- **Transitivity** is the ability to understand that relationships between two objects can extend to a third object. (If Ashley is taller than Justin, and Justin is taller than Thomas, then Ashley is taller than Thomas.)

Language and Reading

At this stage of development, children's improved thinking skills help boost their reading and writing abilities. In kindergarten through second grade, the emphasis is on learning to read. For third- and fourth-graders, mastery of basic reading skills allows them to focus on understanding and thinking about what they read. Children should be able to recognize most words by sight. This allows them to concentrate on meaning. Their ability to identify main points, summarize, and make predictions continues to improve. They learn new ways to figure out unfamiliar words by using context clues and meanings of prefixes and suffixes. Reading skills help improve writing, and writing improves reading. Reading well depends on practice. Children who are encouraged to read for pleasure are more likely to be good readers. Any student who still has difficulty reading needs extra help to catch up.

Social-Emotional Development

Eight- to nine-year-olds mature rapidly in additional ways. They are often eager, friendly, and responsible. They can also be irritable, critical, and careless. Their improving cognitive skills allow them to complete more complex tasks, such as organizing their clothes. Having responsibilities at home and school gives them a sense of accomplishment, 4-7.

Although praise and encouragement continue to be important, children in this stage begin to be sensitive. They do not want to be talked down to or criticized. They are beginning to appreciate reasonable explanations, since they are becoming more rational thinkers.

Peer Relationships

Socially, eight- and nine-year-olds like to be part of a group. They want to have friends. Children at this age may have a best friend. They look for someone who will share in activities and who will give them acceptance and loyalty. It is at this time in their development that children belong to several groups, such as scouts and a sports team.

Experiences such as these offer children opportunities to develop social skills. Children begin to show empathy and caring at a level that was not before possible. They can also show a lack of compassion and may hurt others, intentionally or unintentionally. Some children are excluded from groups, which may result in bullying problems. At this stage, adults can help children learn important skills by identifying other people's

4-7
Children who learn to care for a pet develop responsibility.

viewpoints, talking through possible courses of action, and offering ideas for resolving conflicts. They can also help children learn how to better understand and express their own feelings.

Family Relationships

Children begin to focus outside their families for ideas and activities. This has an impact on family relationships. They still look up to their parents or guardians, but they are more likely to ignore what they are told or to argue. They don't like to be told what to do and are very sensitive to criticism. They are often at odds with their siblings, particularly those who are close to them in age. Children at this stage are in need of consistent rules and limits.

Self-Concept

At this stage, children desperately want to feel a sense of belonging and that they are competent. This primarily depends on gaining skills, especially at school, and on acceptance by others. At the same time, they are full of doubts; not trying may be a way to cope with fear of failure. Dressing just like everyone else is an attempt to ensure acceptance. Criticizing others may be a way to look better in comparison. Competition is exciting, but it brings with it the possibility of not measuring up. No wonder emotions can be close to the surface.

Moral Development

Eight- and nine-year-olds generally remain in Kohlberg's preconventional level of moral development. They may follow rules selectively, depending on whether they see a benefit in doing so. They sometimes like to make deals, essentially saying, "I will behave if you give me something in return." They do not yet see rules as changeable, but they may not always follow them. At the same time, children this age are concerned about fairness. They complain about rules that seem unfair to themselves or others.

Children Ages 10 to 12

As children move into the next stage, even more changes are in store, usually including the move from elementary to middle school. Children in this age span are in fifth, sixth, and seventh grade. They are often tagged as *preadolescents* or *preteens*. As these terms suggest, they have an interesting and challenging blend of childlike and teen characteristics.

Physical Growth and Development

Individual variation in size and maturity becomes apparent at this stage, 4-8. Some children experience a characteristic growth spurt leading up to puberty. Others maintain the looks and size of children. Most show some early signs of puberty, such as increased sweat production and odor.

Growth can be very uneven. A child's hands or feet may grow to about adult size before the rest of the body catches up. Girls tend to develop ahead of boys, and some tower over most of their male classmates. Depending on how physical changes are timed, this can be a time of uncertainty or a time of growing self-confidence.

4-8
Children between the ages of 10 and 12 can vary considerably in size and maturity.

Motor Skills

Muscle strength and reaction time continue to improve. Most children enjoy active play, and organized sports are popular. Often, it takes trying out a number of activities to find those that match a child's personal interests and natural abilities. Activities that require complex skills are now within reach. Children delight in flashy moves, such as skateboard stunts. However, it can take time after a growth spurt to regain coordination.

Similar gains are made in fine-motor skills. At this stage, children write and draw with more skill. They are able to complete complicated projects, such as designing a clay relief map, paper collage, or clay sculpture. Electronic games both require and improve dexterity.

Cognitive Development

In school, 10- to 12-year-olds face new challenges. The move to middle school means adapting to multiple teachers, more independent learning, and additional homework. Teaching also relies more heavily on verbal explanation. That increases the importance of listening skills and note taking. At this stage, students like to discuss topics. They are better able to work in groups.

Thinking Skills

Children between the ages of 10 and 12 become capable of much more complex thought. They master sequencing and ordering, which are skills needed for math. They move past simple memorization to more complex memorization such as memorization of state capitols. Their short-term memory grows, and experiences make longer lasting impressions.

One of the most significant changes in the way older children think is the development of executive strategies. **Executive strategies** are skills used to solve problems. They include assessing problems, setting goals, and developing a plan to meet goals. They also involve implementing and evaluating solutions.

The ability to use executive strategies opens up a world of possibilities for classroom learning projects. Students enjoy using various methods and materials to solve creative problems. Without guidance and encouragement, some older children struggle with the completion of projects. For example, homework may be finished, but is never turned in.

Language and Reading

When children begin school, they know over 2000 words. For the next couple years, they will learn about 1000 new words per year. By fifth or sixth grade, they are learning about 20 new words a day and will know about 40,000 words.

Preteens use more complex sentences in speech and writing. They can understand grammar and the rules of writing. Most assignments involve writing to gain practice for later grades. They know words have multiple meanings. This is just one of the techniques they employ in jokes and riddles.

At this stage, students are often proficient readers. Many spend hours of free time reading for pleasure. Books of fantasy and adventure are popular.

Reading competence is important for learning now and in the years ahead. Some older children may continue to struggle with reading. However, with assistance, older children who are even now experiencing delays can still become proficient readers.

Social-Emotional Development

The ages of 10, 11, and 12 can be a period of calm or a stormy one. Most older children move back and forth as they struggle to deal with new feelings, problems, and expectations. Preteens see themselves becoming independent. They can be eager to please or have a bad attitude, both in the same day. Because adult relationships are important to them, they can develop strong bonds with their teachers, coaches, or club leaders.

Peer Relationships

The importance of peers continues to grow, 4-9. Children at this stage need to feel accepted by others, as friends and as part of groups. A best friend not only provides companionship, but also someone who can be counted on for support and understanding. Group activities give a sense of belonging.

Most 10-year-olds do not interact much with the opposite gender. By the time they reach age 12, however, that may change. Classroom romances and crushes become more common.

The opinions of peers are valued highly. Fitting in becomes very important, and life is difficult for those who do not. Lack of acceptance may be based on anything from level of physical maturity to poor social skills to lack of the "right" clothes. This makes preteens very vulnerable to peer pressure, and peers can be very critical of others.

At the same time, children at this stage are able to understand the positions or opinions of others. They can be caring, empathetic, and nurturing. This makes them better friends. They also respond enthusiastically to projects that help others, such as food drives for the hungry.

4-9
Communicating with peers is an important part of the social-emotional development of 10- to 12-year-olds.

Family Relationships

While children from 10 to 12 generally respect their parents, parent-child relationships are starting to change. At times, preteens defy parental authority by talking back, ignoring what parents say, or doing things they know that their parents would not approve. At home, as at school, they shift back and forth between cooperation and difficult behavior.

The role of parents is very important at this stage. Even though preteens are more capable, they need their parents' time, understanding, and wisdom. It is also important to keep strong lines of communication open as they move toward adolescence. Teachers also provide a source of adult feedback for many.

Sibling relationships can be pleasant or challenging. Preteens tend to be bossy with younger siblings and annoying to older siblings. At around 12 years of age, moodiness increases, and sibling relationships can become more strained.

Self-Concept

By the end of this stage, boys and girls tend to see themselves as capable of functioning quite well on their own. They fail to see their own limitations. They often define themselves in terms of their appearance, their material possessions, and their involvement in activities.

In the meantime, they deal with many worries, including school failures, family problems, and possibly the loss of a loved one. They may worry about world events and natural disasters. Socially, fear may be demonstrated in argumentative, aggressive, or apprehensive behaviors. Preteens often confide in friends, rather than parents, even though the quality of the advice they receive may be questionable.

The terror of rejection is strong. Preteens often become very self-conscious, particularly toward the end of this period. They feel as if everyone notices even the smallest of differences. Riding in their family's older car, a new haircut, wearing less than the latest fad, or an overly enthusiastic greeting from a parent can all cause embarrassment.

Moral Development

Questions about right and wrong become more of an issue at this stage. A number of influences are at work.

Some children are still in Kohlberg's preconventional stage of morality. They still base decisions on the possibility of reward or punishment. If you cheat on a test, you may be rewarded with a higher grade or punished by being caught. Others have moved to Kohlberg's conventional stage of morality. They tend to make moral decisions based on the desire to be perceived as "good" or "bad." Some decisions are based on rules or laws. School rules forbid cheating. "Good" students do not cheat. Unfortunately, some children at this stage have accepted a label of "bad." They base their behavior on this label.

At the same time, preadolescents often begin to question some of their parents' values. This, if combined with negative peer pressure, can lead to experimentation with alcohol, drugs, smoking, or sexual behavior. For a few, crimes like shoplifting and burglary may seem like exciting challenges.

For parents and teachers, this stage can be challenging. Preadolescents want and need guidance, but they do not always accept it. Since they are so sensitive to criticism, it can be hard to offer suggestions. Preteens need to learn to make and live with their own decisions, but they often tackle ones that they are unequipped to handle alone. They need more independence, but too much, or lack of supervision can lead them into serious trouble. The emphasis needs to be on helping children choose good friends, adopt strong values, and develop the social skills to withstand negative peer pressure.

Summary

Most children begin formal school with kindergarten at about age five. In order to have a successful experience, they need to have developed a wide range of skills before that time.

Children from five to seven grow at a steady pace. They are enthusiastic learners, which helps them develop physical, social-emotional, and cognitive skills. Doing so helps them build positive self-esteem.

Children ages eight and nine are settled into elementary school and may show less enthusiasm. Children continue to gain more control over small muscles and fine-motor skills. There is more emphasis on friends.

Children ages 10 to 12 have both traits of childhood and adolescence. Some are entering puberty whereas others are squarely in childhood. They are capable of much more complex thought. The opinions of peers are also valued highly and fitting in becomes very important.

Review

1. What is a developmental delay? Why is it important to respond promptly when one is suspected?

2. Why is stimulating brain development prior to kindergarten important?

3. Give an example of a fine-motor skill that requires hand-eye coordination and dexterity. Explain how the example fits these criteria.

4. Identify at least three things a child must know or be able to do in order to draw a recognizable picture (specifically a house).

5. How does a child's ability to understand a logic problem that involves conservation change between age five and age 11?

6. How does children's sensitivity to criticism relate to Erikson's explanation of the task for this stage of industry versus inferiority?

7. Parents generally dislike it when their children argue with them. How is disagreeing with parents a normal sign of development?

8. Explain how writing a two-page report on some aspect of whales would require the use of at least three executive strategies.

9. Give an example of positive peer pressure and of negative peer pressure that a 10- to 12-year-old might experience.

10. What shift in moral development occurs for some preteens?

Reflect

1. Much emphasis is placed on making sure children enter kindergarten with the skills they need to learn. Choose eight kindergarten-readiness skills from 4-3. As a kindergarten teacher, how would you explain to parents why each of these skills is important?

2. Electronic games have become very popular with young children. Analyze the possible positive or negative impact of frequent game use on each of the following: physical fitness, motor skill development, cognitive development, and social skills.

3. What were the popular fads when you were in elementary school? How were these used as status symbols?

4. Children are very attuned to criticism and praise. Identify something from your own childhood that a peer or adult said to or about you that you still remember today. What was said? Who said it? Why do you think this has stuck with you? How has it influenced your life?

Act

1. Develop a demonstration, for example, to teach a five-year-old how to tie shoes. Begin by identifying the steps involved. Then figure out what you would say and do to demonstrate each step. Pair up with a classmate, and take turns being the "teacher" and "child." Combine the best from each of your plans to present to the class.

2. Ask a librarian for help in choosing a book that would be appropriate for a second grade student and one for a fourth grader. Read the two books. Evaluate how they differ in terms of story, language, length, and difficulty. What did you learn about the development of reading skills from this process?

3. Work in groups to develop a list of the specific social skills a child needs to develop to get along well with peers. Identify ways a teacher could help promote two of these skills.

4. Watch a children's show on television. What is the target age group of the show? Why would it appeal to children that age? What values, positive or negative, were portrayed? What commercials, if any, were shown with the program? Explain why you would or would not recommend this show to parents.

Add to Your Portfolio

Observation is a great technique for learning about children and teaching. Find a place where you can observe parents and children interacting. This may be in a mall, a playground, a children's interactive museum, or your own home. Make notes about what you see. Look for a verbal exchange between a parent and child, preferably about the child's behavior. (This does not need to be lengthy.) Record what the parent said and the child's verbal and nonverbal responses. Also note the circumstances of the observation (date, time, place, and situation) and the child's approximate age. As soon as possible, use your notes to write a factual account of what you saw. Then, write your comments. For example, comment on the effectiveness of the adult response and describe it as positive, negative, productive, or counter productive. Ask for your teacher's feedback. Make any appropriate revisions, and add the observation to your portfolio.

5 THE TEEN YEARS: GROWTH AND DEVELOPMENT

Key Terms

puberty

growth spurts

asynchrony

egocentrism

metacognition

neural connections

multitasking

autonomy

resilience

invincibility

Objectives

After studying this chapter, you will be able to

- **compare** the rate of growth during adolescence to previous periods of development.

- **analyze** the thinking skills commonly required of teens in school.

- **identify** the social skills teens need to develop for adult success and devise strategies for teaching one such skill.

- **identify** the impact of various influences that impact teens' development of personal values.

Tim Jeffers watched students stream into the building for freshman orientation with a mixture of interest, amusement, and empathy. He had been asked to give a welcoming speech as a representative of the faculty.

They were all sizes and shapes. Some students arrived in groups, chatting animatedly, but sticking close together. Others came alone, seeming to know no one and trying to be invisible. Their conversations ranged from bragging to answering questions with only a nod, but it was apparent to Tim that most of his incoming students were very self-conscious.

It didn't seem that long ago that he had been part of that group, although he might well have been overlooked. He still winced when he saw his middle school graduation picture. He was the shortest boy in class. Most of his peers didn't make remarks probably because he was funny, athletic, and a good student. He loved baseball and hoped to play in high school. It seemed like a reasonable hope. His older brother matured early, almost needing to shave in eighth grade. Mr. Jeffers had imagined himself as a power hitter on the freshman baseball team. When the time came, he was too small to even have a chance of making the team.

He actually didn't start growing until his sophomore year. It seemed like he waited forever for his parents to complain that they couldn't keep him in clothes. He grew four inches a year as a sophomore, junior, and senior, plus another three inches in college. Now, at six feet four, he towered over his older brother. He wished that instead of making a formal speech that day, he could whisper in the ear of every undersize freshman, "Don't give up. Your time will come!"

Few birthdays are as anticipated as the thirteenth birthday. Officially becoming a teen seems to open the door to the promise of independent adulthood. In fact, the road is longer and bumpier than it seems at the time.

Teens in the age span from 13 through 18, the focus of this chapter, typically begin adolescence in middle school or junior high. Overall, this is a time of tremendous growth and development. During this period, physical, cognitive, social-emotional, and moral development are significantly interrelated. Seemingly ordinary situations and events may be influenced by what is happening in all of these areas. The reverse is also true. Where teens are in their development influences how they deal with situations and events.

When learning about development, it is important to remember that it is a process that occurs over time. Individuals move through development at their own pace, 5-1. In some cases, they move forward, and then they seem to regress a bit before again making any strides. Although teens

5-1
Remember that teens develop at their own unique pace.

of a particular age or stage may typically have certain characteristics, not all do. That does not mean that those who do not match averages are not normal. There is just a great deal of variation to what is considered normal for teens.

You may recognize yourself or people you know in some of the information about adolescent development. Understanding development is relevant because each stage of development influences the abilities of teens and their interactions. This, in turn, affects teaching and learning. As you learn more, also keep in mind how various aspects of development impact how teachers teach and how learners learn.

Physical Growth and Development

The rate of physical growth and development from ages 13 through 18 is second only to infancy. This is linked to **puberty**, the physical transformation from a child to an adult capable of reproduction. This process begins when the *pituitary gland*, located at the base of the brain, signals the *endocrine system* to release specific *hormones*.

Teens usually welcome this growth as a signal of maturity. However, it also brings challenging adjustments.

Understanding Adolescent Growth and Development

Growth during *adolescence* is marked by **growth spurts**, rapid increases in height and weight. Adolescents can grow as much as three to four inches in a year. Significant weight gains increase both muscle mass and fat tissue.

Growth does not always occur in an orderly way. Growth usually begins with the feet and hands, followed by legs and arms. The arms and legs often grow at different rates. A young teen, for example, may have long legs and short arms, or the reverse. This is called **asynchrony**. In early adolescence, teens often look and feel uncoordinated because of rapid changes in their body proportions.

In addition to changes in size, hormone shifts trigger sexual development. Much of this takes place internally, but there are a variety of external signs, as well. For example, breast development in females begins by about ages 12 to 13 (some as early as 10 or 11). Many girls also begin their periods, although it is not unusual to begin later. Because menstrual cycles are just beginning, they may be unpredictable. On average, boys do not experience a growth spurt until around the age of 14. One characteristic sign of development is when a male's voice begins to change, often called "cracking."

Growth continues even after sexual maturity is reached. Females may gain an inch or two of height in a year. Males, with their later growth pattern, have larger gains in height and still experience significant weight gains. Their physical growth continues until about age 21. Males' shoulders broaden. They build more muscle mass. During these years, the heart doubles in size and lung capacity greatly increases, giving both females and males greater strength and endurance.

Coping with Physical Changes

The timing of puberty is highly individual. It is influenced by a number of factors including heredity, environment, and gender. Girls, as a group, mature before boys. That variability, as well as coping with the process itself, can cause real anxiety. Those who develop early must deal with being out of sync with their classmates. Sometimes adults perceive them as older and have unrealistic expectations. Those who develop late feel left behind. They often fear something is wrong with them and feel conspicuous. At some point in the process most teens wonder if they are normal.

Young teens are dealing with changing bodies and unfamiliar feelings. In fact, during this period, teens seem to see themselves as the main character on the stage of life. They believe that everyone is watching them. This is called the *imaginary audience*. Their own self-consciousness leads them to assume that everyone is paying attention to them.

Since they think that everyone is watching, young teens are often excessively focused on how they appear to others. Are they dressed right? Are they saying the right things? With their strong desire to fit in, they are painfully self-conscious. They hate being compared with others or embarrassed. This self-focus is often called **egocentrism**.

At this age, body image is a major concern. Many young teens worry excessively about their size and shape. Media images feed this concern. Models and stars, whose images are often electronically enhanced, rarely represent achievable reality. For girls, seeing overly thin models at a time when they are sensitive about normal weight gains often leads to dieting, 5-2. Dieting due to

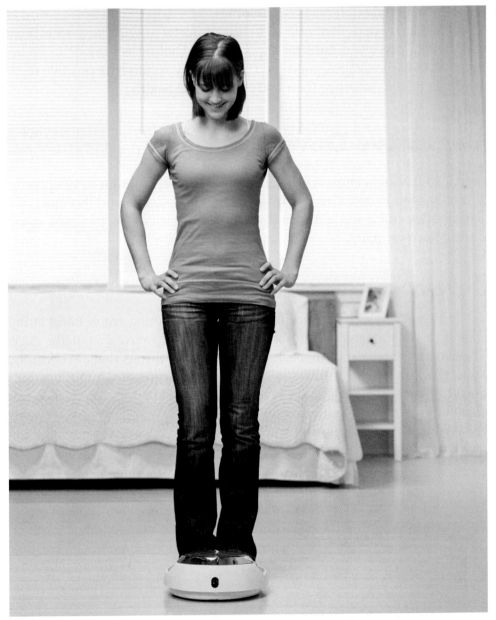

5-2
Concern about body image leads some teens to constantly monitor their weight.

a negative body image can lead to unhealthy habits. Since an increasing number of teens are significantly overweight, many may resort to unsafe and ineffective dieting methods. Their diets already tend to be deficient in calcium needed for bone growth and iron. For both females and males, there is an increased risk of developing serious eating disorders. This increases the probability of related health problems, in addition to negative body image. In addition, some, particularly male athletes, use dangerous anabolic steroids to gain strength and body mass. These, too, can cause permanent physical damage.

By early high school, fewer teens are focused on development, but most remain very concerned about their personal appearance and attractiveness. They spend a great deal of time on grooming, exercising, experimenting with new hairstyles, and choosing clothes.

Older teens may continue to be uncomfortable with how well their body meets perceived cultural expectations. Dieting continues to be an issue. As in earlier stages, good food choices and exercise are positive steps teens can take to improve their body image and health.

Cognitive Development

During adolescence, significant changes occur in brain development. You only need to consider the differences in knowledge and thoughts of a sixth grader and a student in college to get an idea of the progress made during the teen years.

Developing Abstract Thinking

In Piaget's theory of cognitive development, young teens stand at the edge of a stage change. They have been in the *concrete operational stage*. Their thoughts have mainly been limited to those things that are concrete, those that can be experienced with the senses. Teens begin to move into Piaget's *formal operational stage*. This means that they gradually become able to think in more abstract terms.

Abstract thinking is a powerful tool. It includes a variety of skills including the following abilities:

- to grasp abstract concepts such as honor and freedom

- to think about the future

- to consider multiple solutions to problems and the potential consequences of each

- to figure out why things are the way they are

- to understand complex math problems
- to think critically about a person's own thinking, a process called **metacognition**.

It is important to remember that younger teens are just beginning to develop abstract thinking skills. Most of the time, they still use concrete thinking. Teachers can use various types of activities to help teens learn and practice abstract thinking.

As they move into high school, most teens become more skilled at complex thinking skills. They are systematic, rational problem solvers. They can identify and analyze multiple options. They enjoy trying new ideas and possibilities.

By the time teens reach older adolescence, they are better able to solve problems. They can plan, organize, and schedule their own time. They become better decision makers.

Understanding the Adolescent Brain

The ability to precisely document brain activity is a relatively new research tool. It has yielded findings that have significantly altered scientists' understanding of the brain. One outcome has been evidence that the teen years are a window of opportunity for boosting lifetime cognitive ability. **Neural connections**, the links between brain cells, can be strengthened through activities that repeatedly stimulate the brain. For example, when teens engage in the thinking required by challenging classes, playing a musical instrument, or participating in a sport, they are strengthening the brain's ability to function swiftly and effectively. Taking advantage of opportunities to increase the brain's functioning during adolescence can have long-term benefits, 5-3. On the flip side, inactivity wastes this opportunity. Activities such as alcohol use at an age while the brain is still developing can permanently injure the brain.

Adults have long observed the unpredictable emotions and behaviors of young teens. Some days they act like kids, while other days they act more like adults. In the past, these swings in behavior were primarily blamed on hormonal changes. Today, scientists believe that brain development also plays a significant role in this as well. They also seem to think it plays a role in language learning.

Researchers have also found that development continues in some parts of the brain into early adulthood. (Learning, of course, continues throughout life.) Regulation of emotions and impulse control are two areas not fully developed in early adolescence. Younger teens are often thought of as immature, and adults often say, "Act your age." When in fact, their behavior matches their abilities.

5-3
When teens engage in complex activities, they strengthen the neural connections in the brain.

Meeting School Challenges

Young teens in their final years of middle school or junior high are usually curious and anxious to use their new intellectual abilities. They continue to learn best through activities, especially those linked to real life. They like opportunities to work with others.

Beginning high school brings significant new intellectual challenges. Most teens understand that doing well in high school is important to future career options and success. The pace of learning is rapid, and students are expected to be more independent learners. Classes require more complex thinking, including participation in class discussions. Teens can plan and carry out tasks and projects. They are able to research topics and summarize their findings.

By the last years of high school, classes increasingly require abstract thinking. Teens often juggle many things at once including school, work, outside activities, and friends.

Many students' academic performance actually declines during adolescence. Some declines are due to the many distractions and concerns in other aspects of their lives as possible reasons. Researchers are also evaluating the impact of **multitasking**, or trying to do many things at the same time. Most teens would say they can listen to music, text, check their online profile, and write an essay for tomorrow's class at the same time. However, the evidence shows that lack of focus is bound to make writing that essay take longer and lower its quality.

Setting Goals for the Future

In the early teen years, students know they must eventually choose a career path, but their ideas often change. In fact, most know about a fairly limited number of career areas. Learning more about options and opportunities, along with assessing their strengths and interests, can help them begin to sort out career possibilities.

Students in the early years of high school begin to think seriously about career goals, or at least the short-term future. They often hear from parents and teachers about the importance of doing well in high school classes. As teens mature, their improved thinking skills make them better able to understand the long-term effects of their decisions. At the same time, teens this age think in ways that can distort and inflate their opinion of themselves and their own importance. They may believe that they are on their way to becoming a film star, a major league baseball player, or a recording artist. This is called a *personal fable*. Until this phase passes, they may not be realistic in their career plans.

For older teens, the question of what they will do after high school is much more immediate. Is college a goal? Is occupational training a good idea? Will they seek employment? Teachers, school counselors, employers, parents, and other adults play an important role in helping teens navigate the decisions being made during this stage, but ultimately the goals must be the teens' own. The possibilities and importance of these decisions can seem overwhelming.

Social-Emotional Development

As you might expect, major physical changes, combined with brain development, play out in relationships and emotions. Teens are defining who they are as independent individuals. The importance and characteristics of various relationships also undergo changes. The movement toward greater independence increases the importance of relationships with peers and often puts strains on parent-teen relationships. At the end of this period, older teens are more secure in their personal identity and becoming more independent and self-reliant. They can better analyze their own social interactions and those of others.

Redefining Self

As abstract thinking skills develop, young teens begin to question who they are. They work to establish a personal identity, independent of their parents. This is a natural step in the move toward adulthood. Erickson called this quest for identity the most important task of adolescence.

Part of this new identity requires seeing oneself as a male or female. Teens get very conflicting messages about sexual identity and what it means. Media messages are everywhere and are often at odds with those from parents, religion, and a teen's cultural heritage. The issues go beyond how males and females should present themselves. They also include what roles, expectations, rights, and responsibilities are linked to gender. Sexual identity is usually established by the end of the teen years.

All this happens at a time when young teens are extremely self-conscious, 5-4. They base their feelings of worth on their popularity and how they think their peers perceive them. Adults can help young teens develop a positive self-concept based on teens' unique qualities. They can provide positive feedback and emphasize teens' strengths. They can help them learn alternative ways to analyze what is happening in their lives. They can also encourage teens to take part in activities that provide satisfaction and success.

5-4

Teens can be very self-conscious about their looks and how others perceive them.

By early high school, teens try out different roles and integrate opinions of others in formulating their sense of self. These years are the prime time for experimentation with likes and dislikes, values and beliefs, educational and occupational goals, and role expectations.

Older teens are more self-assured. They have fewer self-doubts. They have a better understanding of who they are and what roles they play. However, a sense of self-identity is not completely achieved in adolescence. Most people continue to redefine themselves well into early adulthood.

Moving Toward Independence

In addition to brain development and maturity, the hormones that drive the body's push toward physical maturity also set in motion the drive for **autonomy**—independence that includes personal responsibility and decision making. Teens must become individuals, less dependent on their families. They must develop a personal identity with their own beliefs and goals. Their increasing cognitive abilities help them with this process.

In addition to seeking peer approval, young teens begin to look to adults outside the family for acceptance and advice. They need role models. Teachers often fill these needs, but it is essential that teens realize the importance of those roles. They have opportunities to help students over the rough spots and point them in the right direction, but this comes with real responsibilities, as well. Teachers are responsible for modeling adult coping skills for teens. Teachers should be supportive and provide information about resources and how to access them.

Establishing independence and autonomy from others, especially family, is an important part of establishing identity. Early in high school, teens tend to have the most conflicts with parents and other adult authority figures. They spend less time at home. They are also less likely than younger or older teens to confide in their parents. Breaking rules and accepted standards are often statements of independence that can sometimes have irreparable consequences. Therefore, teens still need parents to clearly explain their own values and the reasons for having them.

During high school, teens still need rules and limits that are applied consistently. However, those limits should gradually loosen as teens show that they are ready for additional independence. They can do so by proving that they are reliable and trustworthy. The freedom to make decisions helps them become better decision makers. They will make mistakes, but need to learn from them.

Older teens often have better decision-making skills. They take pride in their increased ability to be responsible. Although very capable, many older teens are still inconsistent about getting things done.

Gaining independence is just beginning in the late teen years. At this time, they are building the many skills needed to become self-sufficient adults.

Older teens typically feel like they have reached the stage of full maturity. As a result, they expect to be treated as adults, especially in day-to-day decisions. However, as they move into the wider world after high school and are faced with new, complex issues, that confidence often lessens.

Refining Relationships

During adolescence, the relationships teens have with others changes significantly. For children, parental and family relationships provide a stable base for life. With teens' emerging abilities to think critically, and the corresponding push toward independence, the importance of various types of relationships changes. Peer relationships, including those with the opposite sex, take on much more importance. Relationships with authority figures, especially parents, often become more strained.

Peer Relationships

The shift in peer relationships begins during early adolescence. Having friends gives a sense of belonging. Peer relationships can help emotional development, too. Teens bounce ideas off of one another in ways they would hesitate to do with family members.

For younger teens, popularity is very important and is usually measured by the number of friends a teen has. This makes the opinions of peers especially important. Making a mistake in class, tripping, or even having a blemish can feel like a major disaster. On a more serious level, the desire for acceptance often overrides the need to follow rules, meet parental or teacher expectations, or live up to personal values. For example, an otherwise caring teen may go along with a group's hurtful decision to exclude certain people. Teens tend to blame such lapses on the group, rather than taking personal responsibility.

For young teens, being friends with popular classmates can seem important. Other friendships are usually formed because of some similar interest. This may be a common taste in music or clothes, or a specific sport or other activity. Teens begin to have various types of friends, ranging from casual to close. Friendships at this stage still change with some frequency. It takes time and experience to develop mature relationship skills.

Early in high school, teens are still very influenced by peers. They tend to follow friends' tastes, and fads are quite common. They may ask their parents or other adults for advice about values, education, and long-term plans but do not necessarily follow the advice.

Older teens are able to develop friendships with peers that are close and more long lasting. They begin to place less value on appearance when choosing friends and more value on personality, character, and common interests. They often are loyal and care deeply about their friends.

Extracurricular activities provide opportunities for teens of all ages to meet new people and develop social skills. They make new friends, both male and female. Such activities can enhance a sense of social acceptance and may also provide leadership opportunities.

The wide availability of electronic communication is changing the way people interact. Chart 5-5 poses some questions about the impact of these devices on personal relationships.

Romantic Relationships

When the teen years begin, teens are at various stages of puberty and social development. That translates into different levels of interest in the opposite sex. For many young teens, shyness, awkwardness, and fear of rejection are obstacles. Others may show few concerns.

Among young teens, socializing in groups is common. Males still primarily cluster with males and females with females, even in mixed-group activities. There is some pairing off, influenced by differences in physical development and what they see in the media. Teens who are 15 and 16 are more comfortable in mixed gender groups than they were in early adolescence. Group dating is common although some choose to form couple relationships. It is not unusual for girls to date older boys. Older teens still enjoy group social activities, but some are in dating relationships. Some teens become sexually active. Most, realizing the risks involved or conflicts with their personal values, decide to delay sexual relationships, 5-6.

Relationships in the Digital Age
Teens today live in a world where personal communication is almost instantaneous and always available. With the touch of a few buttons, they can communicate with someone around the world as easily as with the person in the next seat. The possibilities seem to expand all the time. This revolution is changing the nature of relationships. Consider the following:
• When people text rather than talk, how does it change the way they communicate?
• How does being constantly available to others impact relationships? Other aspects of life?
• What are the positives and negatives of social networking sites?
• How likely are people to do or say things electronically that they would not say in person?
• How are people without easy access to such technology impacted?
• What restrictions, if any, does your school place on electronic devices? If you were an administrator, how would you change the rules and why?
• Do you know individuals who have been harmed by misuse of this technology? How?

5-5
The digital age is redefining many aspects of relationships.

5-6
Couple relationships begin to develop during the teen years.

In their eagerness for acceptance and love, some teens stay in relationships that are hurtful. They may be the recipients of put-downs, demeaning remarks, controlling behavior, or even violence. Such teens may feel love for the abuser, become convinced that they deserve such treatment, or be afraid to break off the relationship. Such situations are actually emotionally or physically abusive. The abuser may not mean to cause hurt but may lack the skills needed for an appropriate relationship. No one, especially a teen, should stay in such a relationship. Providing love is not enough to bring about change. In addition, accepting such a situation sets the teen up to accept other abusive relationships.

Family Relationships

The teen years are difficult for parents, as well as for teens. With children, parents employ a variety of methods to ensure their safety. They enforce rules, oversee play, teach appropriate behavior, and supervise their actions. In order for teens to learn the skills they need to become independent adults, parents must gradually give them more freedom and less supervision. In doing so, they know their teens will make some poor choices, and poor choices can cause teens harm, even serious harm. It is the nature of teens to constantly push for more independence. They complain about restrictions. It is parents' responsibility to set guidelines that strike a balance between the need for safety and the need for developing independence.

At the same time, the increasing influence of peers, combined with the ability to think more critically, can lead teens to question or reject the views and values of their family. During adolescence, teens must identify their own values and formulate their own ideas. In the end, the values and ideas often look much like those of their parents. Questioning is part of the process. In the meantime, parents are concerned about the choices their children will make.

Dealing with Emotional Challenges

Adolescence is sometimes described as an emotional rollercoaster. Some teens experience a wilder ride than others. It can be a confusing and difficult time, and teens often experience a great deal of anxiety. Causes can range from size or looks to falling behind at school or problems with relationships. Family difficulties, whether they are normal parent-teen conflicts or more serious issues, bring added stress.

Methods of coping vary. Having a good friend, teen or adult, to listen can be helpful. Sports and activities can be good outlets for stress. Some teens keep diaries or journals. Another positive way of coping is developing **resilience**. This means being able to bounce back after a defeat or setback. Others adopt coping behaviors that are self-defeating. Alcohol and other drugs, reckless driving, and sex may seem like escapes, but they only make problems worse. Some teens lash out in violence or seek a substitute family in a gang. Sudden weight loss, not sleeping, a steep decline in grades, prolonged sadness, uncontrolled anger, or lack of interest in life can all be signs that someone needs help. Notifying a counselor or other person in authority can help turn someone's life around. It is better to be wrong in thinking a problem exists than to fail to reach out for help.

Moral Development

Moral development undergoes major changes during the teen years. As cognitive and social-emotional development occurs, teens' beliefs about right and wrong and what is fair and right continue to evolve.

As younger teens move from concrete to more abstract thinking, they begin to think in all-or-nothing terms. This type of thinking may affect moral reasoning. For example, when taking a political view, moral thinking tends to take on a strong stance with no room for variances or exceptions. The concepts of justice and equality become intriguing.

Young teens are just beginning to make moral decisions based on universal principles. Kohlberg termed this *postconventional morality*. Teens may begin to believe that it is wrong to cheat or steal because it is morally wrong. Previously, they may have based that decision on whether or not they were likely to be caught, perceived in a certain way, or breaking rules. However, the transformation is far from complete. Most young adolescents still struggle about whether to report a friend for breaking a rule or law, such as cheating on a test or shoplifting.

Teens have a tendency to see moral decisions in all-or-nothing terms. For example, it is typical for middle teens to label inconsistencies seen in adults as "hypocrisy." Older teens are able to see that many situations do require consideration. They are often idealistic and concerned about their personal impact on the world. They can embrace moral issues with conviction.

Establishing Personal Values

One of the most important tasks of adolescence is development of personal values and a related code of conduct. During childhood, parents must help their children learn positive values and appropriate behavior. Children respond, but they do so mainly to get approval and praise from their parents and other adults. During adolescence, teens must decide for themselves the type of people they will be. This involves evaluating, choosing, and committing to specific values and ideals.

This is not a quick or easy process. It also takes place at a time when so much else is going on in teens' lives.

Establishing values begins with questioning existing ones. Teens' increasing ability to analyze and reason causes them to reexamine their parents' and society's beliefs, rules, and laws. This can be a difficult period for parents. Teens sometimes seem to ignore all that they have been taught about right and wrong. They want and need to understand the reasons behind their parents' beliefs, but teens tend to push them away as a result of their arguments.

To teens, everything often seems contradictory. Media portray a "think of yourself first" lifestyle as personally rewarding. At the same time, teens are developing more empathy and find real satisfaction in helping others, such as through service projects.

Ultimately, teens must consider what kind of adult they want to be. What are their personal goals? Many look to role models, people who have the characteristics they would like to show. Even role models change with more maturity. For a 13-year-old, it may be the latest star. For a 17-year-old, it is more likely to be someone with true character.

Understanding Risk-Taking Behaviors

In early and middle adolescence, teens simply don't believe anything bad will happen to them, regardless of what they do. They think they will never become addicted to smoking or drugs. That only happens to others. This is a feeling of **invincibility**, which means feeling incapable of being defeated or having anything bad happen. This is linked to the personal fable that makes them believe they will be rich and famous.

With more independence and outside influences, including media, there are many opportunities for teens to take risks. Teens complain about parents who check up on them. It is without this supervision that problems are more likely to arise. Many of problems can have serious, long-term consequences.

Many 15- and 16-year-olds are likely to engage in high-risk behaviors. Many teens at this age get a driver's license and have access to a vehicle, 5-7. The combination of lack of driving experience, speeding, and feelings of

5-7
Teens who avoid high-risk behaviors are often responsible drivers.

invincibility can lead to highly dangerous situations. Too often, alcohol and peer pressure are added to the mix. Accidents are the leading cause of death among teens, and most involve vehicles. Another common scenario is participating in unprotected sex while believing that pregnancy or infection will not occur.

High-risk behaviors are more common in later adolescence than ever before. Unlike younger teens, older teens begin to feel more vulnerable and realize that they are mortal. Older teens usually are very informed about the risks of substance abuse. Likewise, they know the risks of unprotected sex include unplanned pregnancy, HIV-AIDS, and other sexually transmitted infections. They have the ability to make informed choices. Why, then, is participation in high-risk behaviors so high? Partly, the increase comes from added independence. Partly, it comes from a greater ease in availability. Older teens want control over more aspects of their life and sometimes engaging in high-risk behaviors gives them a sense of control and independence from society.

Scientists think that brain development may play a role in risk-taking behavior. Even though most brain development is completed by the end of the teen years, some parts of the brain are still developing into adulthood. These include those that regulate judgment, self-control, and emotions. This may mean that teens are not as capable of making as good decisions as they think they are.

Researchers have identified other characteristics associated with teens who are more likely to engage in high-risk behaviors. Those with low self-esteem and those who struggle in school fall into that category. Negative peer influence is a risk factor. Also teens from families with less parent-teen communication and lack of parental supervision are more likely to take risks.

Engaging in high-risk behaviors can have life-altering consequences. Teen pregnancy, a serious car crash due to drinking, drug dependency, and HIV do happen to teens. It takes more than luck to avoid becoming a statistic. Teens need to set clear goals for their future. They know what types of behavior carry high risks and must think through the pros and cons of each in terms of their personal goals and values. Deciding their personal limits before situations actually arise can help them make appropriate decisions when they are under pressure. Many find that preparing an answer for why they choose not to take part in such behaviors helps them deal more easily with difficult situations. Such decision making, planning, and follow through show real maturity in action.

Summary

The growth and development associated with puberty significantly change the size, shape, and functioning of a teen's body. These changes are often difficult to handle.

Teens enter the stage that Piaget termed as formal operational. Significant changes in the brain allow abstract thinking. This allows teens to handle more difficult subjects in school and plan for future careers.

Perhaps the greatest changes in adolescence occur in social-emotional development. Teens must redefine who they are as individuals, develop the skills they will need as independent adults, and form new relationships. Dealing with the many changes and challenges related to development make this a difficult time emotionally for some.

During adolescence, teens decide which values they will adopt as their own. This process can cause conflicts with the family. In addition, teens often engage in risk-taking behaviors. Some of these have potentially serious consequences.

Review

1. How does the rate of growth during adolescence compare with that during childhood? During infancy?

2. What is the impact of wide variations in the timing of teen growth and development on late-developing teens?

3. Do younger teens have the ability to think abstractly? What can teachers do?

4. What type of thinking is related to metacognition?

5. Give an example of an activity that would help a teen take advantage of the window of opportunity in brain development. Explain why your choice would do so.

6. How can adults help young teens develop a positive self-concept?

7. What aids teens in the process of autonomy?

8. Based on what you have learned about teens at different stages (young teens, those in early high school, and those in the last years of high school), which are most likely to bend to peer pressure and why?

9. What is postconventional morality? Give an example of a decision that a teen might make showing use of postconventional morality.

10. Give at least two reasons adults have valid concerns about teens' risk-taking behaviors.

Reflect

1. What messages do teens receive most from the media about what is considered "normal" behavior? Which messages do you think have the greatest impact and why?

2. The section on family relationships includes a list of parental characteristics that match teens' needs. Using that list as a basis, add at least five additional characteristics. Then consider which of these characteristics could also apply to teens. Be prepared to share your reasoning.

3. Identify common causes of stress for teens. Are all related to problems? What are some practical techniques for stress reduction?

4. If even older teens' brains have not yet fully developed in terms of judgment, self-control, and emotions, what implications does that have for the ways parents and teachers give teens more independence? What responsibilities do teens have if this is true?

5. Develop a list of things teachers should remember about teens that would help them teach more effectively. Put your statements in a form that you would find constructive if you were a teacher.

Act

1. Write an open letter to preteens giving advice that you think would be helpful as they enter adolescence. You might include topics such as dealing with worries about appearance, making friends, dealing with peer pressure, and improving relationships with parents. Use a standard letter format.

2. Using a textbook from one of your classes, find examples of 10 questions or activities that require abstract thinking. Write each question or activity on a separate file card. In class, work with classmates to group the cards according to the specific abstract thinking skills required. Which skills occurred most often? Discuss whether such questions and activities generate more learning than other types.

3. Identify at least eight social skills teens need to develop or improve to function effectively in the adult world. Choose one of these skills. Develop an activity that would help teens learn the skill. Write a plan for the activity, identifying the skill, what students will learn, and specific information on how you would present the activity.

4. When deciding on personal values, teens are subject to a variety of influences. Develop a questionnaire to find out which influences really have the most impact. If possible, work with your teacher to arrange for a group of teens to complete the questionnaire anonymously and review the results. Do they match your predictions?

Add to Your Portfolio

School counselors provide a variety of services to students. Use online and print resources to find the following:

- the requirements to become a school counselor in your state

- the main responsibilities of a counselor at the middle school, junior high, or high school levels

- the employment outlook for school counselors.

Compile your findings in a written report. In addition, find out more about the work of a school counselor through one of the following: a job-shadowing experience, interviewing a school counselor, or listening to a presentation by a counselor. Prepare a written summary of the experience. Include a section about whether or not you would consider being a school counselor and why.

Add these materials to your portfolio.

UNIT 3: THE SCHOOL

6 THE EARLY HISTORY OF EDUCATION IN AMERICA

Key Terms

apprentice

dame schools

hornbook

common schools

normal schools

McGuffey readers

Progressives

Montessori method

career and technical education

disposable income

quotas

Objectives

After studying this chapter, you will be able to

- **give examples** of how education during the American Colonial Period reflected local culture and beliefs.

- **trace changes** in the preparation, roles, and status of teachers over time.

- **describe** how educational opportunities changed from colonial times forward.

- **analyze** how key people in early education reform responded to concerns of the time.

- **research** how education developed in your community.

Have you ever wondered how schools came to be the way they are today? Who decided which subjects should be taught? Where did textbooks originate? Has school attendance always been required? In the next two chapters, you will learn more about the history of schools in America. That history is divided into periods characterized by historical events and social trends that have significantly affected education.

The early history of education in America formed the foundation for things to come. From the time of the first immigrants to the Great Depression, a system of free public education by qualified teachers developed. Education had to adapt as the world changed significantly.

Looking back is more than an interesting exercise in history. How American schools developed from their earliest roots helps explain much about today's schools. As you read, think about how people in your own community were educated through time. In every period, the availability and quality of education are shaped by society, history, and government. The education students receive also impacts society, events of the time, and government institutions.

The American Colonial Period (1600–1776)

European migration to what would later become the United States began in the seventeenth century. In education, the time period between about 1600 and 1776 is known as the American Colonial Period of education.

What motivated Europeans to come to a new land? Their reasons varied. Some were seeking economic opportunity. Many were looking for greater religious freedom. Others were motivated by the idea that they could produce a better society. Some were simply adventurers.

Educational opportunities here were as varied as the motives for immigrating. They reflected the beliefs and circumstances of the immigrants. While some similarities existed, options for education also differed by location, since there was no overall educational system.

At first, most education took place in the home. Those parents who were able, taught their children basic reading and arithmetic skills. Daily life and work provided many additional opportunities for the practical learning needed for adulthood. Even after schools began to be established, they were available mainly in well-populated areas.

The schools that did exist were primarily for elementary grades. A few universities and colleges, including Harvard University and the College of William & Mary, were founded during this period. However, very few students had the opportunity to attend them. Most older children worked on their family farms or businesses. Others, including some girls, learned a trade in an *apprenticeship*. An **apprentice** is someone who learns a skilled trade by watching and helping someone in that trade. In early America, some apprentices worked without pay for an agreed-on period in exchange for their learning, 6-1.

Most colonists in the New England colonies (Massachusetts, Connecticut, New Hampshire, and Rhode Island) came from England. The majority of them were Puritans. This religious group believed in the importance of religious education and valued each person's ability to read the Bible. They viewed schools as a way to reach those goals and also to teach basic skills for farming. Education was a way to ensure their beliefs and way of life would be safeguarded. As early as 1642, Massachusetts enacted a law requiring every town to establish a school, although this was not always followed.

In the middle colonies (New York, New Jersey, Pennsylvania, and Delaware), people came from a number of different backgrounds. Many emigrated from Ireland, Scotland, Holland, and Germany, as well as England. Because their backgrounds were more diverse, there was no one common school system. Instead, cultural groups developed their own schools. The Quakers, a religious group from England that settled around Philadelphia, believed that everyone should be educated and were tolerant

6-1
Working as an apprentice in a blacksmith shop was a way to learn a skilled trade in early America.

of others' religious beliefs. They established the first school there that welcomed all, regardless of religion or race. Quaker schools were open to girls, African Americans, and Native Americans.

Social and economic class divisions were more rigid in the southern colonies (Virginia, Maryland, North Carolina, South Carolina, and Georgia), and education was not considered a function of government. Sons of wealthy plantation owners received a formal education that prepared them for college in the colonies or Europe. Plantations were geographically separated, so many boys were educated at home by tutors. The middle class was much smaller in the southern colonies than in other areas. Middle-class and poor children, especially girls, had fewer opportunities for formal education. Enslaved people (slaves) were only taught skills that were useful to their owners.

Dame schools also existed in the colonies. Students were taught by women in their own homes. Parents paid a fee for their children to attend. Such schools were open to both boys and girls.

The Role of Teachers

Throughout the colonies, teachers ranked just below religious leaders in importance. Both groups of men were better educated than the general population. Both were expected to teach and to act as examples of moral behavior.

Being a role model brought with it many expectations. Teachers could not drink, smoke, date, or marry. Regular church attendance was required, along with participation in civic events. Teachers were expected to be industrious and honest. A teacher routinely cleaned the school and often visited the sick or performed other charitable acts to set a good example.

School Curriculum

In most schools, teaching focused on basic reading, writing, simple math, and religion. Some students were educated beyond elementary school, although few formal schools existed. In the middle and New England colonies, training was available for trades, such as shoemaking. Sons of wealthy parents often learned Latin, Greek, and more advanced math. Those in the South also studied astronomy for navigation and plantation management skills.

In addition to basic skills, girls learned sewing and other home management skills. Girls from wealthy households sometimes had the opportunity to study literature and learn poetry, in addition to their basic subjects.

Books were rare and expensive. Schools used hornbooks for instruction. A **hornbook** was a flat wooden board with a handle. A sheet of paper—usually containing the alphabet, a prayer or two, and Roman numerals—was pasted on the board, 6-2. Since paper was scarce, a thin,

6-2
Since paper was scarce, hornbooks were used throughout the colonies.

flat piece of clear animal horn was attached to cover and protect the paper. Hornbooks were used widely throughout the colonies until the 1800s when books became less expensive.

The American Early National Period (1776–1840)

The second period of education began with the American Revolution. People of the time believed they could make a better society and were eager to try out new ideas.

During the American Early National Period, America was still primarily a rural nation. Most children grew up on farms or in small towns and expected their adult lives to be much like that of their parents'.

Change occurred more quickly in cities. Their population was more diverse, and people freely shared and discussed new ideas. Educational changes began in cities, eventually spreading to rural areas.

During this time, educators came to believe that people could improve their lives and society through the use of reason. People able to think critically would be able to find rational solutions for problems. Schools were seen as a vehicle for making a better society.

As America continued to grow and prosper as an independent nation, the ideas and traditions of Europe had less of an influence. Education was considered a way to promote the new nation's ideals of freedom and liberty. Religion played less of a role in education. Instead, growing communities focused on teaching skills to help students enter fields such as agriculture, business, and shipping.

Benjamin Franklin and Thomas Jefferson were two influential political leaders of the time. They also helped to shape the development of schools during this period.

Benjamin Franklin

Benjamin Franklin was one of the most important early leaders in the colonies, urging independence from England. He signed the Declaration of Independence and the Constitution. In addition to being a politician, he was well respected as a scientist, writer, and inventor.

Curious about everything, Franklin experimented with all sorts of scientific concepts, from electricity to the common cold. He believed that understanding science helped people understand people and societies. He read every book he could find. Wanting others to have this opportunity, Franklin began the first public library.

Benjamin Franklin also worked to expand educational opportunities. He started a secondary school, or academy, in Philadelphia that offered a broad range of subjects, including practical ones. The school was open to anyone who could pay the tuition and attend, regardless of their religious beliefs.

Because of Benjamin Franklin's influence, schools to this day teach good citizenship. Public schools are available to everyone and teach a wide variety of subjects. Although Franklin himself was primarily self-educated, he had a lasting impact on how the American education system developed.

Thomas Jefferson

Thomas Jefferson, the third president of the United States, is often considered one of the most brilliant individuals in history. He was a politician, an architect, a philosopher, an inventor, a farmer, and a writer. His interests were limitless, and his accomplishments were vast.

Jefferson also played a major role in establishing the current American educational system. He believed that education was the key to making the newly formed democracy a success. If common people were well educated, they could take part in democratic government, and it would thrive. Others countered his views. Alexander Hamilton, for example, believed only those who were wealthy and educated were suited to rule.

Jefferson introduced legislation to divide counties in Virginia into smaller districts that were responsible for education—a public system of education. He wanted to make sure that elementary schools were available without cost. While he was only partially successful, in the next century, his dream became the way America's public schools were organized. Another of Jefferson's major educational achievements was the establishment of the University of Virginia.

The Role of Teachers

During the American Early National Period, teachers continued to be positive models of good citizenship for their students. They were expected to be involved, making the community a better place through both church participation and involvement in community issues. Teachers taught that citizenship involved obeying laws and rules and respecting authority.

School Curriculum

Schools continued to teach the basics of reading, writing, and math, along with Christian principles and citizenship, 6-3. Students learned Greek, Roman, and English history, and now American history, as well. However, educational opportunities remained limited, especially in less populated areas.

6-3
In a typical classroom from the American Early National Period, slates and chalk were often used instead of paper.

Wealthy boys went on to study Greek, Latin, and English grammar plus advanced math, geography, literature, and science in preparation for university entrance. If girls received additional education, it was often through a tutor at home or in schools designed specifically for girls. Education, at that time, was mainly limited to those of European ancestry.

The American Common School Period (1840–1880)

The American Common School Period in education extended from 1840 to 1880. These years were marked by events that significantly altered the American way of life. In the 1840s, the Oregon Trail was opened. After gold was discovered in California, the expansive west gave many people new hopes and dreams of finding their fortune and starting a new life. Labor-saving devices, including sewing and washing machines, gave people more time for other interests and pursuits.

Throughout the 1850s, the country moved closer to the internal split of the Civil War. Some Americans realized the injustice of slavery and worked actively to end it. In the South, the economy was still based on slavery. In the 1860s, the Civil War claimed many lives in both the North and South. Ultimately, the freeing of slaves and the triumph of the Union cause altered American life.

At the beginning of the American Common School Period, most American children received minimal schooling, if they received any at all. By the end of the period, education—including free public education for many—was much more widely available. One reason for the improvement in educational opportunity and quality was the influence of Horace Mann.

Horace Mann

Horace Mann served as the first secretary of the State Board of Education in Massachusetts. In this role, he made an impact on education nationally, as well as in his state.

Mann worked hard to establish free, public education for every boy and girl in Massachusetts. He believed that everyone had the right to an education. The first public state-supported schools were called **common schools**, giving the same education to people from different levels of society.

Horace Mann tried to improve and standardize schools. One key innovation was the establishment of teacher-training schools called **normal schools**. (The term "normal school" reflected the hope that through teacher training, all schools would become *normalized*, or similar, to each other to improve quality.)

Mann advanced education in other ways, as well. He successfully advocated the establishment of free libraries. He increased state funding for public schools by using state taxes to pay for education. This provided money to raise teachers' salaries and improve educational materials and equipment.

Because schools were funded by taxpayers' dollars, Mann believed they should be nonsectarian. They should not teach any specific belief system. His reasoning was that people should not be required to pay for education that might teach religious principles contrary to their own religious beliefs. However, since the country was overwhelmingly Christian, morality based on general Christian principles was still taught, 6-4.

Other states copied Horace Mann's efforts. Many of his ideas are still part of today's educational system.

African American Education

In the years before the Civil War, very few enslaved African Americans were able to read and write. Most who learned did so in secret. Laws existed in many places in the South prohibiting educating African Americans. Whites feared that education would lead to rebellion.

Former slaves in northern states faced tremendous obstacles to education, both social and economic. Not many African American schools

6-4
Early American school buildings were often one-room schoolhouses.

existed, and Quaker schools were among the few other schools that allowed African American students to attend. In addition, African Americans, as a group, usually struggled with very low wages. Children often found work as soon as they were old enough to do so.

After the Civil War, there was a real effort by many to improve educational opportunities. Educated African Americans set up schools. Some northern churches sent missionaries to the South to start schools. It was then that the first African American colleges were founded, including Howard University and Spellman College for women. At the same time, there was real debate among African Americans about what type of education was best.

Many of these efforts were short-lived. All were hampered by the fact that most schools remained strictly segregated. African American schools lacked the funds to provide a truly equal education for those who attended.

The Role of Teachers

At the beginning of the American Common School Period, the country was still primarily rural. Most children were educated at home or in small country schoolhouses where one teacher taught all grades. Teachers in these schools were paid by community members. Often, their salaries were quite low. It was not that education was not valued, but running schools was expensive, and people had little money to spare.

Because of Horace Mann's impact on education, teachers trained in normal schools were better prepared to teach. To gain entrance to a normal school, applicants had to take a test to show they had been properly educated. As a result, people had higher expectations of teachers' knowledge and teaching abilities. More women enrolled in normal schools and entered the teaching profession. This provided an opportunity for them to make a living on their own.

School Curriculum

The American Common School Period brought more change in how subjects were taught than in which subjects were taught. Significant changes included the establishment of kindergartens in public schools, the use of McGuffey readers, and the passing of the Morrill Act of 1852.

Kindergarten

Friedrich Froebel, a German educator, developed the idea for kindergarten. He believed that young children learned best through play. Although his ideas were not widely adopted in Germany, American educators were interested in the concept.

The first kindergarten classes established in America were intended to help poor children succeed in school. Using Froebel's ideas, songs and games were used in schools. His creative and social approach to learning worked well with young children. Educators and parents noticed the success of his methods. In the 1870s, public schools began to offer kindergarten programs. Prior to this time, young children did not attend school until they were about seven years of age.

Today, educational programs for young children are still based on play and social interaction. Preschoolers and kindergarteners have opportunities to choose their own activities, express their creativity, and interact with one another. This helps expand and reinforce their learning.

The McGuffey Readers

Textbooks became much more widely available during the American Common School Period. Reverend William Holmes McGuffey was asked to write a textbook. This was the beginning of the **McGuffey readers**, a series of books that were used in schools across the country. The books taught moral lessons along with reading, spelling, and other subjects. A reading story, for example, might show the importance of being honest or kind. Subsequent McGuffey readers taught other subjects, such as history, biology, botany, literature, and speech, along with lessons on proper behavior. Because they were used in so many schools, the McGuffey readers contributed to the standardization of American education.

The Morrill Act

In 1862, the Morrill Act, also known as the Land-Grant College Act, gave federal land to establish colleges in every state. These colleges were to provide practical education in agriculture, home economics, and other useful professions to people from all social classes. Land-grant colleges made higher education available to Americans nationwide. Many well-known universities of today began as land-grant colleges. A second Morrill Act in 1890 expanded the system.

The American Progressive Period (1880–1921)

The American Progressive Period in education bridged the nineteenth and twentieth centuries. The United States had been divided by, but survived, the Civil War. Women were gaining more rights. European immigrants poured into the nation's cities. At the same time, the Industrial Revolution continued to change the nature of both work and society.

The Progressive Era was a time of business expansion and reform in the United States. Members of this reform movement called themselves **Progressives**. They wanted to regulate big business that often took advantage of both workers and consumers. Corrupt government officials were another target. Progressives wanted to make America a better and safer place to live, and education had a key role to play, 6-5.

Between 1880 and 1920, half of the rural population in America abandoned farming and moved to towns and cities to find work. In addition, over 15 million new immigrants came to the country, most from Ireland, Italy, and Eastern Europe. They, too, settled primarily in cities. The Industrial Revolution held the promise of work for many. However, urban areas became overcrowded. Many of the new city dwellers lacked education, practical skills, and financial resources. Few social, charitable, educational, or government services were available to help these people meet basic needs. Poverty and disease became widespread.

Those who did find work in factories found their lives profoundly changed during that time. Work hours were long. Working conditions were often hazardous. Many children worked alongside their parents,

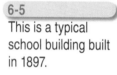

6-5
This is a typical school building built in 1897.

limiting their educational opportunities. Urban schools quickly became overcrowded, and conditions in the schools were poor.

Progressives expected to make the world a more democratic place. They fought for better pay for women. They passed laws reducing the number of hours children could work in factories. By 1920, all states had laws requiring children to attend elementary school. Many policies and institutions from the Progressive Era remain central to American life today.

Segregated Education

Schools during the American Progressive Period were still highly segregated. African American children attended separate public schools that received less funding. Educational materials were scarce and inferior, often the cast-offs from the "white" schools. African American teachers could only teach in African American schools, and they received significantly lower pay than their counterparts.

The Role of Teachers

During the American Progressive Period, teachers were considered professionals. Teacher preparation programs in colleges replaced normal schools. More emphasis was placed on educational theories. Teachers were well trained and qualified to both run a classroom and teach a variety of subjects.

Many teachers grew unhappy with the emphasis on standardization. They wanted more freedom in the classroom. As a result, the first teachers' labor union was formed to protect the working rights of teachers. The union fought to improve the pay, status, and working conditions of teachers.

During the Progressive Period, women entered the workforce in greater numbers. Many became teachers, and a few rose to positions as school principals. By the end of the Progressive period, women had achieved the right to vote. Many believe that this change was a direct result of women's presence in classrooms.

School Curriculum

Progressives believed that schools should focus on students more as individuals. Many felt that the curriculum was too standardized. They felt that students should be encouraged to think critically and independently, rather than simply memorize information and accept facts. These changes were significant for education. Progressives believed that citizens trained to think and question would work to clean up corrupt city governments, improve working conditions in factories, and create better living conditions for those who lived in poverty. Schools could set students on this path. For example, a science class might focus on the need for water sanitation.

One notable change during this era was the opening of thousands of public high schools. In 1880, there were only about 800 such schools. This movement allowed students to continue their education and prepare for a career, even if they were not attending college. A high school diploma became more important in finding a job.

John Dewey

John Dewey, an educational philosopher, psychologist, and writer, was a leading voice for progressive education during this time. His influence on what was taught and how it was taught should not be underestimated.

Dewey believed that classrooms were too rigid and inflexible, did not adapt to the needs, interests, and abilities of individual students. Like Progressives in general, he believed that schools should place a greater emphasis on the development of problem-solving and critical-thinking skills. He saw these skills as a means of improvement of society.

Dewey promoted the link between learning and experience. He believed that students learned best through real-life activities that linked new information to previous experiences. He also believed social interaction—working together on projects and discussing topics—aided learning. Other educators, influenced by his work, began focusing on the role of the teacher as guiding learning, rather than simply providing information. You can see evidence of John Dewey's theories in today's educational system.

Maria Montessori

Maria Montessori, Italy's first female doctor, tried to find ways to help children who had difficulty learning. The students with whom she worked had medical conditions that may have kept them from learning. The teaching program she developed had a significant impact on young children during the American Progressive Period. Her program remains well-recognized and accepted today.

Montessori believed that young children are capable of great discovery and motivated to explore the world. She believed that sensory experiences should come before learning to read and write. The educational program Maria Montessori developed is known today as the **Montessori method**.

How is it different? The Montessori method considers all of a child's needs, not just intellectual needs. Montessori classrooms are stimulating environments. There are many opportunities for large- and fine-motor development and sensory exploration, along with language, science, art, geography, and math. Children direct their own learning with teachers as their partners. Teachers encourage children to judge their own progress and choose their own interests.

Career and Technical Education

The Smith-Hughes Act of 1917 established federal funds to support vocational education (now called career and technical education). **Career and technical education** prepared (and still prepares) students for the many career opportunities in specific trades and occupations where skilled workers were needed. The funding provided greatly influenced the spread of the career and technical classes in public high schools.

The 1920s and the Great Depression Era (1921–1940)

Following World War I, many Americans turned away from concerns about political reform. America was the most industrialized country in the world and economic prosperity and growth were strong. However, the influence of the Progressive movement in education continued throughout this period.

The economic prosperity of the 1920s increased the size of the middle class. More people had **disposable income**, money to spend on things they wanted, not just needed. Americans became consumers, rather than producers, of their own consumable goods. The introduction of the automobile became the stimulus for industrial growth in the nation. Consumer credit issues surfaced for the first time as credit became more widely available, so consumer education became a need.

There were concerns about the rate of immigration. **Quotas** (government limits) were set on the number of immigrants allowed in the country.

Many economists believed the economic prosperity would continue. Few had concerns when, on October 14, 1929, the New York Stock Market crashed. That day, known as Black Thursday, caused an economic panic that put the country into The Great Depression.

Impact of Economy on Schools

In good economic times, schools expand both in number and what they offer. This was true during the 1920s. In hard economic times, schools had to respond to lost revenue. During the Great Depression of the 1930s, the situation for schools was bleak, 6-6. Public schools faced a shortage of cash, since many citizens were unable to pay their taxes. Some school districts ceased to operate. Other districts shortened the school year. Teacher pay was often decreased or eliminated, and course offerings cut back to basic subjects.

For families finding it difficult to keep their children fed and dressed, there often was not enough money for books and school supplies

6-6
This is a Great Depression-era classroom. How does it compare to the classrooms of today?

necessary to attend school. Many were simply unable to attend. Children who could work, often did so to supplement the family income.

The federal government stepped in to help. Funds helped support some schools to hire teachers and purchase supplies. With federal money, schools began offering free hot lunches for children. As part of the program to employ others, better schools were built in some communities.

By the end of the 1930s, the Great Depression was starting to ease. Families were trying to get back on their feet. Social institutions, including schools, were also working to recover from a decade of hardship. Americans were inward focused. However, rumblings in Europe would eventually lead to the beginning of yet another world war.

"Dick and Jane" Readers

In spite of the Great Depression, in the early 1930s, a new set of reading textbooks for beginning readers began publication. Often known as the "Dick and Jane" books, these books taught basic reading skills with simple stories about a family. From the 1930s to the 1960s, over 85 million students used these textbooks. As with the McGuffey readers before them, their widespread use helped standardize education.

Summary

During the American Colonial Period, the type and availability of education varied considerably by region and the local population. Children were educated in the basics of reading, writing, and math, along with religion, at home or in elementary schools.

After the Revolution, in the American Early National Period, many believed that education could prepare citizens to participate in a democracy, make the economy grow, and society to succeed. Benjamin Franklin and Thomas Jefferson were two significant contributors to educational innovations that took place.

During the American Common School Period, schools became more standardized. Horace Mann was influential in establishing free public education. The first programs for formally training teachers were established.

The American Progressive Period occurred about the turn of the twentieth century. Immigrants and people from rural areas moved to cities to find work, overwhelming schools. The Progressive movement pushed for educational reforms to improve society.

The twentieth century brought with it hope and better economic conditions. Progressives believed that education was the place to start teaching citizens to create better living conditions.

In the 1920s, after World War I, Americans enjoyed economic prosperity. Educational reforms continued. However, during the Great Depression of the 1930s, education, like other aspects of life, was pared back to basics.

Review

1. Various sources of education existed during the American Colonial Period. Identify at least four.

2. Describe at least three ways schools changed during the American Early National Period.

3. What did Thomas Jefferson contribute toward how schools are viewed today?

4. Common schools and normal schools developed during the American Common School Period. What were they?

5. How did educational opportunities for African Americans change during the American Common School Period? What were they like during the American Progressive Period?

6. Who developed the idea for kindergartens? Why were kindergartens first used in America?

7. Who were the Progressives, and what did they believe about the importance of education?

8. What are two of the educational changes advocated by John Dewey?

9. Describe the Montessori method.

10. What was the purpose of career and technical education?

11. How did the Great Depression impact classes offered in schools?

Reflect

1. In the American colonies, there was great individual variation in schools from town to town and region to region. Today, schools must meet both state and national guidelines and laws in an effort to standardize schools even more so. What are the pros and cons of each approach?

2. One-room schoolhouses with a single teacher responsible for all grades developed in rural areas with limited population. A few of these schools still exist. If you were teaching in such a school now, how could technology help you manage to teach students at so many different levels?

3. During the Great Depression of the 1930s, some teachers continued to work for little or no pay. What do you think motivated them? How do you think you would react, as a teacher, if a similar situation occurred? What factors would you weigh as part of your decision?

4. Develop a list of at least eight questions that you would use to interview one of the following key people in the early history of education: Benjamin Franklin, Thomas Jefferson, Horace Mann, John Dewey, or Maria Montessori. Your questions should reflect your interest in how the period in which the person lived influenced his or her ideas about education.

5. Throughout the early history of education in America, teachers were held in great respect and were expected to be role models for students. In your opinion, how are teachers regarded today? Give reasons for your views.

Act

1. Research the history of education in your community. Where was the first school located? Who started the school and for what purpose? What grades attended the school? If it still exists, how has it grown or changed?

2. Visit your local library. Find out how far back local newspapers are available. Choose a four-month period from a previous decade and read through the papers. Note specific examples of how schools, teachers, and students were portrayed. Report your findings, using examples from the papers. Compare attitudes then to the ways school, teachers, and students are viewed today. How are they similar? How are they different?

3. The Morrill Act is linked to the establishment of land-grant colleges and universities. Use the Web to gather more information about the original purpose of these schools. Identify a land-grant school in your state and find out whether it still carries out any of its historical purpose. What is the current relationship between land-grant colleges and universities and the Cooperative State Research, Education, and Extension Service (CSREES)? What services does CSREES provide?

4. Montessori schools still exist today. Work in groups to research and report on Montessori schools, each person taking responsibility for a particular aspect, such as the philosophy behind the schools, teacher preparation, teaching/learning methods, and classroom environment.

Add to Your Portfolio

Arrange to interview someone who was in school before 1940. Develop a series of questions to find out more about the schools the person attended, what they learned, how teaching and learning compared to that of today, how information was presented, a typical day's schedule, and what life was like at that time. Ask permission to record the interview or take careful notes. After the interview, prepare a summary of the interview, using actual quotations where appropriate. Include a section on what you learned from the experience. Add your paper to your portfolio.

7 THE MODERN HISTORY OF EDUCATION IN AMERICA

Key Terms

baby boom

Project Head Start

bilingual education

illiterate

back-to-basics movement

global economy

educational standards

national standards

competency-based education

accountability

standardized tests

charter school

career clusters

Objectives

After studying this chapter, you will be able to

- **identify** links between key federal education legislation and perceived threats to national security or prosperity.

- **trace** the impact of the civil rights movement on American education.

- **give examples** of ways the civil rights movement prompted improved educational opportunities for other groups.

- **research** and evaluate the impact of educational reforms on teachers and students.

- **identify** how educational changes in recent decades continue to shape education today.

Why are math and science so important? Why do you take so many exams? When did schools start offering classes in languages other than English? Why did it take so long for schools to become desegregated? Who decides what should be taught in schools? In this chapter, you will learn the answers to these questions as you read about the history of schooling in America from the 1940s up to today.

In the previous chapter, you learned about American education from the settlement of the colonies through the Great Depression of the 1930s. These beginnings shaped the structure and the role of the educational system that exists in the United States today. This chapter provides an overview of education from 1940 to the present. What happened during these more recent decades has had a direct effect on the policies, procedures, and issues of education today.

During every era, historical events and changes in American life impact expectations of the educational system and the public's perception of it. New initiatives are tried, then revised and made in reaction to perceived problems. Presidential beliefs and priorities determine their degree of federal involvement in education. Some presidents have believed in the importance of shaping educational policies, while others believed this should be left up to the states. During some periods in history, international conflicts or major problems within the country may deflect attention away from educational concerns.

American Education During the 1940s and 1950s

The first half of the 1940s was dominated by World War II. Production of war-related material, from tanks to uniforms, helped pull the country out of the Great Depression. Thousands of young men left each month to fight the war overseas. This created job vacancies in factories, offices, and classrooms. These positions were filled by women and African Americans. Both of these groups also had expanded roles in the military during the war. Never before had so many women worked outside of the home.

With the end of the World War II (1945), the troops flooded back into civilian life, 7-1. They looked forward to returning to normal life, but they, and society, had changed. Many war workers had to give up their jobs for veterans. Other soldiers took advantage of what was known as the *GI Bill*, federal legislation that included money for veterans to attend college or train to learn new skills. Young people married in record numbers. The result was a surge in the birth rate over the next years. This is often known as the **baby boom**.

After the war, neither African Americans nor women were willing to again accept the lower status they held during the prewar years. They had proven their capabilities in the workplace and in the armed forces.

7-1
Following World War II, significant changes took place in American education.

Long-held ideas began to change. Photographs and stories of the Holocaust made people more aware of the tragic effects of prejudice. These changes aided the subsequent civil rights movement.

The period after World War II was a time of new ideas and technology. As factories stopped producing products for the war effort, consumer goods finally became more available. There were new options in housing, home technology, fashion, and even food. Industries grew, jobs were available, and Americans were hopeful. It was also a time of social and political conservatism and a fear of the spread of communism.

Education was not immune to this era of change. The children of the baby boom began to enter the public school system. Their sheer numbers resulted in the need for more schools and teachers. In addition, world events and social change had significant impact on American education.

Keeping America Competitive

After World War II, tensions and competition increased between the Soviet Union on one side and the United States and its allies in Western Europe on the other. While no actual fighting broke out, this came to be known as the Cold War. This standoff continued for decades.

Both America and the Soviet Union had programs to develop and test missiles. Americans were alarmed when the Soviets launched the first satellite, Sputnik, in 1957. There was a fear that the Soviets' emphasis on math and science in their schools was giving them a technological advantage that could later translate into a military advantage.

In 1958, Congress passed the *National Defense Education Act*. This made money available to improve scientific equipment for public and private schools and to provide college scholarships and student loans. It encouraged schools to strengthen their math, science, and foreign language instruction.

Schools responded by requiring students to take additional math and science courses. Foreign language programs were improved. Homework requirements increased in an effort to spur learning.

Brown v. the Board of Education

In the early 1950s, many schools in America were still racially segregated based on "separate but equal" policies. Yet, African American schools still were not equal in funding. Educational materials were inferior and usually outdated. African American teachers were only allowed to teach in African American schools, and they received significantly lower pay. School buildings were often in disrepair.

In 1954, the Supreme Court agreed to hear the case of *Brown v. the Board of Education of Topeka, Kansas*. The court ruled that racial segregation of schools violated the Constitution because segregated schools were, by nature, unequal. As a result, public schools were ordered to desegregate. Some districts did so. Others used delaying tactics.

Although school desegregation has gone through many phases since 1954, this initial Supreme Court ruling was critical to the civil rights movement. The civil rights movement sought to gain equal rights regardless of race. The push to integrate schools was the most radical, and potentially influential, aspect of the movement.

Behaviorism

Chapter 3 described a variety of learning theories, including B. F. Skinner's behaviorism. Behaviorism is the belief that how a person behaves is determined by that person's experiences. Skinner's book *Science and Human Behavior* was published in 1953.

Many educators embraced Skinner's theory during the 1950s. They believed that by controlling the classroom environment and experiences, they could produce educated, well-behaved students, 7-2. Appropriate behavior and achievement were rewarded. For example, young students were often given gold star stickers when they performed well. Punishments were also common. This way of approaching learning was widely accepted. It influenced American education for decades.

American Education During the 1960s

The 1960s were a time of change. Those born during the baby boom were becoming teenagers and young adults. Many in this new generation

questioned the conservatism of the 1950s and challenged the values, policies, and way of life of older adults.

The sixties were a decade of contrasts. They began with the optimism of newly elected President John F. Kennedy. Neil Armstrong walked on the moon in 1969. However, it was also the decade America became involved in the Vietnam War. John Kennedy, Dr. Martin Luther King, and Robert Kennedy were all assassinated.

The civil rights movement was especially active during this period. Its leaders favored peaceful methods, such as sit-ins and marches, to protest discrimination. In 1963, more than 200,000 people of all races marched in Washington, D.C. in support of civil rights. They heard Dr. Martin Luther King's famous "I Have a Dream" speech.

The civil rights movement spurred other groups to work for their own equality. These included women, Hispanic Americans, Native Americans, and people with disabilities. Like African Americans, all had been discriminated against in various ways.

The 1960s were a time of educational innovation. Schools and teachers had the freedom to try creative ideas in an effort to improve education. On the national level, the most significant changes affected students who were disadvantaged economically or educationally.

The Civil Rights Act

Although the Supreme Court decision in 1954 called for an end to segregation, many schools, especially in the south, were slow to comply. Even a decade later, many African American children were still being educated both separately and unequally.

The *Civil Rights Act of 1964* formally outlawed segregation in the United States public schools and public places. School districts were ordered to end segregation. They were called to "undo the harm" segregation had caused by racially balancing schools. Federal guidelines were issued. However, some school districts continued to stall, and problems remained.

The Elementary and Secondary Education Act

President Lyndon Johnson, who succeeded President Kennedy, pushed for wide-ranging reforms with his "War on Poverty" and "Great Society" programs. The *Elementary and Secondary Education Act of 1965* sought to improve the schools most in need. Federal education dollars were given to school districts based on the number of poor children enrolled. This was a major boost to struggling schools and helped equalize educational opportunities.

Project Head Start

Project Head Start, still in existence today, also began in 1965 during the Lyndon Johnson administration. It was designed to help preschool children from low-income families develop the skills they needed for success in kindergarten and beyond. Students who begin with a good start in school are less likely to experience academic problems later.

Some Head Start programs are coordinated with other social programs. They may, for example, provide all-day child care. These programs provide a positive, high-quality environment for preschool children. Today, the program is open to more families. Hundreds of thousands of children are served each year.

American Education During the 1970s

During the 1970s, America had many foreign and domestic preoccupations. On the international front, after years of protests, the Vietnam War finally drew to a close. President Nixon visited the communist countries of the Soviet Union and China. At the end of the decade, United States citizens were killed and held as captives in the American Embassy in Iran.

At home, America was changing, and people faced many concerns. The divorce rate rose, and the number of single parents increased. Overall, there were significantly more women in the workforce in a broader range of jobs. An oil crisis sent prices soaring and created shortages. There was a push for conservation and finding alternative sources of energy.

Unemployment went up during the 1970s. So did prices as inflation hit home. People had less disposable income and were less willing to spend on education. Many schools suffered from inadequate funding.

Desegregation and Busing

The civil rights movement continued to push for equality. Desegregation at the school level had not solved unequal education. The problem stemmed partially from the tradition of neighborhood schools. By choice or lack of opportunity, neighborhoods tended to be divided by race. That meant that schools often had little racial diversity, and those with primarily minority populations often had inferior facilities and lacked sufficient, up-to-date educational materials.

School districts were mandated to look at desegregation at the larger district level, rather than just school by school. This led the way to forced integration. School districts assigned students to schools in proportions that would achieve integration and bused them to those schools.

This plan certainly was not without controversy. Many families of all races objected to having children forced to take long bus rides to schools outside their neighborhoods, 7-3.

Congress voiced the opinion that busing was not the issue, and that desegregation was not necessarily the answer to making schools equal. Injustices still existed, even in desegregated schools. The issue of inequality would continue for years ahead.

7-3
Busing was a
controversial plan
aimed at achieving
desegregation.

7-3
Busing was a controversial plan aimed at achieving desegregation.

Bilingual Education

Amid the controversy over school busing, the Supreme Court ordered that a group of Spanish-speaking students be granted **bilingual education**. That is, classes would be taught in two languages, both English and Spanish. In 1971, the Supreme Court ordered the joining of two school districts in Texas, one that had primarily Spanish-speaking students and the other mostly English-speaking. The Court found that language was a barrier for equal education. All students were taught both Spanish and English.

In 1974, the Supreme Court acknowledged the problems students face when they have limited English skills. The Court ordered schools to provide basic English language classes for children who had limited English skills. This ruling was based on the difficulty Chinese students were facing in San Francisco.

Gender Equity

The Civil Rights Act affected education in many ways. It stimulated a variety of subsequent laws that provided equal opportunities for other groups. For example, in 1972, *Title IX* or the *Equal Opportunity in Education Act* was passed. It prohibited discrimination based on gender in all programs and activities receiving federal financial assistance. If a school, even a college, receives federal funds, every program and activity must be open to all, regardless of gender. One impact of this act was opening sports, even those formerly designated for boys only, to girls. However, the overall influence of the law was much more far-reaching.

Tradition and discrimination had long limited the career options of women. This began to change in the 1960s and 1970s. Prior to that time, nursing and teaching were the two professions most available to women. It was unusual for women to enter professions dominated by males, such as law and medicine. Even when women held comparable positions, they were usually paid considerably less than men. Due to the combination of job options and pay discrepancies, in 1970, women earned 59 cents for every dollar earned by men. In 1978, more women than men enrolled in college for the first time.

Children with Disabilities

In 1975, Congress passed the *Education for All Handicapped Children Act.* For the first time, it guaranteed a free public education for children with disabilities. Further, it mandated that the education provided for each child be appropriate and take place in the least restrictive environment. Parents were to be involved in decisions about their child's placement.

Previously, most children with disabilities had been segregated in special classrooms. With this legislation, children are able to spend part or all of their school day in regular classrooms, 7-4.

7-4
In 1975, Congress passed legislation that guaranteed free public education for children with disabilities.

American Education During the 1980s

During the 1980s, there was less national emphasis on education. President Ronald Reagan believed the federal government's role in education should be reduced. His Vice-President, George H. W. Bush, who succeeded him, held similar views.

The 1980s were a time of growth and prosperity for some people, but the gap between rich and poor widened. Consumerism was at an all-time high. Buying on credit was a way of life for many. Those born during the baby boom had reached adulthood and many were raising families of their own. However, those families, on average, had fewer children. There were more single-parent families as the divorce rate rose. In addition, two-income families were more common than in previous decades as women gained more career opportunities.

The Back-to-Basics Movement

In 1983, a report called *A Nation at Risk* was published by a federal government agency. The report asserted that America's competitive edge was at risk. It said that the United States was falling behind other countries in business, science, and technology. There was concern that creative innovations in schools in the 1960s and 1970s had left many students lacking a good foundation of basic knowledge and skills in reading, writing, and math.

A number of indications of this gap were cited. American students fell behind students of other developed countries in math and science scores. College graduates were scoring lower on general knowledge tests than in prior years. The military reported that recruits had poorer reading and writing skills than the previous generation. Millions of Americans were **illiterate**. They could not read or write.

There were calls for school reform. Many Americans believed that schools again needed to emphasize reading, writing, and math. This was called the **back-to-basics movement**. Critics of the movement believed that students needed more than basic reading, writing, and math skills to succeed in a complex world.

American Education During the 1990s and Beyond

The 1990s were about technology. The Internet changed the way people communicated, received information, shopped, and conducted business. It played a key role in education, as well.

The economy was booming and unemployment was at an all time low. At the same time, the United States became involved in conflicts around the world, including in Bosnia and the first Gulf War.

The first decade of the twenty-first century brought new challenges to the United States. After the terrorist bombings in New York and Washington, D.C. on September 11, 2001, the United States went to war in Afghanistan and Iraq. At home, the economy seemed strong, with rising real estate values and high consumer spending, much of it on credit. However, in 2008, a financial crisis began that plunged the country into a period of financial uncertainty. Some financial institutions failed. Jobs were lost as spending slowed.

What was striking about this financial crisis was how quickly it spread around the world. It confirmed the existence and impact of the **global economy**. Finance, international corporations, and trade link the economies of nations around the world—particularly those of major countries. For example, computer links had made it possible to move many of a business' functions to any country with an educated, but less expensive, workforce.

The Computer Revolution

With computers such an integral part of education today, it is hard to believe that they played a minor role in learning until the development of smaller versions (very large by today's standards) in the 1980s. It was not until the mid 1990s that most classrooms were equipped with a single computer.

As more educational programs were developed and the price of computers declined, they became more available. It was the development of the Internet and search engines that turned computers into the powerful and essential learning tools of today. The ability to use computers skillfully soon became a key career skill. Today, education, as well as information, is readily available via computer. This makes it available at a time and place convenient to the student.

Educational Standards and Accountability

State governments and local school districts largely control the public educational system. Consequently, there has always been a great deal of variation in what is taught at various grade levels, in different courses, and in individual schools. Uniformity was promoted by state curriculum guidelines and textbooks used in schools across the nation. Beginning in the 1980s, the call for more demanding and uniform educational standards grew louder. *Standards* are agreed-on levels of quality or achievement. **Educational standards** refer to guidelines defining what students at various levels should know and be able to do.

In 1991, Congress established the National Council on Education Standards and Testing (NCEST). This group began asking questions. What should be studied? How should learning be measured? What standards of performance should be set?

In addition, teacher associations for various subject areas (such as history, physics, math, and others) voluntarily began to develop standards for what should be taught in school. They answered the questions about what should be studied and how it should be measured. They also set standards for performance in their subject areas. These are commonly referred to as **national standards**.

The teaching toward standards is often called **competency-based education**. That is, schools teach toward students demonstrating ability in subject areas. Many people who support standards believe that they provide an objective way of evaluating student learning. Many who object to standards believe that real learning and creativity is lost and only memorization of facts is gained.

In 1999, President Clinton made it clear that the role of the federal government was to establish guidelines for achieving excellence in education. Individual states, on the other hand, would establish specific standards and objectives, testing to evaluate whether standards were met, and ways to measure whether schools met the standards. Although this seemed like a reasonable plan, it soon became complicated by politics.

Setting standards naturally led to the next question of how to measure whether or not students had met the standards that had been set. There was a move toward educational **accountability**—proving that schools and teachers were providing high-quality education. Beginning in the 1990s, many states began using standardized tests to measure success.

Standardized tests are designed to give a measure of students' performance compared with that of a very large number of other students. For example, they may measure reading comprehension skills of third-grade students across the country.

Standardized tests are used for a variety of purposes in addition to measuring student achievement. They can be used to compare different groups of students or schools. They can help educators make decisions about which teaching programs are working and which are not. They can report on an individual student's progress.

Goals 2000

The impact of the back-to-basics movement was felt by most Americans during the 1990s. After the report was widely distributed, President George H.W. Bush and the nation's governors established six educational goals to be reached by the year 2000. These goals, listed in Figure 7-5, gained wide approval and Congressional support in the *Goals 2000 Act of 1994*.

National Education Goals
By approving the *GOALS 2000: Educate America Act*, Congress reaffirmed the six National Education Goals agreed to by the nation's governors under the leadership of Governor Clinton and then-President George H. W. Bush in 1990. In the Act, which passed with strong bipartisan support in 1994, Congress also added two Goals—one on teacher learning and one on parent partnerships. Every major parent, education, and business group endorsed the National Education Goals and GOALS 2000 across the country. The goals stated the following:

By the year 2000
- All children in America will start school ready to learn.
- The high school graduation rate will increase to at least 90 percent.
- All students will leave grades 4, 8, and 12 having demonstrated competency over challenging subject matter including English, mathematics, science, foreign languages, civics and government, economics, the arts, history, and geography, and every school in America will ensure that all students learn to use their minds well, so they may be prepared for responsible citizenship, further learning, and productive employment in our Nation's modern economy.
- Students from the United States will be first in the world in mathematics and science achievement.
- Every adult American will be literate and will possess the knowledge and skills necessary to compete in a global economy and exercise the rights and responsibilities of citizenship.
- Every school in the United States will be free of drugs, violence, and the unauthorized presence of firearms and alcohol and will offer a disciplined environment conducive to learning.
- The Nation's teaching force will have access to programs for the continued improvement of their professional skills and the opportunity to acquire the knowledge and skills needed to instruct and prepare all American students for the next century.
- Every school will promote partnerships that will increase parental involvement and participation in promoting the social, emotional, and academic growth of children.

7-5
The *Goals 2000 Act of 1994* tried to remedy complex problems in education.

However, implementation was left up to the states and local school districts. Translating the goals into specific plans took time, and there was little opportunity to remedy complex problems within the last years of the twentieth century.

No Child Left Behind Act

In January 2001, just three days after taking office, President George W. Bush announced his plan for educational reform. The *No Child Left Behind Act* was passed later that year. The goal of this act was to improve the performance of schools in the United States. Increased accountability, more choices for parents when choosing schools for their children, and an increased focus on reading were important components of this act.

Underlying the act was the belief that high expectations and goals would result in success for all students. One of the most controversial features was the expectation that every child should meet state standards in reading, math, and science. One method of measuring achievement was the use of standardized tests at specific grade levels. Standardized tests and other measures of evaluation were encouraged. Receipt of federal educational funds were tied to school performance. Schools demonstrating success in meeting high standards would receive more money. Parents would have the opportunity to move their children from low-achieving schools to higher-achieving schools.

While few argued with the need for higher achievement, many expressed concerns about the provisions of the *No Child Left Behind Act*. Some pointed out that the characteristics of students and funding levels varied widely among schools. Those schools starting with a higher percentage of students already behind grade level would have difficulty meeting the goals, especially if they were poorly funded. There were complaints that teachers were encouraged to spend much of their time specifically preparing students for the standardized tests at the expense of other content information and educational experiences.

One impact of the *No Child Left Behind Act* was an increase in the variety of school options. In some states, more charter schools were established. A **charter school** is a public school that operates with freedom from many of the regulations that apply to traditional public schools. Charter schools often use innovative teaching practices. Each has a charter that establishes the school's mission, goals, students served, programs, methods of evaluating programs, and ways to measure success. Parents must specifically choose to send their children to charter schools.

Not all states have approved charter schools. Proponents believe parents need choices and competition among schools will improve public education. Opponents worry that as schools become competitive in nature, some students may be left out. Others worry that experimental methods will not work or that funding will be reduced for long-established, traditional public schools.

Competing in the Global Economy

Schools play a crucial role in preparing future workers with the necessary skills to compete in a global economy, 7-6. In the United States, even before the financial crisis, many jobs formerly performed by American workers had shifted abroad. Part of the reason was that wages and benefits in the United States were higher than those of other nations. However, the availability of many highly educated workers was also a major factor. In

many countries around the globe, students and societies see education as their best hope for a better life.

With falling math and science scores and many students not even completing high school, there has been real concern that the United States may lose its competitive edge. It may be one of the countries that fall behind economically. The most important factor in remaining competitive in a global market is having a skilled and well-educated workforce. This is the job of schools. As in earlier times, there has been debate about how education must change to meet these challenges.

Career Clusters

Since a skilled workforce is a key to prosperity, one essential goal of education is to prepare students to succeed in the workplace. The United States government partnered with business and industry professionals, colleges, trade schools and high schools to discuss how to help students prepare for successful careers. Based on predictions that today's students will change careers a number of times during their working life, the group developed a system of career clusters. **Career clusters** are 16 general career areas, each having a wide range of related opportunities. By developing the necessary academic and technical skills identified for a cluster, students can pursue a variety of career options within the cluster. Educators can use career clusters to create curriculum that will prepare students for successful transition from high school to postsecondary education and employment. The career clusters are listed in 7-7.

Sixteen Career Clusters

The Career Clusters icons are being used with permission of the States' Career Clusters Initiative

www.careerclusters.org

7-7

The Career Clusters model lists the 16 areas that include a variety of career options.

Summary

During the 1940s and 1950s, America fought World War II. Then the decades-long Cold War with the Soviet Union began. The African Americans and women who assumed new jobs during the war wanted to retain their improved status. This pumped new life into the civil rights movement. The Cold War prompted increased emphasis on American education, especially science, technology, and foreign languages. In the 1950's, Skinner's theory of behaviorism made punishments and rewards common tools in American schools.

The 1960s brought demands for change. *The Civil Rights Act* became law. A war on poverty was declared and schools began focusing on meeting the special educational needs of children living in poverty.

In the 1970s, educational issues focused on equity. Busing was one technique used to integrate schools that had remained segregated. Two Supreme Court cases sided with special accommodations for those with limited English skills—bilingual education and special courses to teach the English language. *Title IX* legislation made it illegal to restrict participation in activities based on gender. Legislation guaranteed children with disabilities a free public education with the least restriction possible.

In the 1980s, concern deepened over students' perceived lack of basic knowledge and skills. This was fueled by a government report titled *A Nation at Risk*.

In the 1990s and the beginning of the twenty-first century, concerns about America's international competitiveness continued to affect education. The emphasis was on developing national and state goals and standards and holding schools accountable. Global financial instability in the first decade of the new century translated into budget concerns for schools.

Review

1. How did World War II spur the development of the civil rights movement?
2. What was the impact of the baby boom on the educational system of the 1950s?
3. What is the purpose of the Project Head Start program? Give one possible reason that it is still in existence.
4. Explain the intended purpose of busing. Why was it unpopular with many parents?
5. Describe the *Education for All Handicapped Children Act.*
6. Explain what prompted the back-to-basics movement. What subjects were considered to be basic?
7. Identify one aspect of your education that relies on computers. How would it have differed before computers were widely available in schools?
8. How were standardized tests used with the *No Child Left Behind Act*?
9. What are charter schools?

Reflect

1. Teacher education programs at the college level generally include classes on the history of education. Identify as many benefits as possible that future teachers can gain from studying the past.
2. In small groups, discuss what factors can contribute to attitudes of prejudice. Once you have made a list, determine what methods are most effective in minimizing prejudice. Why is it so difficult? How should teachers deal with prejudicial attitudes in the classroom?
3. The *Elementary and Secondary Education Act of 1965* gave more federal education funds to schools with higher enrollments of children from low-income families. The *No Child Left Behind Act* imposed penalties on under-performing schools, many of which had large low-income populations. What is the reasoning behind each approach's attempt to improve education for low-income students? With which method do you agree most and why?
4. Review the descriptions of major educational changes since 1980. Which do you feel has the greatest impact on your education today? Give specific reasons for your choice, including examples.
5. As education changes, how can teachers learn about new ideas, methods, and laws? What can they do if they disagree with changes mandated by their school or a state or federal law?

Act

1. Create a timeline showing significant events in the civil rights movement's push for equal education. Use information from your textbook and other resources. Identify some of the reasons it took so long to deal with this complex issue.

2. On the Internet, access and print an example of national or state standards for a particular subject area and level (such as health education grades K-4). How are the standards organized? Are they written in language that is clear enough that teachers would know what to teach and how to evaluate learning? Do you think teachers are limited to teaching only what is in the standards? What questions do you have about this process?

3. Often concerns about education focus on math and science knowledge and skills. Why is this so? Write an essay making a case for the importance of at least three other types of knowledge and skills that you feel are key to career success in a global economy. In class, discuss what role courses preparing students for careers such as child care, building trades, and agriculture have in schools today and should have in the future.

4. Attempts to change education have very real consequences for students' lives. Choose two educational reforms. Research the main implications of those reforms on the classroom experiences of students. Use your research to write imaginary accounts of the experiences of two students. In the first, show how one reform positively changed the life of a student. In the second, relate how the other reform had a negative impact on the student's life.

5. Research how much and what type of impact a new president can have on education. Consider the status of existing laws, government policies, funding of programs, and new legislation. What roles do Congress and the Supreme Court play in educational policy?

6. Ask a person from another country, such as a foreign exchange student, how education in the United States differs from the person's home country. What does the person see as pros and cons of each system? Report on your interview, telling whether or not you agree with the person's assessment and why.

Add to Your Portfolio

Arrange to interview a teacher or administrator who has been in education for some time. The purpose of the interview is to understand someone's personal experience in dealing with changes in the field of education. Prepare questions prior to the interview to determine what shifts in education the person has seen, the effects of those changes on teachers and students, and any patterns of change the person has identified over time. Take accurate notes. If possible, and with the person's permission, record the interview. Write a summary of the interview, including a section with what you learned and your personal thoughts about educational change. Add the document to your portfolio.

8 SCHOOLS AND SOCIETY

Key Terms

spending per pupil

school funding gap

achievement gap

corporate-education partnership

at risk

mentor

cyberbullying

zero tolerance policy

expulsion

Objectives

After studying this chapter, you will be able to

- **explain** how public schools are governed and funded.

- **identify** the structure of education in your state.

- **give examples** of how schools and communities interact.

- **describe** societal problems that impact schools and learning, along with possible solutions.

Schools are tools a society uses to help its children acquire the knowledge, skills, and values they need to carry society forward. As such, schools both reflect a society and shape it.

Around the world, countries understand the power, influence, and importance of education. Many countries have put great emphasis on improving educational opportunities as a way to boost the economy of their nations and the lives of their citizens. In other countries, leaders have used educational policies for their own motives. Some have tightly controlled education, restricting what could be taught. By regulating access to information, they sought to limit dissent. In other countries, education—or quality education—is available only to those who can afford to pay for it.

How does the United States compare to other countries? Its educational system is not based on a national system, which has real advantages and disadvantages. However, less uniformity also results in variations related to quality and opportunity. American schools rank well compared with other nations in some regards, and not so well in others. This fuels the push to do better, 8-1.

As in schools everywhere, American schools and learners are influenced by problems the country as a whole faces. In order to help students learn as effectively as possible, they must find ways to deal with such problems. Caring and creative teachers help to do this every day.

8-1
The power, influence, and importance of education are recognized by countries around the world.

Who Is Responsible for Schools?

In the United States, millions of students are enrolled in public schools. Who is in charge of their education? Control of public education actually falls under three levels of government: individual state governments, local communities, and the federal government. Each plays a different role. The scope and degree of their control varies.

In the United States, powers not assigned by the Constitution fall under the jurisdiction of individual states. Education is not specifically addressed in the Constitution. Consequently, states have primary control of public education.

This chapter focuses on education from kindergarten through high school, often abbreviated as K-12. All states also have public colleges and universities. These, however, are controlled and funded separately from the K-12 system.

State Governments' Role

Each state has its own method of organizing and controlling K-12 education. However, there are some similarities. Although their names and titles may differ, almost all states have the same following key people:

- *The legislature.* The state legislature passes laws and makes major decisions related to education. The state government also decides how much it will spend each year for education and from where those funds will come.

- *The state board of education.* The job of the state board of education is to provide leadership in educational policymaking. It promotes state education standards and advocates for equality of access to schools. Most importantly, the state board of education advocates for continued citizen support and public funds. Members of the state board of education may be appointed or elected.

- *The superintendent of public instruction (or commissioner of education).* In most states, one person, usually an elected official, acts as the link between the state legislature and the state board of education. This person serves as a spokesperson for the state legislature and communicates expectations to the state board to execute.

- *The state department of education.* This agency is responsible for the operation of schools within a state. It performs many essential functions. For example, it is the state department of education that certifies teachers. It allocates money to school districts and checks that they follow state and federal regulations.

Local School Districts' Role

Early in the nation's history, local school districts were formed to organize and run local schools. Today, states are still divided into school districts. These districts have direct responsibility for providing education for the students within their boundaries.

As with state government, there is organizational structure at the local level, dividing responsibilities for schools in the district. The most common structure includes the following:

- *The school board.* This group of elected people sets policies and makes decisions about how schools within the district should be run, 8-2. Some school boards oversee education from kindergarten through high school. Other boards may oversee a specific level of education, such as the high schools in a district.

  The school board works with the school administration to set the vision for the school district. It controls or approves school curriculum (the courses taught), funding, and other policies that affect local schools. The board determines the budget and issues financial reports. It negotiates contracts with employee unions and oversees hiring practices and decisions.

  School boards hold regular meetings that are open to the public. The agendas for these meetings must be publicly posted in advance. School board meetings generally include an opportunity for citizens to express opinions. In many communities, board meetings are broadcast on television.

8-2
Members of school boards are elected to make decisions about how schools in their districts function.

- *The district superintendent.* For each school district, a district superintendent acts as the connection between the school board and the individual schools. The district superintendent acts much like the president of a company. The superintendent answers to the school district board much as a company president answers to the board of directors. The superintendent makes sure that the school board's policies are carried out in the schools.

- *School administrators.* Individual schools utilize administrators to oversee daily operations. In each school, a principal acts as the top executive with the help of assistant principals in larger schools. Other key personnel, such as deans and department heads, have specific responsibilities and provide administrative assistance to the principal.

   School principals set the tone for their schools. They are responsible for carrying out day-to-day activities. They oversee a budget for the money allocated by the school district board for their school and provide leadership for curriculum development and educational updates.

   School principals hire (with school board approval) and supervise teachers. They advise, support, and provide professional growth opportunities to foster teaching excellence. They visit classrooms to make sure that educational goals are being met.

   School principals also spend time with parents, students, and community representatives. They act as the spokesperson for the school. They also deal with difficult issues, such as those related to discipline and personnel.

The Federal Government's Role

Although the states play the primary role, the quality of the nation's schools is also a concern of the federal government. The federal government has a compelling interest in making sure that its citizens receive a good education and become productive members of society.

Over the years, Congress has passed federal legislation to assist states in providing quality education for all students. As you learned in the previous chapter, sometimes legislation focuses on a particular group, such as students from low-income families or those with disabilities. Other times, legislation is passed in response to perceived problems, such as the United States falling behind in math and science education.

These programs generally come with federal funds, if the states and local school districts follow the specified legislative guidelines. States must comply in order to receive these supplementary funds. Many school districts express concern that they do not receive sufficient reimbursement for many programs mandated by the federal government.

The United States Department of Education originated in 1867 with the job of collecting information on education. Today, the head of the department, the Secretary of Education, sits on the President's cabinet. The agency's mission is to ensure quality education for all children. It establishes priorities, focuses national attention on these priorities, and collects data to see how schools are achieving them. It evaluates what educational programs work most effectively. The agency also acts as a watchdog to prevent discrimination in schools.

Funding for Education

In the United States, every child has the right to a free public education in grades K-12. Of course, the process of education is actually quite expensive. Salaries must be paid, books and materials purchased, and buildings built and maintained. State governments, local school districts, and the federal government all contribute toward the cost of education. Sometimes private funds are also available. The proportion varies somewhat, but the pie graph in 8-3 shows the average split of educational funding.

8-3

Funding for education is often allocated as indicated here.

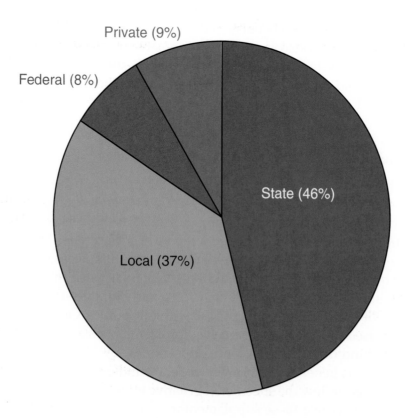

Private (9%)

Federal (8%)

State (46%)

Local (37%)

Source: U.S. Department of Education

State Funding

Each state determines how to fund its own educational system. Most states use taxes—generally sales taxes and income taxes—for the state portion of educational costs. The state pays the largest share of education expenses, with local funding a close second. Educational spending varies from state to state.

Local Funding

Local dollars also make up a substantial portion of educational funding. Local funding comes from the community, usually from a portion of local property (real estate) taxes. Some districts have a higher educational tax rate than others, even in neighboring districts. These differences are often due to building projects, such as the need for new schools, or special programs a district offers.

The use of property taxes to fund schools is often controversial. When property values increase rapidly, property taxes can rise sharply. For many people, such as retirees on fixed budgets, escalating taxes can cause real hardship. In addition, the use of property taxes means everyone, even those without children attending school, are taxed to pay for education. On the other hand, those who rent or lease housing do not directly pay property taxes. Districts with large businesses or industries within their borders may collect large amounts of property taxes from those, often giving homeowners lower taxes for education. These and other issues have led some districts to look for other sources of income, such as sales taxes.

Federal Funding

Because of the federal government's interest in making sure its citizens are well educated, it contributes money to states for use in education. This is termed *national* or *federal funding*. These funds are usually designated for specific special programs. Common examples include Project Head Start, providing school lunches for low-income students, and remedial reading programs. However, federal funding provides less than 10 percent of the total money needed to operate schools.

The federal government has been involved in providing supplementary financial support for education for many years. The *Elementary and Secondary Education Act of 1965* made federal money available to schools with low-income students to help equalize educational opportunities. The *Carl Perkins Vocational and Technical Education Act of 1984* helped fund career and technical education. The *No Child Left Behind Act of 2001* used federal money to help schools close the gap in student achievement among schools.

Besides the funds linked to major education legislation, the federal government often includes additional funding to support education in its annual budget, 8-4. However, these funds are never meant to cover basic educational costs, because they are the responsibility of states and communities.

8-4
Federal funds for education are often linked to education legislation.

Private Funding

Some private funding is available for education. Some private charitable foundations award grants to schools for special projects or to help solve problems related to the goals of the foundations. In addition, individuals and groups help schools. For example, a civic group might raise funds to buy safety equipment or new band uniforms.

The Problem of Unequal School Funding

With the enormous costs involved in education and varying characteristics of students and schools, it is no surprise that school funding raises many issues. One of the most controversial is the gap in school funding among school districts. The amount of spending per pupil for education varies greatly from district to district. This is true not only when states are compared to one another, but also between school districts within the state. **Spending per pupil** refers to the average amount of money a school district spends to educate one student for one year. This figure is often used to compare school funding.

While the quality of a child's educational experience depends on various factors, schools that have more money can provide more teachers, materials, services, and opportunities. In one recent year, the spending per K-12 pupil in one state ranged from about $4,300 to $28,000.

What causes these differences? One major factor is the use of local property taxes as the primary source of local funding for schools. School districts with lower property values have difficulty generating income for schools. Districts that include higher-priced homes and businesses often have higher local funding.

Unfortunately, school districts with lower levels of income from property taxes tend to be in urban areas. The schools in these districts often have a higher proportion of students who are low-income and need a higher level of services. This problem, often called the **school funding gap**, is not easy to solve. Some states and school districts are changing the way they allocate funds to schools. They take into account how many students in a school need extra educational services and provide some additional funding for these students. This method does not equalize spending, but it narrows the gap among schools somewhat. Many of these same schools also have lower test scores and higher dropout rates. This is often referred to as an **achievement gap,** which is the differences in learning and graduation rates among schools, often linked to differences in school populations and funding. Opponents of plans to change funding argue that additional spending does not necessarily translate into improved academic achievement.

Private Schools and Home Schooling

Not all K-12 education takes place in public schools. Throughout the country, private schools educate about 6 million students. In addition, countless more are home schooled.

Private schools are quite varied. Many are associated with a specific religion. Students learn religion and moral behavior along with reading, math, and other academic subjects. Many religious private schools are open to students of other faiths. Other private schools are not based on religion. Examples may be one that offers an advanced course of study, more individualized attention, or have a specialized purpose, such as a military school or one for students with autism.

Private schools do not receive public funding. Instead they depend on tuition and private support, such as donations and grants. A few private schools operate as for-profit companies.

Private schools are also free from many laws that govern public schools. They set their own policies. For example, they are not required to hire certified teachers, although most do. They are not required to accept every student.

In recent decades, more parents have chosen to home school their children. That means they are responsible for determining what will be studied, preparing and teaching lessons, and evaluating learning. Quality home schooling takes a major commitment of time and effort. Some parents rely on textbooks and published materials, while others develop their own materials. Internet courses are sometimes used, especially for more advanced subjects. State laws regarding home schooling vary, but many have little oversight.

Communities and Schools

Schools have long been a focal point for communities, 8-5. That remains true today. Citizens take pride in the accomplishments of students and schools, from spelling bee champions to winning sports teams. Even those people without children in school may attend school programs or run for a position on the local school board. Positive school-community relationships benefit both sides. When they are strained, both the schools and communities lose.

Parents and Schools

Parents are the community members most closely tied to schools. They want their children to receive the best possible education. Some even base decisions about where they will live on the reputation of the schools in a particular area.

8-5
Schools are vital parts of communities.

Effective schools usually have good relationships with parents. They encourage teachers to communicate with parents on an ongoing basis, not just when problems arise. They create opportunities for parental involvement. Parents can serve on committees, participate in parent-school associations, help with sports and activities, or volunteer in many other areas. When parents are involved with schools, they are more likely to be strong supporters of education.

Business and Industry Links

The businesses and industries in a school district also care about education. They need potential workers who have the knowledge, skills, and attitudes needed for successful employment. A capable local workforce is important to a community's economy. In addition, companies that recruit workers from outside the area are more likely to attract good people if the school system is highly regarded.

Businesses and industries can be important partners in developing and maintaining effective schools. Company leaders can help schools design or upgrade programs related to business and industry. They can help identify the types of skills workers will need in the future. Sometimes a group of business professionals join together to raise money to pay for a specific school improvement project.

Occasionally, businesses, especially large corporations, enter into an expanded and more formal relationship with a school. This is often called a **corporate-education partnership**. The business essentially "adopts" a school and may help it in a variety of ways. Sometimes the business plays a significant role in working with the school to improve facilities or educational opportunities or offer grants for worthy projects. Employees may be allowed time to volunteer at the school, including during working hours. There are many ways such a partnership can work to benefit both schools and the community.

Schools and Community Resources

Schools depend on the resources of their communities to educate and serve their students. In turn, schools can share some of their resources with community residents.

Although schools have personnel and services to help students with some learning-related problems, other problems require different types of assistance. School counselors and administrators may refer families to community social services for appropriate support.

Other community facilities and organizations also help support teaching and learning. For example, public libraries typically have more resource materials than school libraries. Museums and other community resources offer ways to expand learning beyond the classroom. Some schools benefit from links to area colleges or universities. These offer their expertise, while the schools may serve as student teaching sites for college students studying to become teachers. Other times, schools and colleges develop programs to offer more advanced courses for students still in high school. Career and technical programs at secondary and postsecondary levels may coordinate what is taught at each level so that students can transition smoothly from one level to the next.

Many K-12 schools offer programs outside of the school day to benefit citizens. They may provide adult education classes, open their facilities for community groups and recreational activities, or offer before- or after-school care for students with working parents. Schools sometimes buy supplies from local businesses. This practice, along with teachers' salaries, helps pump school tax dollars back into the community. There are many ways schools and communities can support and strengthen one another.

Social Problems Affect Schools

Because schools reflect the communities where they are located, they are not immune to societal problems. These can affect students' learning to a significant degree.

Unfortunately, many of those problems are serious and difficult to solve. Schools must work to minimize them in order to maximize learning. Students caught up in these difficulties are much more likely to fail academically or to drop out. Even students who do not experience such problems directly may be negatively affected in their education. The situations and problems of their classmates take time away from learning. Schools that have been most effective in minimizing the impact of social problems on learning have found that it takes the efforts of everyone—administrators, teachers, students, parents, and the community—to truly make a difference.

This section highlights some of the most common of the serious problems affecting education today. As you learn more about them, think about how they have influenced your experiences as a student and those of others in your school. Also consider how you might best respond to them in a teaching situation.

Poverty

The majority of Americans living in poverty are children. Such children face a long list of challenges that can affect their learning. For example, they are more likely to have inadequate nutrition and suffer from hunger. Limited access to health care means they are sick more often or have untreated conditions, such as poor eyesight. Their living conditions may make it difficult to get adequate rest. They are less likely to have books or computers at home. Because of a lack of resources, children living in poverty are less likely to have had enriching life experiences, such as travel and museum visits.

Children from families living in poverty are among those labeled as **at risk**. What does this mean? Basically, at risk students or groups have characteristics that make them more likely to fail academically.

Children become aware of social and economic status differences at a very young age. Students who are poor often struggle with emotional security and self-esteem issues. School may not feel like a welcoming environment, and they may develop negative attitudes toward learning and school.

Older students living in poverty have similar disadvantages. However, access to computers and other technology also becomes more of a concern. Finding a time and place to do homework may be difficult for children living in poverty. High school students may feel responsible for providing additional income for their family members. Some may be the sole providers for their families.

Families who live in poverty often move from place to place. Some are homeless. Without a permanent address, children may not be eligible to register for school or may change schools often. Friendships are severed during moves. Relationships with teachers are lost. There may be no place to study or even to sleep. Learning is difficult when feelings of embarrassment, worry, anger, or fear limit concentration.

What Can Schools Do?

Education provides the best opportunity to break the cycle of poverty. Today, a high school diploma is the minimum needed to find employment, and most jobs require more advanced education or training. Those who fail to finish school are unlikely to be able to provide adequately for themselves in the adult world.

Schools need to draw on diverse resources to help students living in poverty succeed in school. Some have made school the place where students and families can find the various types of help they need for stability. The school works with social service agencies and refers families to the services they need. These may range from helping parents find job training or housing assistance to signing students up for free meals and providing them with clothing. In addition, schools closely monitor individual students' progress to help keep them on track. Tutoring is available for students who need it. Community members may act as mentors to students. A **mentor** is an adult who commits to a long-term relationship with a student to provide support, guidance, and help. Often, having a caring relationship with another adult helps students see their strengths and set goals for the future. Many schools also find that getting students involved in school activities helps keep students in school.

Violence

As violence has escalated in society over the years, it has become more prevalent in schools as well. It is not just actual incidents of violence, but also fear regarding safety, which hinder teaching and learning.

Violence is pervasive in the media. Students watch it on television, see it in the movies, hear about it in songs, and participate in it by playing video games. It is not surprising that it spills over into schools. Children learn by example, mimicking what they see and hear. All too often, students also experience some form of violence in their homes or neighborhoods. It may be verbal abuse, fights, or gang activity. There is special concern about the impact of violence and fear of violence on schools and learning. When a person lives in fear or is intimidated, it is difficult to concentrate on learning. Some students become withdrawn. Others have increased school absences. For teachers, dealing with violence takes time away from teaching.

Violence exists in many forms. It ranges from name calling to intimidation (real or implied threats) to physical violence. Sometimes violence is random in nature. Other times, a specific individual or group is targeted. In all cases, far more people than the individuals involved are affected. Some of the most common areas of violence in schools include the following:

- *Bullying and intimidation.* A child's lunch money is stolen on the way to school. Another student is not allowed to sit in a certain row on the school bus. False rumors are spread about someone. Bullying and treating someone in an intimidating way are common problems in schools. Bullies usually direct their behavior toward a weaker, younger, or less resourceful person, 8-6.

8-6
Teachers who observe bullying or are made aware of it should put a stop to it immediately.

Bullying and intimidation are usually physical or verbal in nature. However, **cyberbullying**, intimidation through e-mail, social networking sites, and texting, is a growing problem.

- *Sexual and racial harassment.* Similar to bullying, one person or a group tries to intimidate someone. Sexual harassment can take many forms, including unwanted touching, comments, rumors, and pictures. The victim usually feels uncomfortable and unsafe. Sometimes such harassment leads to sexual abuse or rape. Similarly, racial harassment can take many forms, but it is based on a person's race, color, or ethnic background. It, too, can precede more violent attacks.

- *Physical violence.* For some students, physical fights are the only way they know how to resolve conflict or to release frustration and tension. They need to learn alternative methods of resolving conflicts. Incidents of violence against students and teachers are all too common in schools.

Unfortunately, the presence of weapons in schools, as well as in society, makes it easy for disagreements to become even more violent. Some students who carry weapons say they do so for self-protection. For others, weapons are a symbol of power or status. Others carry weapons specifically to threaten or intimidate classmates or teachers.

Gang activity adds significantly to problems of violence. Although only a small percentage of students actually belong to gangs, violence and crime escalate significantly in areas where gang activity occurs.

What Can Schools Do?

Schools must develop programs that combine maximizing safety with working to change circumstances that make violence seem like a reasonable option. Parents and communities need to be involved in these efforts in order for them to be effective.

Most schools have established zero tolerance policies regarding violent behavior. A **zero tolerance policy** means that the prohibited behaviors and actions will not be tolerated—no exceptions. In zero tolerance policies, expulsion is usually the only acceptable result. **Expulsion** means that a student no longer has the right to attend school for a specified period of time.

In addition, schools may use other measures to minimize violence. For example, in schools where weapons are an issue, metal detectors may be installed at building entrances. Other schools have eliminated permanent lockers and require students to carry see-through bags to transport their personal items. Dress codes are one way to combat the effects of gang activity. Security personnel and security cameras are common on many campuses.

School administrators and teachers must establish strict standards and expectations for nonviolent behavior. Such policies go beyond forbidding physical fights. Other policies include any form of intimidation.

Changing attitudes is the other key. This means creating an atmosphere where tolerance, acceptance, and fairness are valued. Students must learn nonviolent alternatives for dealing with anger and frustration. Conflict-resolution skills can help students learn how to state their needs, negotiate, and collaborate. Students must be encouraged to break their informal code of silence. When they stand up for their own safety, campus crime and violence decrease.

Many communities support school antiviolence policies by promoting public awareness campaigns. Partnerships with community agencies that enhance school resources and activities are also effective. By partnering with local law enforcement, fire and police departments can help schools deal with safety issues more efficiently. This includes education, response, mental health resources, and identification and monitoring of potential threats.

Sexually Active Students

As their bodies change, young teens become more aware of their sexuality. They become sexually curious. Some teens become sexually active, often because they think "everyone" else is. (The actual number of teens who are sexually active is fewer than half.) Others, realizing the risks involved in sexual activity or because of personal values, decide to delay sexual relationships.

As with violence, media's coverage of sex seems astounding. The media is also often at odds with parental, community, and even personal values.

Teens who are sexually active usually know the risks, including unplanned pregnancy, HIV-AIDS, and other sexually transmitted infections. Even so, American teens have one of the highest rates of sexually transmitted infections of any developed countries. Teen pregnancy rates have been rising. In spite of teens' beliefs, the chances of contracting a sexually transmitted infection or becoming pregnant can be quite high. Both can have devastating effects for a student's future.

Sexually transmitted infections can be treated, but not all can be cured. HIV-AIDS can result in early death. Pregnancy brings with it enormous long-term responsibilities for both the mother and father. Many teen parents drop out of school to care for their child. This involves physical and financial responsibilities. Teen parents can often experience a life of poverty. Teen parents who stay in school are more likely to experience academic difficulties because of their increased responsibilities. Even though the responsibilities of teen parents are many, those who finish their education are in a better position than those who do not.

What Can Schools Do?

Schools have taken several approaches to stem premature sexual activity and its effects. Some focus on helping younger students develop positive self-esteem and decision-making skills. Students learn how to resist peer pressure. Making peers and older students part of these efforts can increase their effectiveness.

Schools often involve parents and the community in efforts to reduce teen sex, infection, and pregnancy. Health and social service agencies can share their expertise. Some schools offer health services on campus.

Supporting pregnant and parenting teens is another way to keep students in school. Some schools help teens find social services, monitor their academic progress, offer parenting classes and child care options, and arrange for a mentor or counselor to provide ongoing support. Such efforts can pay off in terms of the career opportunities for the parents and the parenting skills they need to successfully raise a child of their own.

Alcohol and Other Drugs

Student use of alcohol and other drugs are real problems. Use of these substances can adversely affect learning. It can also have devastating personal consequences.

Alcohol is illegal for minors for a reason. Even in small amounts, it can impair judgment and create difficulties in learning. In larger amounts, it can cause blackouts. Longer-term heavy alcohol use can cause permanent changes to the brain that hinder learning. Students who have been drinking have difficulty learning, and especially students who drink on a regular basis. A drinking-related car crash or sexual encounter can have life-altering results that can jeopardize a teen's whole future. Substance abuse is linked to a rise in violence.

The use of illegal drugs or misuse of prescription or over-the-counter drugs can lead to similar consequences. Responding to a "just try it once" dare can quickly become an addiction, 8-7. Research shows that adolescents are more likely to become addicted than older drug users. A family history of any type of addiction adds to the risk. Parental supervision and discussions between parents and students are among the most effective means of minimizing these problems.

What Can Schools Do?

Parental communication, management, and discipline can reduce the risk of substance abuse. Peers often play a part in encouraging substance abuse. However, they can also be among the best deterrents. Active groups, such as Students Against Destructive Decisions (SADD), help teens take ownership of the problem and work toward solutions.

8-7
Encouraging
students to avoid
the use of illegal
drugs or misuse of
prescription drugs
can save lives.

How Can Teachers Make a Difference?

Teachers are in a unique position when it comes to helping students who find themselves facing significant problems. Because they interact with students on a daily basis, teachers are often the first to see signs of difficulty. Addressing problems as quickly as possible improves students' chances of getting back on track. Problems often snowball the longer they go on, and learning losses accumulate if students are preoccupied with the difficulties of their lives. Personal or social and academic problems often go hand in hand.

How can teachers identify students in trouble? The symptoms can be quite varied. They include aggression, violence, irritability, and a decrease in interest in grades and school activities. Changes in behavior, such as irregular school attendance, social withdrawal, or depression can also be clues.

Once problems are detected, teachers can provide warm and caring relationships with both students and their parents or guardians. Sometimes it is the home environment that makes it difficult for students to concentrate on school. Teachers can help students and families by linking them with school and community resources.

Other effective techniques for helping students cope with difficulty also benefit the whole class. These include the following:

- having high expectations for all students
- encouraging ambitious but realistic goals
- providing consistent class routines
- making learning meaningful and linked to the real world
- providing students with opportunities to help others
- communicating respect and caring
- showing a willingness to listen
- being even-tempered
- having conflict management and mediation skills
- conveying a sense of hope and optimism
- suggesting positive choices and alternatives

As students work through their difficulties, teachers can help them remain focused on learning. Creative teachers can find ways to incorporate important life skills and issues into any subject. With an education, students have choices. Without one, their options are even more limited.

Summary

Schools are institutions that society uses to prepare the next generation and keep the society strong. Those who control schools can determine who attends, what is taught, and the quality of education.

In the United States, responsibility for schools officially belongs to states. They transfer some duties to local school districts. The federal government also plays a role, primarily through legislation.

While states vary somewhat in how they handle education, it is generally the legislature that passes laws, determines policies, and funds education. A state board of education, state superintendent, and state department of education translate the legislature's guidelines into policies and procedures for schools. Day-to-day operations at individual schools are determined by local school districts.

States must pay for basic school funding through state taxes. Local taxes also make up a major share of the cost. Private funds may be available for special projects. The federal government makes some money available for carrying out its education programs and helping to respond to specific educational initiatives.

Schools are part of communities. When good relationships exist between schools and parents, business and industry, and the community, everyone benefits. Schools draw on community resources to meet students' educational needs. In turn, schools may share their resources with their communities.

As part of society, schools are affected by societal problems. Issues such as poverty, violence, sexually active teens, and drug and alcohol abuse all negatively impact students' learning. Schools that partner with parents and their communities are more successful in minimizing the impact of these problems. Teachers play a vital role in helping individual students overcome obstacles so that they can gain the education and skills needed for future success.

Review

1. Why do states have primary responsibility for education?

2. How are the roles of the state superintendent of public instruction and a district superintendent similar?

3. Indicate who is responsible for each of the following:
   a. allocating money for individual schools
   b. certifying teachers
   c. recommending which teachers should be hired
   d. determining how money will be spent within a school
   e. deciding how much money will be spent for education within a state

4. Identify one drawback of relying on property taxes for the local portion of school funding.

5. Give an example from your own community and schools of how parents can be involved in the schools.

6. What does it mean when students are described as "at risk"?

7. Sometimes those accused of bullying say that they are only teasing. How would you explain the difference? How can bullying disrupt learning for the person being bullied?

8. What are zero tolerance policies? Why are they used?

9. Why is parental involvement a key to cutting down on drug and alcohol use among students?

10. Why do teachers play such a key role in helping students who are experiencing problems?

Reflect

1. Serving on a local school board is often an unpaid position. Why do you think people want to be on such a board? Identify at least eight qualities you believe an effective school board member should have.

2. Think about the issue surrounding school funding gaps and the idea of giving schools with students who have extra needs more funding. Using two columns, identify valid arguments for and against this proposal.

3. Think of an issue or problem within your school. How, specifically, could involving students help better identify the causes of the problem and possible solutions?

4. Some experts believe that by helping strengthen students' self-esteem and decision-making and communication skills, the students can avoid many difficulties. Why do you think they have identified these particular skills as crucial? Do you agree with their assessment? Why or why not?

Act

1. Create a visual aid that explains how your state organizes responsibility for education. Identify the people or groups involved and their responsibilities. Are individuals elected or appointed? Does your state fit the general model described in this chapter? Your visual should be similar to one you would use to teach this information to a class. It may take any appropriate form, such as a diagram, poster, or PowerPoint presentation. The Web site for your state's department of education may be a good resource for information.

2. Use your school district's Web site to find out more about the district. Make a list of the types of information available on the site. Then record at least 10 things you learned about the district from the site. Make suggestions for improving the usefulness of the site.

3. Choose one of the societal problems identified in the chapter or another that impacts your school. How does the presence of the problem affect the learning of students who do not experience it directly?

4. Interview a teacher to discuss how he or she responds to students who are dealing with problems. Develop a set of questions to use for the interview.

Add to Your Portfolio

Attend your school district board meeting. Write a newspaper article for your classmates on the issues discussed and the decisions made at the meeting. Consider how the issues discussed or the decisions made will affect your education. Add the completed article to your portfolio.

UNIT 4:
THE TEACHER

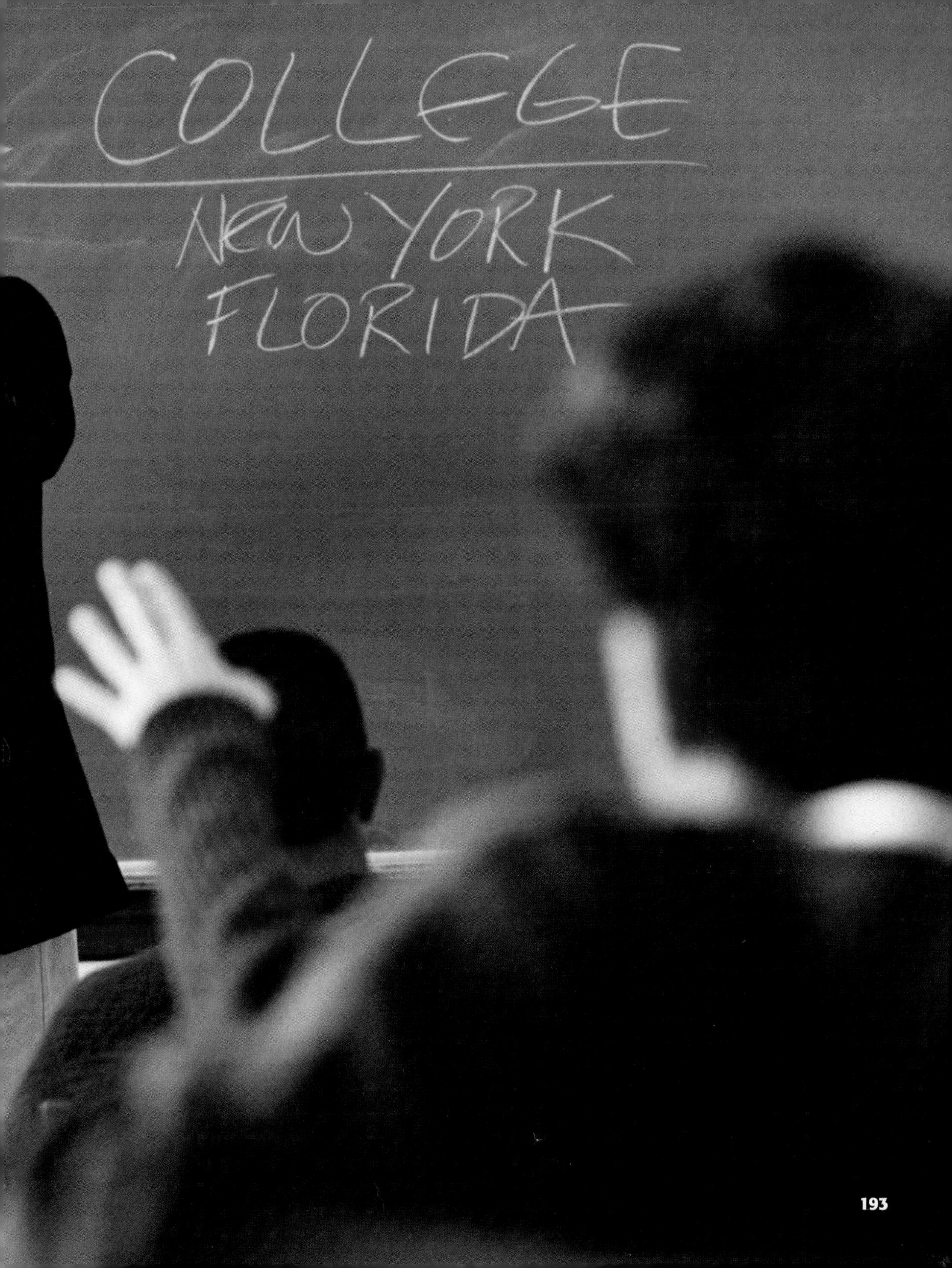
COLLEGE
NEW YORK
FLORIDA

9 TEACHING DIVERSE LEARNERS

Key Terms

learning diversity

learning styles

visual learners

auditory learners

kinesthetic-tactile learners

multiple intelligences

exceptional learners

self-paced learning

magnet schools

pull-out programs

special needs

Individualized Education Program (IEP)

accommodations

mainstreaming

inclusion

special education

ethnicity

stereotype

limited English proficiency (LEP)

English language learners (ELL)

differentiated instruction

Objectives

After studying this chapter, you will be able to

- **analyze** personal learning styles and intelligences.

- **identify** methods schools can use to help gifted and talented learners and students with special needs reach their potential.

- **develop** classroom strategies for ensuring an atmosphere of respect for all students.

- **identify** the difficulties English language learners face and how classroom teachers can help them.

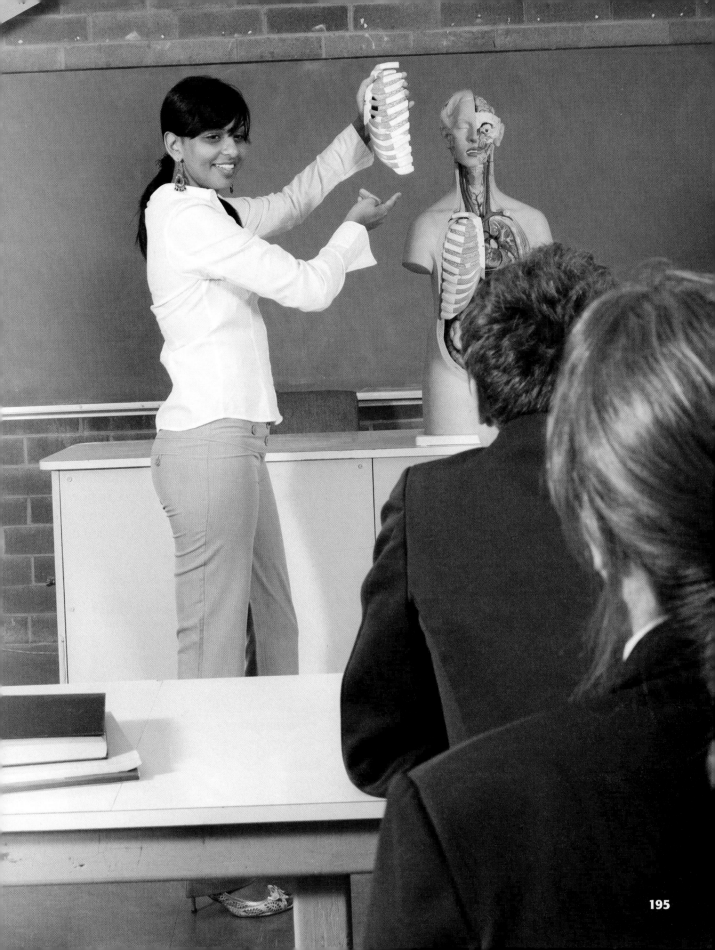

I magine that you and your family just moved to a new country that has a culture very different from your own. When you start school, you don't speak the language or understand much about the culture. It is difficult not knowing what teachers expect of students. The teaching style is quite different from that in the United States. The daily struggle to understand and learn creates constant stress.

For a variety of reasons, many students do not feel like they fit into schools in the United States. Sometimes it is because the way that they learn best does not fit well with the way that schools teach. Other students have physical, social, emotional, or mental challenges that make learning difficult. Highly intelligent students may feel bored or unchallenged. Others may find that language barriers or differences in ethnicity or cultural customs set them apart.

Every student comes to the classroom with a unique combination of experiences, expectations, and abilities. This presents challenges for both learners and teachers. Too often, feeling that they do not fit into the expected mold hinders learning. However, **learning diversity** (differences in learning based on abilities, interests, or experiences) is also what gives schools their richness. If everyone were alike, little learning would take place. The variety of backgrounds, knowledge, skills, and perspectives encourages learning.

It is up to schools and teachers to help every student feel comfortable, accepted, and valued. Teachers who are sensitive to the differences in how students learn best provide varied learning experiences, 9-1. Schools have the responsibility to create a climate where acceptance and appreciation of differences are encouraged.

9-1
Varied learning experiences encourage success among diverse learners.

Learning Styles and Multiple Intelligences

Educators and researchers are continually analyzing the complex factors that affect learning and achievement. There is a continual desire and push to improve education.

One of the biggest concerns today is how to help *all* students learn effectively, not just most. There is better recognition that each student is an individual. While the majority of students function in regular classes, many fail to reach their real potential. When teachers better understand the differences in how students learn, they can more effectively teach in ways that maximize learning for more students. Information about learning styles and multiple intelligences are two helpful guides to gaining insight into such differences.

Learning Styles

Imagine that you just got a new game. How would you choose to learn how to play? Would you read the directions? Perhaps you would ask a friend to explain the rules of the game. Maybe you would learn best by jumping in and playing, learning the rules as you went.

People learn in different ways. **Learning styles** are the methods individuals prefer and find most effective to absorb and process information. Some people are **visual learners** who learn best by seeing. **Auditory learners** learn most easily by hearing or listening to information. Those who learn best by performing hands-on or physical activities are often called **kinesthetic-tactile learners**. Most people learn in all three ways, but one style is often dominant.

Learning styles is an important concept for teachers. When they realize that the ways students learn most effectively varies, they can plan their lessons to incorporate different modes of learning. Knowing how each student learns best allows teachers to help individual students. Also, when teachers know their own preferred learning style, they can make certain they do not emphasize only that style in teaching or favor students with a similar style. There is no one right way to learn. The characteristics of people with each of three learning styles, along with which learning strategies typically work best for them is shown in 9-2.

Visual Learners

Visual learners learn best when they can see the information to be learned. When presented with a spoken math problem, a visual learner

Learning Styles			
Learning Styles	Visual	Auditory	Kinesthetic-Tactile
Characteristics	• Prefers written and visual materials • Remembers details of how things look • Takes detailed notes • Often distracted by movement • Doodles • Prefers written directions	• Prefers to listen to information • Sounds and songs stimulate memory • Takes incomplete notes • Often distracted by sounds or talking • Prefers oral directions	• Prefers to learn by doing • Remembers how things were done • May not take notes • Often distracted by movement • Finds it difficult to sit still • Prefers directions with examples
Learning Strategies	• Reading • Photos, diagrams, charts • PowerPoint presentations • Films, television • Flashcards	• Lectures, explanations • Discussions • Listening to recordings • Films, television • Reading aloud • Repeating information	• Demonstrations • Hands-on activities • Models • Projects • Field trips • Dramatizing • Labs, experiments • Singing, clapping • Games

9-2
An understanding of learning styles helps teachers plan their lessons effectively.

often responds by saying, "Wait a minute, let me write it down." Seeing the problem on paper is a key to comprehending and processing it.

Imagine that you are learning about the main battles of the Civil War. As a visual learner, you could learn the material visually in several ways. You might read about the battles (seeing written words) and take notes. You might draw a timeline to be able to visualize the sequence of the battles. You could view pictures, watch a movie about the battles, or see someone act them out. When studying, you could highlight the main points in your notes, assigning a different color to each battle. Each of these techniques could help you visualize the information and help you recall it when assessed.

Auditory Learners

Can you sit in a class and, without taking notes or looking at the board or computer, learn by simply listening? Do you find it easy to remember spoken directions? Auditory learners learn best when they hear information. Although lecturing is generally considered the least effective teaching method, auditory learners get the most from lectures.

Auditory learners often say, "Can you explain that to me?" They find information presented orally easiest to understand and remember.

To learn about Civil War battles, as an auditory learner, you would prefer to listen to a teacher explain when and where important battles occurred. Discussing the significance of each battle would further reinforce learning. You might study by reciting the battle sequence out loud. During a test, mentally pretending to tell someone about the battles might help you as an auditory learner formulate answers.

Many auditory learners can easily recognize song tunes and rhythms. Young children who are auditory learners often find it easy to repeat lines from a movie or a television show. Young auditory learners are often praised for their ability to remember what they have been told to do.

Kinesthetic-Tactile Learners

You have just purchased an item that requires assembly. If you open the box and attempt to put the item together without instructions (the trial-and-error method), you are probably a kinesthetic-tactile learner. (*Kinesthetic* refers to using bodily movement. *Tactile* refers to touch.) Kinesthetic-tactile learners learn best by doing or through hands-on activity. They often say, "Let me play around with it for awhile."

A kinesthetic-tactile learner would find it hard to sit still during a lecture. Reading a textbook chapter might be punctuated with breaks. To learn the sequence of Civil War battles, as a kinesthetic-tactile learner, you might physically place numbers on a map showing, in sequence, where the key battles occurred. Another technique would be to use an object to represent each battle and place them in order by date. Briefly dramatizing the battles could also serve as a memory aid. Studying with others, particularly other students with a similar learning style, might be helpful. During a test, you might visualize the memory of placing the numbers on the map or objects in order.

Young children are especially open to kinesthetic-tactile learning. Babies explore their world through touch. Dancing to the rhythm of a song can help a child learn the alphabet. A special clap may help a young child remember to quiet down. As with older kinesthetic-tactile learners, the physical actions reinforce the learning.

Multiple Intelligences

The term *intelligence* is often used to mean learning ability. In the 1980s, Howard Gardner of Harvard University published his theory of **multiple intelligences**. His research and observations led him to the idea that individuals have a broad range of types of intelligence, each to a different degree.

Gardner identified a variety of types of intelligences, shown in 9-3. The list is still evolving. Gardner believes that each person possesses all of these types, but to different degrees.

Schools typically focus on just a few of these types of intelligences. If you have strong logical intelligence, you may get high grades in math. However, you are not graded directly on strong interpersonal skills or dramatic abilities.

Gardner's work has prompted many schools and teachers to take a broader view of intelligence. They have found that by using activities that draw on more types of intelligence, students learn more, all areas of intelligence improve, and behavior problems are reduced.

Tapping Individual Learning Strengths

As you read about learning styles and multiple intelligences, you may have noticed similarities. Although they look at different aspects of learning, teachers can use many of the same techniques to incorporate both into their teaching. Experienced teachers who have made such changes have reported increased enthusiasm for teaching and significant gains in both attitude and learning among their students. Specific benefits include the following:

- *Understanding student potential.* When teachers begin to evaluate students' potential on more than whether they score well on written tests or contribute to class discussions, a change often occurs in their own attitude. They look for other strengths, particularly in underperforming students, and begin to devise ways to use these to improve learning. This, in itself, can improve students' attitudes toward learning. Feeling that a teacher has confidence in their abilities makes them want to try harder. When activities take into account diverse learning styles and intelligences, students are more likely to connect to the material.

- *Using varied teaching techniques.* Good teachers know that they cannot teach a concept in just one way, and that different topics lend themselves to different teaching methods. Incorporating learning styles and multiple intelligences simply builds on this. Teachers can consciously expand their choices so that more learning styles and intelligences are included.

A third-grade teacher who is introducing the concept of the free enterprise system could assign students to read the related chapter in their social studies textbook and fill out a worksheet. Both of these activities match the strengths of visual learners and those with linguistic intelligence—often the same students. An alternative would be to introduce the concept by asking

Gardner's Multiple Intelligences			
Type of Intelligence	**Strengths**	**Student Characteristics**	**Preferred Learning Activities**
Logical-mathematical	Good with logical problems and math	Performs well in math and science, abstract thinking, classifying	Strategy games, experiments, math problems, logic exercises, problem solving
Spatial	Good at visualizing	Has artistic skills, imagination, can think in three dimensions	Drawing, picturing, making models, seeing patterns, visual puzzles
Bodily-kinesthetic	Good with movement, hands-on activities	Coordinated, athletic, may like art, crafts, or building	Drama, dance, crafts, experiments
Linguistic	Good with words	Has good written or oral communication skills and large vocabulary, learns languages easily	Reading, story telling, writing, note taking, summarizing, word puzzles
Musical	Good with rhythm and sound patterns	Understands rhythm, tone, sings or hums to self, emotionally sensitive	Music, auditory activities, those requiring emotional sensitivity
Intrapersonal	Good analyzer of self, own strengths and weaknesses	Reflective, goal-oriented, instinctive, makes good personal decisions	Journaling, reflection exercises, self-paced work, personal projects
Interpersonal	Good with communication	Communicates well, leadership, sensitive to others, understands others, resolves conflicts	Group activities, discussions, group projects
Naturalistic	In tune with and analyzes environment	Observes, classifies, visualizes	Collections, observations, journaling, creating charts
Existentialist	Good at asking philosophical questions	Learns best through seeing the "big picture" of human existence	Interactive communication tools, such as e-mail, teleconferencing

9-3

Gardner's theory of multiple intelligences encourages using activities that draw on a variety of intelligences.

questions to generate students' interests and determine their knowledge of the topic. "Does anyone have a savings account?" "How is that different from putting money in your piggy bank?" "What happens when everyone wants a popular video game, and it is in short supply?" Questions such as these can set the stage for learning. The teacher might still have the students read the textbook, but perhaps aloud as a class, discussing points and filling in a worksheet together as they read. Students could work in groups to develop a plan to sell an item other students might want to buy, deciding such things as what to sell and how much they would charge. They could develop an advertising skit, a song, or a rap. The second plan draws on a wider range of student strengths and learning styles. Students are also likely to learn and remember much more about the free enterprise system because of the following:

- *Allowing more student choice.* Sometimes teachers can allow students to choose how to explore a topic in more depth. The teacher may give a limited number of options or allow students to suggest their own alternatives (that meet certain criteria and are approved by the teacher). For example, a health lesson on the importance of exercise for people of all ages would lend itself to this approach. Students could work individually or in groups. Possible projects might include developing brochures, a videotape of exercises for seniors, an interview with a health professional, a radio ad promoting exercise, posters, charts with possible weight-loss calculations, media presentations, a game incorporating physical activity, a personal exercise journal, or a design for a fitness trail. When students work on projects of their choice, they often produce amazing results because they can draw on their strengths. At the same time, the whole class learns more when individuals and groups share the range of projects they have developed.

- *Helping individual learners.* Teachers can help students better understand their specific strengths and how to use them effectively. For example, a teacher can help a student understand that learning styles vary and discover which style is personally dominant. The next step would be assisting the student in finding learning, study, and test-taking techniques that match his or her personal strengths.

- *Helping all learners.* Both learning styles and multiple intelligences are based on the premise that everyone uses all styles and possesses all intelligences to some extent. By improving the areas that are not natural strengths, learning becomes easier and more complete. When teachers incorporate many techniques, students gain practice and skills in more of these areas. Those with a predominately kinesthetic-tactile learning style can learn to take better notes. Given practice, a person with high *intra*personal intelligence who is not outgoing can gain more *inter*personal intelligence and function more effectively in groups.

One key that many teachers miss is incorporating tips and techniques for gaining such skills into regular lessons. For example, a teacher might suggest three good ways to study for an upcoming test, each appropriate for a different learning style. Teachers at every level can help students better understand how their textbooks are structured and how to use them effectively. If students are asked to make a display or poster, briefly reviewing the aspects to consider will help more students succeed. Often, teachers take for granted that students have learned and remember how to successfully tackle a wide range of tasks. Simple reminders, explanations, examples, checklists, and organizational aids help students fill in the gaps and become more effective learners.

Exceptional Learners

For most students, the regular classroom with a caring and competent teacher can provide sufficient opportunities to learn well. However, some students require special educational modifications and, perhaps, other services matched to their abilities and potential. They are often called **exceptional learners**. There are two main groups of exceptional learners—gifted and talented students and learners with special needs.

Gifted and Talented Learners

Do you know someone who can solve complex problems quickly? Perhaps you know a young child with exceptional language skills or a classmate who always gets top scores on tests. You may have a friend who is a natural leader or a talented artist. Students who have abilities that are significantly greater than those of others their age and have exceptional potential are often referred to as gifted or talented. *Gifted* most often refers to those who excel academically. *Talented* is more often used for those who have outstanding skills in other areas, such as music, art, theater, dance, or leadership, 9-4. The terms are often used together and sometimes interchangeably.

Although gifted students are usually described as "smart," there is no one definition or test to determine who qualifies. Some students seem to have high intelligence that helps them do well in most subjects. Others excel in one or two areas, such as math or writing. Some students who make high grades may not have exceptional intelligence but succeed mostly because of motivation, good organizational skills, and hard work. In general, those who are at the very top of a school's population or have scored in a designated range on an indicator (standardized) test are often considered gifted.

9-4
Talented students
are often called
exceptional learners.

Howard Gardner's multiple intelligence theory has been influential in increasing the recognition of students who have talents or intelligences in other areas. A student who plays in a youth symphony may have exceptional talent. A teen who can turn a pile of miscellaneous parts into a helpful invention would seem to deserve as much credit as someone who excels at physics. Many school districts now find ways to support both gifted and talented students.

Supporting the Gifted and Talented

Within society and education, people have different views about schools' responsibilities toward gifted and talented students. Some believe that since these students usually excel with little special training or support, no special programs or efforts are needed. Others feel that it is important to help gifted and talented students reach their highest potential so that they can better help society in the future.

The wide variation in the types of gifts and talents raises other issues. Schools and teachers are faced with real challenges in determining how to best help students with so many different exceptional potentials and abilities. Over the years, many options have been developed. They include the following:

- *Providing in-class enrichment.* Students remain in regular classes but their teachers tailor some learning opportunities and projects to their special interests and abilities.

- *Using self-paced learning.* Students learn at their own rate. **Self-paced learning** allows students to spend the amount of time they personally need to master concepts. Students who are more advanced can move on to more difficult concepts as soon as they are ready. Students progress at individual rates, rather than as a class.

- *Skipping a grade.* Gifted students sometimes skip one grade and move on to the next. This approach is less common today than in the past. Students, particularly younger ones, often lack the social and emotional skills to handle this successfully. They may also miss out on concepts taught at a particular grade.

- *Attending special schools.* Some larger school districts have schools for academically gifted students. Some also offer magnet schools. **Magnet schools** are organized to emphasize a particular subject area, such as science, or promote an area of talent, such as the arts. High-achieving students from throughout the district may enroll.

- *Providing pull-out programs.* Students attend regular classes for part of the day. During other periods, they participate in a **pull-out program**. Students leave regular classes to participate in educational sessions geared toward specific needs. Gifted pull-out programs can provide advanced learning and opportunities to work and socialize with other gifted students.

- *Participating in extracurricular programs.* Most schools offer opportunities outside of the regular school day for students to pursue interests. Sports, clubs, special-interest classes, and similar options all give students possibilities for improving knowledge and skills in areas of interest.

- *Taking advanced classes.* Community colleges in many states offer high school students the opportunity to take college courses while still in high school. Some colleges and universities allow gifted students to enter early.

Although some teachers specialize in teaching gifted and talented students, regular classroom teachers usually have gifted and talented students in their classes as well. Students with high academic ability in one or more subjects often need enrichment to the curriculum and assignments to keep them learning and interested. Technology allows techniques such as self-paced learning to be used within the classroom. Gifted students can be given assignments with more rigorous requirements. Sometimes students join the class in a higher grade for a particular subject. Grouping gifted or talented students for some projects and activities may be appropriate. Students with talents in other areas can be encouraged to use them to complete projects and activities. Depending on the student and the situation, classroom teachers have many options.

Learners with Special Needs

The term **special needs** includes a broad range of physical, mental, social, and behavioral challenges that impact learning. Students with speech, vision, and hearing disorders are also considered to have special needs. The effects of these conditions can range from minimal to severe.

As you learned in Chapter 7, Congress passed the *Education for All Handicapped Children Act* in 1975. This required public schools to provide students with a free appropriate public education in the least restrictive environment possible, 9-5. The law was renamed the *Individuals with Disabilities Education Act (IDEA)* in the 1990s.

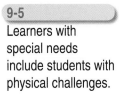

9-5

Learners with special needs include students with physical challenges.

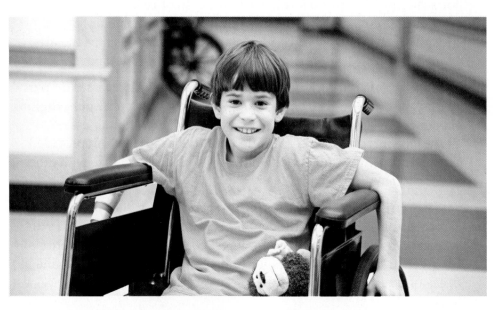

Part of the *IDEA* requires that public schools create an **Individualized Education Program (IEP)** for each student who meets specific requirements. The IEP is developed by a team that includes the child's parent or guardian; one or more regular classroom teachers; a special education teacher; and a school counselor, psychologist, or administrator.

An individualized education program is a written plan for providing a student with the most appropriate opportunity for learning. It describes the student's level of performance and how the child's disability affects academic performance. Academic goals and objectives are set. The plan describes specific **accommodations** or modifications to the environment, learning strategies, or materials that are made to help students with particular special needs succeed in the classroom. (For example, a student who is blind might need Braille copies of textbooks.) The IEP specifies services needed for the student to succeed in the classroom. The goal of an IEP is to provide the least restrictive, most effective learning environment for the student.

Meeting the Needs of Students with Disabilities

Depending on the individual student, schools may use various educational placements or a combination of them. These include the following:

- *Mainstreaming.* In **mainstreaming**, students are placed in one or more regular classes based on their expected ability to keep up with the standard curriculum. They may have extra learning aids, but they are not treated as special students. For example, a student who is hearing impaired may have an interpreter in class, but is responsible for all regular class assignments. Mainstreaming works for many special needs students.

- *Inclusion.* Sometimes students with special needs are placed in regular classes, even if they are not able to keep up academically with class requirements. In **inclusion**, the only requirement is that the student will benefit from the class. For example, a student with Down syndrome might be placed in a regular classroom, even if unable to keep up academically, to gain social interaction skills. A student included on this basis would complete modified assignments. Special education teachers serve as resources for classroom teachers when students are placed for inclusion.

- *Special education classes.* Students with special needs may spend part or all of their day in classes with other students with similar disabilities. **Special education** provides adapted programs, extra staff, and specialized equipment or learning environments or materials to help students with special needs to learn. Special education teachers are trained to adapt and individualize learning for many different special needs. Students with severe disabilities often spend the whole day in special education classrooms to best meet their learning needs.

Cultural Diversity

Part of this nation's strength comes from the fact that people with different backgrounds, languages, races, and religions have come together to form one society. The United States is a country of immigrants. From the first colonists to those who have come recently, individuals and groups from many countries have added vitality and energy, as well as skills and knowledge, to their new country. Schools reflect the diversity of the United States, 9-6.

Many people identify with a specific ethnic group based on their heritage. **Ethnicity** refers to a particular racial, national, or cultural group including that group's customs, beliefs, values, and often language and religion. Racial diversity is just one component of diversity. Some people identify with a racial group. Others identify with their country of origin or that of their ancestors. Many people simply see themselves as American.

9-6
Teachers should be aware that a student's culture, background, and experiences affect his or her learning.

Using Diversity to Enrich Learning

It is natural to gravitate toward people with whom you have things in common. However, listening to different ideas and opinions, learning to understand others, and trying new experiences all stimulate thought and learning. This happens when you are part of a diverse learning environment.

To schools that see diversity primarily as a source of conflict, it presents an arduous challenge. It may be viewed as something that requires extra effort and resources. To those who embrace diversity, it can offer a competitive edge. Diversity is woven into the school's vision, mission, values, and student learning. Together, this unified climate delivers a rich learning environment.

School administrators set the overall tone for a school regarding diversity. Teachers who model acceptance, develop policies of tolerance, and incorporate interest in culture into learning create a positive atmosphere for learning. In classrooms where students know they are respected and treated as individuals, learning is enhanced. In such an atmosphere, students develop the skills they need to succeed in the adult world. Employers rely on employees who can collaborate with one another, using their individual strengths and experiences as positive forces. **Stereotypes**—preconceived generalizations about certain groups of people—and prejudice have no place in schools or the workplace.

A student's culture, background, and experiences affect his or her learning. All of these factors create a context in which a learner grows and develops, and they have an important impact on learning.

Teaching requires sensitivity to each student's personal situation. For example, some cultures discourage competition. Learning about students' cultures may come from meeting with parents, listening to the students' personal stories, and studying cultural traditions. As with other students, family structures and financial situations should be taken into account. (Students from low-income families may not be able to participate in activities that require extra fees.) Not all students have two parents. For example, instead of making Mother's Day cards, a sensitive teacher might introduce a class project of making thank you cards as a way of thanking someone who has been helpful.

Language Diversity

Language is linked to culture, but students from other cultures who are not proficient in the English language face additional challenges in school. Such students are described as having **limited English proficiency (LEP)**. They are sometimes also referred to as **English language learners (ELL)**. They must learn English while also mastering the content of their regular classes.

The process of learning English is not an easy one. It involves developing reading and writing skills, as well as verbal communication. In addition to general vocabulary, every subject area has its own specialized terms. Understanding also depends on learning about popular culture, such as holidays and traditions, television and movies, music, magazines, and fashion.

There is debate about how to best help these students. States and school districts have tried a variety of approaches. On one end of the spectrum, *bilingual* programs teach all classes in two languages, English and students' native language. On the other end, students spend the school day in regular classes taught in English and receive some additional help outside of class. Sometimes students attend regular classes part of the day and a pull-out *English as a Second Language (ESL)* program for other periods. ESL programs concentrate on teaching English language skills.

Many variables are involved in decisions about how to structure programs. Some school districts have a large percentage of English language learners. One language may be dominant, or students may speak dozens of different languages. Other districts have few students not proficient in English.

Helping English Language Learners

Classroom teachers who have students with limited English proficiency must be innovative in finding ways to help them. Younger children pick up the oral skills of a new language more quickly than older students. Older students also must deal with more difficult school subjects and a faster pace of learning.

Many techniques for these situations mirror those of good teaching in general. For example, when teachers use several methods to teach concepts, the English language learner has multiple possibilities for understanding.

Other techniques are based on common sense. Speaking clearly, printing assignments on the board, summarizing, demonstrating, and giving step-by-step directions can all be helpful. Students often benefit from working in pairs and groups. Teachers may provide study guides emphasizing key points and vocabulary. Working collaboratively with experts in the school, such as an ESL teacher, to alter instruction is often helpful.

The Challenge of Teaching Diverse Learners

Perhaps, after reading this chapter, the idea of meeting the needs of so many different types of learners seems a bit overwhelming, 9-7. There is no doubt that teaching is a challenging profession, but that is part of

9-7
Meeting the needs of diverse learners means learning about students as individuals to maximize learning for all students.

its appeal. Putting forth your best efforts to help all students succeed is worthwhile and can be immensely satisfying.

Meeting the needs of individuals does not require separate teaching plans for every student. It starts with the belief in each student's potential. It means learning about students as individuals, their knowledge, abilities, strengths, challenges, interests, and learning styles. Effective teachers plan their teaching to target a wide range of students. Classes of students often include individuals with special needs, gifted students, and English language learners, in addition to other types of diversity.

Many teachers use a philosophy of teaching called differentiated instruction to maximize learning for all students. With **differentiated instruction**, a teacher often provides options for learning a topic or skill. Either the teacher or the students may choose options that fit the students' needs or learning styles. For example, if students are to learn about the metamorphosis of caterpillars into butterflies, the options might include reading about it, performing an experiment, using a computer simulation, or creating a model of the process. For each option, the teacher would provide guidelines for learning and identify how that learning will be evaluated.

Teachers who use differentiated instruction often divide students into groups, but not always the same groups. For example, for one lesson, students might be divided according to how much they already know about the topic. For another, English Language Learners might work together, supported with important vocabulary translated into the first language. Sometimes the teacher might have learning activities suited to different learning styles.

Learning more now about the spectrum of students who may one day sit in your classroom gives you a head start. You can pay attention to how your current teachers deal with learning diversity. As you study to become a teacher, choose projects, activities, and experiences that will prepare you well for this aspect of teaching. Commit to being a creative and caring teacher.

Summary

Students vary in the ways they learn most easily. These preferred methods are known as learning styles. Howard Gardner has also theorized that people have many types of intelligences, although schools typically focus on only a few of these. By understanding learning styles and multiple intelligences, teachers can help students learn more effectively.

Both students who are considered gifted and talented and those with special needs are called exceptional learners. Gifted students usually excel in one or two academic areas, not necessarily all areas. Talented students excel in other areas, such as fine arts. Schools can provide opportunities for these students to build their gifts and talents.

Students with special needs may have any of a variety of problems that impact learning. These range from physical, mental, emotional, and social disabilities to speech, vision, hearing, and learning disorders. The effects of these problems can range from minimal to severe. Schools work with parents and professionals to determine the best learning situation for students with special needs.

Cultural factors, background, and experiences also can impact students. Schools must provide environments that are free of bias. When diversity is seen as a positive force in schools, it can enhance learning and prepare students to work effectively in the diversity of society.

Students just learning English face additional learning challenges. Schools use different techniques for helping them learn the language and content. Classroom teachers can use a variety of methods, as well, to help these students.

Effective teaching requires identifying the characteristics of individual learners and devising ways to meet their needs. A commitment to doing so can have a long-lasting impact on lives of the learners.

Review

1. What does the term *learning diversity* mean?

2. What learning style would be linked to the following ways a young child might learn the alphabet?
   a. Singing the "ABC" song.
   b. Placing magnetic alphabet shapes on a refrigerator door and identifying them.
   c Creating letter shapes with the fingers.

3. Which two multiple intelligence areas are most closely linked to success in core school subjects? Give a rationale for your choices.

4. How could analyzing an underperforming student's strengths using multiple intelligence theory help a teacher improve the student's learning?

5. What do magnet schools emphasize?

6. How are pull-out programs used in gifted education?

7. Who makes up the team that develops an Individualized Education Program (IEP) for a student?

8. What is the difference between mainstreaming and inclusion programs?

9. How does a school environment that treats diversity as an asset prepare students for the workplace?

10. Identify three strategies classroom teachers can use to help English language learners. Explain why each technique can be helpful for these students.

11. Why do some teachers use differentiated instruction? How do they do this?

Reflect

1. What would you consider your primary and secondary learning styles? Which do you think are your top four intelligences? Give your rationale for these selections. How are your preferred learning styles and top areas of intelligence related? How has having these particular traits affected your school experiences?

2. Why do you think that schools have historically put more emphasis on academic giftedness over talents in other areas? Identify some specific ways that schools could be more supportive of talented students.

3. Develop a list of five key classroom rules you would use to foster respect for all learners in the classroom. Identify the grade levels for which these rules would be appropriate.

4. Compare and contrast the experience of learning a foreign language as a subject in school with learning English for the first time while a student in a school in the United States.

Act

1. Observe a group of young children at play. Try to detect the preferred style of learning for at least two children. In your report, identify the specific examples that support your conclusions.

2. Choose one way to find out more about education for students with special needs. For example, you might interview a special education teacher or a parent of a student with special needs, observe a class, or conduct online research. Write a brief proposal with specifics of your project for your teacher's approval. Include a paragraph on whether your choice draws on specific types of intelligence that are your strengths or will help you improve skills in other areas of intelligence.

3. Work cooperatively in a small group to identify the responsibilities of each of the following groups in making diversity a positive aspect of education: parents, community members, administrators, teachers, and students. How can each group disrupt such efforts?

4. Interview someone who immigrated to the United States. Develop questions you will ask that relate to the experience of dealing with differences in language, customs, and schools. Share the results of your interview with the class.

Add to Your Portfolio

Choose a grade level and subject that you may be interested in teaching. Identify a specific topic you might teach for three to five days. Develop a plan of teaching and learning activities for that topic that incorporates various learning styles and provides opportunities to use different types of intelligence. Identify the specific learning styles and types of intelligence linked to each activity. Add your plan to your portfolio.

10 WHAT MAKES AN EFFECTIVE TEACHER?

Key Terms

facilitator

assessment

ethics

organizational culture

mission statement

chain of command

lifelong learners

professional development

mixed message

active listening

assertive communicator

aggressive communicator

passive communicator

mediator

mediation

Objectives

After studying this chapter, you will be able to

- **describe** the major roles that teachers perform.

- **identify** teachers' professional qualities that have had an impact on your life.

- **compare** your school's written information on organizational culture to your observations.

- **explain** the importance of subject-matter knowledge to teachers and how they can stay updated.

- **demonstrate** your ability to produce clear, professional, written communication.

- **identify** the steps in constructive conflict resolution and describe the goal of mediation.

"Another crazy day!" Anna reflected, as she rode the subway home. There were no boring days teaching fourth grade. Today's lessons included reading, long division, spelling, state history, and folk dancing. Students worked in groups for reading. Some struggled with long division, others with spelling. A few didn't want to dance with a partner. Other students were excited about everything. Those were the planned topics, but the day, like most, didn't go entirely according to plan.

Today, there was a long fire drill with everyone standing outside in the cold wind. After lunch, two boys came close to trading blows. A normally shy girl told a funny joke that made everyone laugh. The twins brought a picture of their new baby sister. Another student cried when he missed the bus. One boy remembered his homework for the first time in a week. Another gave her a big smile when he passed his spelling test.

It had been a day of familiar routines, dealing with the unexpected, and quickly adapting her teaching plans. She had smoothed over disputes, given feedback, and shared emotions. Anna knew tomorrow would bring a new set of challenges and rewards.

You, like every person thinking of becoming a teacher, want to be a great one. Perhaps you were inspired by a wonderful teacher who made a real difference in your life.

If you put a group of highly effective teachers together in a room, you might be surprised by their obvious differences. They would, for example, vary in personality. By looking deeper, however, you would find they have much in common. They are comfortable in the numerous roles that teachers play. They display important characteristics of professionalism. They understand how to work effectively within their school. Everyone respects their knowledge and teaching skill. They are effective communicators and are able to deal effectively with conflicts that arise.

This chapter will help you learn more about what it takes to become that great teacher. Many of the topics explored here will be discussed in greater detail in other chapters. As you read, think about how you can start now developing the attitudes, skills, and knowledge you will need to have a positive impact on students' lives.

Teaching Roles

If you were asked what teachers do, how would you answer? In the most simplistic terms, they teach. How that plays out on a daily basis is infinitely varied.

Teachers have many roles. These change quickly, sometimes minute by minute. Although the roles may change, all focus on helping students learn. The following five key roles deserve a more in-depth look:

- information provider
- facilitator
- planner
- learning evaluator
- role model

Teachers Provide Information

Students know that teachers are great sources of information, and providing information is an essential teaching role. Competent teachers know the content of the subjects they teach well. A middle school math teacher may not have the depth of math knowledge that a math professor at a university may have, but that makes sense. A teacher's knowledge base should be appropriate in scope and depth for the level taught. Today, the problem is often that there is an overload of available information. Knowing their subject matter well helps teachers evaluate information. It allows them to choose what is most accurate and relevant to present to their students, 10-1.

10-1
Teachers who know their subject matter are a great source of information for their students.

Parents and students expect teachers to provide appropriate, current information. If you are learning the abdominal thrust (Heimlich maneuver) for choking victims, you want to be confident that your teacher knows the technique and guidelines and correctly demonstrates the procedure. At the very least, providing inaccurate information wastes everyone's time. In cases such as this, it can be the difference between life and death.

At the same time, considering teachers only as information providers would not be accurate. Information is readily available, especially with today's technology. If you want to know more about English grammar, you could easily read a grammar book or find a tutorial online. However, most people learn better when the best information at the right level is presented in a variety of interesting ways. Interaction, feedback, review, and practice are also keys to learning. That is where some of teachers' other roles come into play.

Teachers Facilitate Learning

Teachers play the role of **facilitator**. This means they create situations that help students learn by actively involving students in learning, rather then just presenting information. They do this in a variety of ways. They plan what will be taught and figure out how to best present the material. They lead discussions. They ask questions. They suggest alternative ideas. They devise and guide student activities. They help students to work together. Simply put, teachers guide students' learning.

Leading by facilitating is not the same as directing learning, however. Teachers who use direct learning tell students what to learn and provide all the structure for the learning to take place. Facilitators guide, rather than direct. Both methods are appropriate in certain situations. For example, having students follow set directions carefully is appropriate in a science experiment that involves chemicals that could be dangerous if combined incorrectly.

When teachers act as facilitators, they require that students do the work of learning. For example, when students ask questions, the teacher helps and encourages them to find the answers for themselves. Not every student is comfortable with the open-ended nature of facilitative learning. Some prefer knowing exactly what they are supposed to learn and the steps needed to understand.

One benefit of facilitated learning is that it can unleash students' creativity and self-motivation. They often feel more pride and ownership in their learning. Students who are motivated and engaged in the learning process are also less likely to exhibit problem behaviors.

Facilitation is a learned skill. Teachers who facilitate well know the difference between "getting the job done right" (the teacher's way) and making sure that students are learning. As a new teacher, you will develop this skill with practice.

Teachers Plan for Learning

In planning for instruction, teachers determine what information will be learned, how it will be presented, and what the outcomes should be. They plan ways to assess whether or not learning took place. They utilize resources to adapt lessons for different types of learners. They devise ways to make learning challenging, fun, inspiring, and effective.

Although teachers put a great deal of time into planning, they know that plans will not always work out. Emergencies arise and unexpected events happen. Sometimes unforeseen teaching opportunities (teachable moments) come along in the course of a lesson, and teachers decide to take advantage of them. Experienced teachers learn to adapt to the unexpected. Changes in plans can enhance learning and teach students flexibility.

Teachers Evaluate Learning

Another important role of teachers is to evaluate students' learning and progress. Sometimes this process results in a grade. Other times it does not.

When teachers assign grades to students' work, they are evaluating how much or how well the students have learned. (Actually, learning itself cannot be accurately measured. Teachers look at how well students can demonstrate what they have learned.) Grades are usually a letter (**A, B, C, D,** or **F**) or a number. Letter grades have standard meanings. An **A** is excellent, a **B** is above average, a **C** is average, a **D** is below average, and an **F** means failing. Report cards typically show letter grades, sometimes with a plus or minus sign.

Students need to understand their teachers' grading policies. With older students, grades are often a point of conflict. Having clear, consistent policies helps minimize disputes. With younger children, understanding what "counts" helps them know what kinds of effort a teacher expects so they can benefit most from learning. For example, Anthony, a bright but shy third-grader, rarely raised his hand to answer a question. Once he found out participation counted toward his grade, he was more willing to volunteer. The class benefited from his contributions, and he gradually became more outgoing.

Assessment is a related, but somewhat different, type of evaluation. It involves determining how much a student or class has learned or is currently learning. When teachers assess student performance, they are simply reporting on achievement. There is no judgment or consideration of quality, as there is in grading. For example, if the lesson is on the impact of good nutrition on the growth of a baby chick, the teacher may use discussion to assess students' understanding. If that shows students haven't understood main points, the teacher might review or add an activity before moving on to another topic.

Both types of evaluation—grading and assessment—involve monitoring student progress. They vary primarily in purpose.

Teachers Are Role Models

Schools are one of the first, and most important, places where behavior and future educational success are shaped. Teachers are important role models for their students, 10-2.

Being a role model comes with a great deal of responsibility. Teachers' behavior can have either a positive or negative effect on students' behavior and future success. The best teachers live in ways that demonstrate the values, attitudes, and behaviors that go with the roles of learner, professional, and citizen.

10-2
Many students look to their teachers as positive role models.

Whether they are at school or in the community, teachers must show honesty, respect, and responsibility. Effective teachers do not simply talk about examples, they act as examples. They live the expectations they have for their students by coming to class well prepared. They show competence, commitment, and integrity. They model how to handle disagreements. They set high standards for themselves, as well as others.

Developing Professional Qualities

Qualities related to professionalism are critical to teaching success. The term *professional* is used frequently to indicate a high degree of skill, competence, and **ethics** (conduct based on moral principles). Your reputation as a professional is important to being successful as a teacher. This section identifies some of the important skills, habits, and attitudes professionals exhibit.

Be Dependable

In the workplace, dependability is highly valued. For teachers, it is doubly important. Each school day, students rely on their teachers to be there on time and to be prepared to teach. People who are dependable are reliable and loyal. Others know they can be counted on to do what they say. Think about what would happen if a coach does not show up for a game or a teacher is three days late turning in grades. One employee's lack of dependability can have far-reaching consequences.

Be Responsible

Imagine that you are a kindergarten teacher. You are gathering up your things to leave school on a Friday afternoon when you receive a call from the mother of one of your students. She is obviously upset. She tells you that her daughter may not be in school on Monday because the family has just been evicted from their home. She does not know if or where they will be able to find a place to stay. It would be easy to just say that you are sorry and ask the mother to notify the school office on Monday. Instead, you alert the school counselor to the issue. She is able to secure a place for the family at a shelter. You assure the mother that you will be especially sensitive to her daughter's needs as she adjusts to an abrupt lifestyle change. Because you took the time to follow through, you will be a bit late for dinner with friends. Taking the time to aid this family is worth the minor inconvenience. You feel a responsibility for your students that goes beyond the classroom.

Being responsible means being committed to your obligations, relationships, and actions. It means not blaming someone else when things do not go exactly as planned. When working on a team, you commit to doing your best, which may result in personal satisfaction. Facing difficult challenges will earn respect from others and a reputation for accomplishment and trustworthiness.

Responsibility means carrying a task through to the end, whether or not the process is easy. You commit to being the person who has the ultimate responsibility to get the job done. Those who handle responsibility well are usually asked to take on more. They find that facing difficult challenges can bring real satisfaction.

Be Committed to Students

As you read in the previous chapter, effective teachers come to the classroom believing that all students can learn, though how they learn best may differ. Through careful observation, teachers can better understand each student's abilities, skills, interests, strengths, and relationships. In addition to helping students gain specific content knowledge, teachers also help foster self-esteem and motivation to learn. This requires a real commitment to each individual.

Show Respect

Showing respect involves showing regard for others' dignity, ideas, and expectations. As a student, you show a teacher respect by being courteous and meeting his or her course requirements or standards. Teachers treat students with respect when they show regard for each individual's needs, feelings, and potential.

For teachers, showing respect within their school or other workplace is a key skill. They expect respect from their students. At the same time, they need to show respect for their students and for everyone on staff.

Many new teachers fail to understand and acknowledge their place in the workplace organization. Even the most casual, unstructured schools have organizational structures, although they may be difficult to identify. You owe respect to those above you, but a professional treats everyone well. Too often, the roles and importance of *support staff*, all the nonteaching personnel from bus drivers to food service personnel and counselors, are underestimated. You show that respect through your attitude, how you communicate, and the courtesy you show others.

Be a Team Player

In survey after survey, employers list effective interpersonal skills as the primary characteristic they look for in potential employees. People with good interpersonal skills get along well with others in the workplace and are good team players.

Almost all jobs require *collaboration*—working cooperatively with others. Because so much of work is accomplished through teams, it is essential to be a team player. In effective teams, members encourage one another and utilize the skills and talents of individual members, 10-3. They focus on group success, rather than on taking individual credit. Ineffective teams are usually due to a poorly defined task or, more likely, a lack of teamwork.

10-3
Sharing computer skills with other staff members is an example of being a team player.

Teachers not only work with students, they also work with fellow teachers, staff, administrators, and school board members. Effective teachers work in collaboration with other school personnel on everything from curriculum (what is taught) to developing school policies.

See the Big Picture

"Seeing the big picture" means looking past the small details and remaining focused on the larger purpose. Some people get so bogged down in their own tasks or day-to-day problems that they lose sight of the real goals. For example, if a teacher is so focused on getting through a lesson, the special learning needs of individual children may be overlooked.

Seeing the big picture does not mean overlooking the details of a job. In fact, many jobs require a high level of attention to details. However, the larger purpose should always be kept in mind.

Develop a Positive Attitude

Why do some people love their work and others do not? Two factors are usually involved. They have a positive attitude, and they get satisfaction from what they do.

Having a positive attitude means having the optimism and energy to positively relate to others and to complete a job. It is the desire to make something happen.

Keeping a positive attitude has many benefits. When you can see the potential good in situations, those around you will be energized by your enthusiasm. Conversely, constantly complaining drags you and others down. While individuals often have a tendency toward optimism or pessimism, each person can make a conscious choice to try to keep a positive attitude.

What if you find yourself in a difficult work situation? Being proactive in finding solutions will help improve your attitude. Take a step back to note what you like most about your job. Are you excited about helping students learn? Focus on the positive strides your students are making, rather than on an administrator who isn't as supportive as you would like. If you are dealing with students whose behaviors are getting you down, network with colleagues for a new approach to discipline. Try to find out if the environment may be restructured to minimize the negative behaviors. What is within your power to make your job more personally rewarding?

Think about the benefits of establishing these habits—thinking positively and improving difficult situations—now. They will help you through rough spots in school, work, and life. Most of all, you will enjoy life more and have a positive impact on others. You cannot control life, but you can control your reactions to it.

Working Effectively Within a School

You have landed your first teaching job. You are off to the back-to-school picnic for teachers, wearing shorts and flip-flops. When you arrive, all of the other teachers are dressed in coordinated sportswear, mainly khaki pants, and pressed shirts. Is it all in your mind or is everyone a little guarded in conversations with you? Did you miss a memo about what to wear, or do you not understand the organizational culture?

What is **organizational culture**? It is the "personality" of an organization based on the assumptions, values, standards, behaviors, and actions of people, as well as the tangible signs of an organization. For teachers, the organization is the school. Some signs of organizational culture are easy to recognize. They include the things you can see or observe, such as the "look" of the space, the way people dress, and which accomplishments are highlighted. Others are intangible, or less concrete. These include people's assumptions, values, and the reasons behind their behaviors and actions.

How can you figure out the culture of a school? A good place to start is with the school policies and procedures and how the school or school district is structured. Many schools and school districts have a manual for new teachers. This may include a **mission statement**—the official version of an organization's purpose and goals, along with policies and procedures. Official Web sites may give information about the **chain of command**. This is the official organizational structure that tells who reports to whom. For example, department heads may report to the principal who reports directly to the superintendent. What responsibilities do those in various positions have? Understanding the chain of command and how it works in your school is important. In many workplaces, you are expected to discuss problems and issues with your immediate supervisor, rather than go directly to people above that person. Look for how the school values and uses people, facilities, space, and other resources, such as technology. Do the school's stated goals match what you observe?

The next step in understanding organizational culture is to ask questions. Fellow teachers are usually willing to share information. Pay attention to conversations and how people negotiate issues. How do things get done? Who has the most influence? (Remember that the official chain of command does not always reflect what is really happening.) Understanding and assessing the organizational culture can mean the difference between success and failure in the workplace.

Subject Knowledge and Teaching Skills

Teachers must have a thorough understanding of the subject that they teach. A Spanish teacher must know Spanish through speech and written text. A kindergarten teacher must understand the developmental abilities of five- and six-year-olds.

The best teachers have a broad understanding of their subject matter. They understand how it is organized, how it has changed over time, and how it may change in the future. They know how their subject matter relates to other subjects such as reading, math, and writing. Teachers also need to understand how their subject matter relates to careers students might later pursue.

New discoveries and information are added continually, so teachers must be **lifelong learners**. This means that they commit to staying up to date in their knowledge and skills, 10-4. Some of this requires reading and study. Effective teachers also take advantage of opportunities for **professional development**. Professional development involves taking part in professional organizations, attending seminars and conferences, pursuing an advanced degree, or other activities meant to improve your professional knowledge and skills.

10-4

Effective teachers stay up to date by seeking opportunities for professional development and being lifelong learners.

It is not enough for teachers to just know their subject matter. They must also know how to teach it. A driver's education teacher must be able to demonstrate and quickly communicate accident-avoidance techniques.

Teachers must be skilled at many teaching techniques and know which work best with particular topics and students. One class may have great discussions and learn effectively from them. Another may have few people who volunteer ideas. In every class, individual students have unique combinations of learning abilities and styles. An effective teacher adapts the teaching techniques accordingly.

Teachers must utilize many different creative teaching methods to capture their students' interest. Not all students learn in the same ways, so variety helps enhance learning. Choosing the best technique for particular material and adapting it skillfully is the sign of a good teacher.

Communicating Effectively

Virtually every aspect of teaching is based on communication, 10-5. Teachers determine what content to communicate and decide how best to convey it. The act of teaching depends on effectively communicating with students. Teachers, administrators, school boards, and community members all must exchange ideas. Parents, too, are part of the communication loop. This process can work well, but communication is complex, and there are many ways it can break down.

10-5
Communication between teachers and students is vital in order for learning to take place.

People communicate continually, even when they are not aware they are doing so. Your best friend ignored you at lunch. Did you offend her, or is she worried about her mom's health again? Every word spoken, gesture, action, and facial expression sends a message that is interpreted by the receiver. The person who transmits a message or messages is called the *sender*. The *receiver* in communication is the person who accepts a message from another. Normally, communication involves being both a sender and receiver.

For effective communication, the sender's spoken words and nonverbal messages must match. The nonverbal messages may come from a person's posture, tone of voice, facial expressions, eye contact (or lack of it), and many other things. When there is a discrepancy between verbal and non-verbal messages, it is called a **mixed message**. Mixed messages confuse receivers. A teacher who laughs while scolding a child for breaking a rule is sending a mixed message.

While there are many components of effective communication, two key ones will be explored here. First, communication must occur in the context of positive relationships. Second, each form of communication—verbal, nonverbal, written, and electronic—depends on specific, but related, skills.

Creating Positive Relationships

Good communication begins with positive relationships. Negative relationships create barriers that impede effective communication. For example, you are angry with your brother. He asks if you will swap chores with him, and you snap back that he is just trying to get out of work. His message was about a trade of jobs, but all you hear is that he wants you to mow the lawn so he doesn't have to do it. Because of your feelings, you put a negative spin on even a neutral message from him.

Several factors go into building positive relationships. These include the following:

- *Take ownership in the relationship.* This means taking responsibility for your own feelings and behaviors, rather than blaming others. For example, if you are feeling sad, acknowledge "I feel sad," rather than thinking "You make me sad." Your feelings are your own. They may be influenced by events, but another person does not cause them.

Understanding this difference will help you to realize that although you can influence others, you cannot control the feelings of others. For example, you can encourage young children to act appropriately in the classroom, but you cannot force them to want to behave. Rewards, encouragement, or punishments may influence a child toward a particular behavioral goal, but the motivation must come from the child.

- *Be an active listener.* **Active listening** involves asking questions and restating ideas to discover the true message of the sender. By giving verbal feedback, you tell the sender that you are listening and understanding the message. Look at the conversation between a teacher and student in 10-6. Each time the student makes a statement, the teacher demonstrates that he or she is listening by asking another clarifying question. By the end, it is clear that the student is feeling left out and friendless. From actively listening to the student, the teacher can then help solve the problem. Listening requires that you focus on the other person. It will help you to stay in the present moment and increase the exchange of clear communication.

- *Use assertive communication.* **Assertive communicators** freely express their thoughts, ideas, and feelings. However, they do so respectfully and allow others to do the same. **Aggressive communicators** aim to hurt or put down other people. They show disrespect. A third group, **passive communicators**, are unwilling to say what they feel, think, or desire. They want to avoid all conflict.

Improving Communication Skills

Effective teachers rely on exceptional communication skills. They are able to communicate clearly through speech and writing. Their nonverbal messages are consistent with what they say. They also use electronic communication to their advantage.

Speaking

Even though effective teachers are good listeners and involve students in activities, the many aspects of teaching involve a great deal of talking. Unlike casual conversation, teachers must speak with thought and purpose.

In the classroom, time is a limited commodity. Teachers must be conscious of using it effectively. Lesson plans help them figure out how to

Example of Active Listening
Chaney: I don't want to go to recess.
Mr. Griggs: Are you unhappy when you go to recess?
Chaney: Yeah. People are not very nice.
Mr. Griggs: What do they do that isn't nice?
Chaney: No one includes me.
Mr. Griggs: You feel left out of games?
Chaney: Yes. I wish I had more friends.

10-6
Teachers who are active listeners can better understand their students.

achieve as much learning as possible within a class period. Experienced teachers do not need to write out exactly what they will say, but they do identify the points to be learned and key questions to discuss. This allows them to achieve their goals while staying flexible enough to improvise based on what actually happens during the lesson.

Effective speaking requires tailoring what you say to your particular audience. What are their needs and interests? What motivates them? What will keep their attention and interest? Think about how what you say will affect your listeners. Simplicity and clarity are important. Choose words that your audience understands. When using words that are unfamiliar, briefly explain their meaning. As you speak, check your audience for signs of understanding and interest. It is important to tailor your message and how you present it to the specific audience.

As representatives of their school and role models for their students, teachers must remember they are almost never "off duty." A conversation with a friend while waiting to check out at the supermarket may be overheard and repeated. As professionals, teachers understand that it is never appropriate to speak badly about coworkers or students. Similarly, teachers have an ethical responsibility not to reveal personal information about students or confidential work-related information to anyone else, except as part of their job.

The old saying "Think before you speak" is a wise one. Words are powerful, and once they are spoken, they can never be taken back. It only takes a few seconds to think about what you will say before you speak. No one will notice the slight pause. Making it a habit to do so can save you and others much embarrassment, hurt feelings, and perhaps even your job.

Writing

In these days of dashing off text messages, formal writing may seem too time-consuming. However, important information, particularly in business and education, is still conveyed in writing. It is essential that teachers are able to write well.

Most of the guidelines for effective speaking also apply to good writing. A few additional points are important to remember:

- *Avoid trying to impress people with complicated words and long sentences.* Sometimes people think that complex writing full of difficult or trendy terms will make them seem more intelligent. Actually, this type of writing frustrates readers and may make them feel like the writer is trying to put them down. It is best to convey your message clearly and concisely. Consider your tone. Remember that your purpose is to communicate your message.

- *Organize your writing effectively.* Make sure your main points are clearly stated. Check to see whether you move logically from one topic to another. If what you have written is long, use headings to divide sections, and provide a brief summary.

- *Check your grammar and language.* Never rely on your computer's spelling- and grammar-checking features. They often miss problems or suggest incorrect solutions. Learn the rules of good grammar, keep a grammar reference at hand, and proofread what you have written (preferably more than once) before you send anything in writing. Always use formal standard English, not slang or texting abbreviations. Poor grammar and writing keeps many people from getting or advancing in jobs. If you are unsure of your writing skills, have someone else proofread your work and learn from your mistakes.

- *Realize that anything you write may be permanent.* Once you deliver a printed document, you have no control over where it goes. Think carefully about what you put in writing, and make sure it represents you and the school professionally.

Nonverbal Communication

While words can be powerful, so are other aspects of communication. Your facial expressions, body posture and movements, your tone of voice, and appearance are all forms of nonverbal communication. They can reinforce your words, take away their power, or confuse your listener. Even when you are not speaking, your body is.

You can improve the effectiveness of your communication by becoming more aware of your nonverbal cues. For example, you can make sure you are dressed appropriately for situations. Make an effort to speak calmly, even when you are upset. Pay attention to the messages your body is sending.

Nonverbal cues account for a major part of miscommunication and often cause stress in relationships. For example, a teacher's facial expression may communicate anger, even when the words do not. A smile may mask a message of seriousness.

Electronic Communication

While e-mailing and text messaging may seem like private forms of conversation, they illustrate some of the special problems that can come with electronic communication. Because it can seem so spontaneous, it is easy to quickly translate your thoughts and feelings into words and hit the Send button. The problem is that once you have sent them, you have no control over what happens to them. A message can be forwarded to others without your permission. Information posted on the Web, such as on a personal Web page, may stay there indefinitely.

Jacob found that out when he applied to be a camp counselor after his sophomore year in college. He was studying to be a teacher and thought the job would give him great experience working with middle school students. Unfortunately, the camp staff checked to see if applicants had personal Web pages. Jacob's included obscene language and pictures of him at a drinking party. He had posted these after high school graduation, and he had forgotten they were still on the site. He did not get the job.

Electronic communication has enormous benefits for teachers. It allows them to stay in touch with students and parents. It can be a great link to other teachers. However, it comes with additional potential pitfalls. Suggestions for effectively using e-mail, the most common form of electronic communication, are identified in 10-7.

Resolving Conflicts

Conflict is inevitable in any active relationship. People simply have different ideas, beliefs, and priorities. When they communicate, it is easy for these differences to surface.

People react to conflict in different ways. Some people view all disagreements as negative and try to avoid them. Others find conflict positive

10-7
These tips can help you to avoid electronic communication pitfalls.

Tips for Effective E-Mail
• Before you send a message, think what might happen if someone forwarded it without your knowledge or permission. Remember that your identity as the sender goes with your message.
• When you start using e-mail for any professional purpose (such as job applications or work-related correspondence), make sure you have an e-mail address that sounds professional.
• E-mails should have a descriptive subject line.
• Briefly summarize any necessary background information.
• Remember that all communication with teachers, potential employers, and the public should use formal standard English—no abbreviations.
• For professional messages, include your name, title, and contact information.
• Proofread your message carefully before sending it.
• Never say anything in an electronic message that you would not say in the same way directly to the recipient.
• Avoid large attachments.
• If you are replying to an e-mail, never "Reply to All" unless you really mean to do so. Your unflattering comment could go to those you don't intend.
• In most work situations, your employer can monitor your e-mails and computer use. Inappropriate use can be grounds for dismissal.

and enriching. Be aware of your own feelings about conflict, and remember that others' feelings may be different.

Certain situations increase the likelihood of conflict. It is common in close relationships. This is especially true when one person is comfortable communicating (especially communicating feelings) and the other is not. Conflict is common when people are under stress. They often say things they regret later.

Teachers routinely encounter situations where disagreements or miscommunication leads to conflict. They can help those involved deal more effectively with their differences.

Constructive Conflict Resolution

When two (or more) people work through a conflict in a constructive way, the result is greater understanding and relationship growth. When it is not handled well, conflict can lead to continued conflict. One effective approach is known as *constructive conflict management.*

Constructive conflict management is a step-by-step method of coming to a solution. Conflict can be thought of as a process that moves from decision making to problem solving to crisis resolution. The following are the steps in the process:

- *Step 1: Clarify the issue.* The process begins with identifying the problem. Remember that when two people are in conflict, they often identify the problem differently. Each person must honestly and clearly state the problem from his or her perspective. Each also must listen carefully to the other person.

- *Step 2: Find out what each person wants.* Each person in the conflict must identify and express what he or she wants or needs in order to resolve the situation.

- *Step 3: Identify various alternatives.* The next step is to identify various ways the conflict might be resolved. In constructive conflict resolution, both parties are open to suggestions. They are willing to brainstorm creative solutions. They try to focus on finding a solution, not just on meeting their own needs.

- *Step 4: Decide how to negotiate.* Decide on a resolution strategy. Will the areas of conflict be discussed in hopes one person will change his or her mind? Will each person give up part of what is wanted? Will they toss a coin? The people involved need to agree on how to proceed.

- *Step 5: Choose the best alternative.* There is rarely a solution that makes everyone happy. It is usually a matter of agreeing on which alternative both can accept. Sometimes a compromise just isn't possible, and the two sides simply agree to disagree.

- *Step 6: Solidify the agreement.* The parties must accept the choice they have made and agree to implement it.

- *Step 7: Review and renegotiate.* What happens when an agreement does not solve the problem? Perhaps one person does not follow through or accept the agreement. In that case, the decision should be reviewed and compliance requested. As a last resort, the conflict may need to be renegotiated.

Mediation

Of course, disagreements are not always easily solved. Often, the people involved are so emotional or convinced they are right that they will not negotiate. That is when a third party who is neutral—a **mediator**—can often help the process. A mediator tries to help those in the dispute reach a peaceful agreement. This process is called **mediation**.

Teachers frequently act as mediators, especially with students, 10-8. For example, two young children argue over whose turn it is to play with a toy. Their teacher may help them figure out a way to take turns. Older students may disagree over perceived personal rights.

When acting as mediators, teachers play the role of an objective third-party (not directly involved). They help each participant move through the process of reaching a settlement or agreement.

10-8
Sometimes teachers serve as mediators when students are experiencing a conflict.

Summary

Teachers play a variety of roles, but all relate to helping students learn. They must be adaptable as they shift from one role to another throughout the day.

Effective teaching depends on developing key personal habits and attitudes. These are linked to supporting students, school, and community. Establishing a good personal reputation is critical to teaching success.

Understanding how a school works helps a teacher effectively function within it. Every school has its own goals, culture, chain of command, and expectations. Teachers who learn and adapt to the organizational culture of their school are more successful and productive.

To teach well, teachers need not only a thorough background in their subject area, but also the skills to motivate students to learn. Teaching techniques must fit both what is being taught and the characteristics of the students. Teachers must be committed to lifelong learning.

Excellent communication skills are essential for teachers. They begin with positive relationships to minimize barriers to communication. Teachers also need to maintain professionalism in their speaking, writing, nonverbal communication, and electronic communication skills.

Conflict is inevitable in any active relationship. Constructive conflict management involves actively pursuing a solution. Teachers often act as mediators when conflict arises between students.

Review

1. Identify the five main roles performed by teachers. Tell which you think is most important and why.

2. How are grades and assessment different?

3. Identify three of the personal and professional qualities needed for teaching success. For each, briefly describe a teaching-related situation that would require this quality.

4. Explain why understanding the organizational structure of a school (how different positions are related) is important for teachers. Identify at least two ways a new teacher could learn about the organizational structure.

5. How can teachers stay up to date with the information in their subject area?

6. What are two reasons teachers should use a variety of teaching techniques?

7. How does active listening differ from just hearing what someone is saying?

8. What causes a mixed message? Give an example.

9. Name the steps to conflict resolution.

10. What role does a mediator play in resolving a conflict?

Reflect

1. Think of an example of a lesson in one of your classes in which the teacher acted as a facilitator. What planning do you think the teacher did to prepare this lesson? How might it have been taught in a directive way? Would it have been as effective?

2. Reflect on the teachers you have known who were positive role models for their students. Without using names, describe two ways they led others by their example.

3. Think of a teacher who you have had who showed both strong knowledge of his or her subject matter and exceptional teaching skills. What impact did this teacher have on you and other students?

4. Decide whether your spoken or written communication skills are stronger. On what did you base your decision? What are some specific ways you could improve your skills in the other area?

5. Identify five common causes of conflict among students in your school. Most people do not use a formal process, such as constructive conflict management for everyday disputes. However, if students used just one of the steps, which one do you think would help resolve problems more quickly and with less ill will? Be prepared to explain your choice.

Act

1. Using your school's student handbook and Web site, describe what you were able to learn about its organizational culture. Note any ways in which the official version varies from your perception.

2. Interview a school employee who is not a teacher. In preparation for the interview, develop a list of questions that will help you learn more about the person's position, responsibilities, and the skills and qualities needed to do the job well. What does the person contribute to the school? Summarize your interview to share with the class. Discuss the importance of the people you and your classmates interviewed in the overall functioning of the school.

3. Students interested in teaching often visit classrooms to observe, assist teachers, or present lessons. Develop a list of guidelines about appropriate dress for such situations. Include pictures of two outfits that would be examples of good choices. How is dress related to respect? How is it a form of nonverbal communication?

4. Write an article for a parent newsletter about an event in your school. This can be an interesting class or school activity, volunteer opportunity, or other topic that would be of interest. In developing your article, keep parents' needs and interests in mind. Communicate the information clearly and concisely. Proofread your work carefully. Make sure that the tone is positive, enthusiastic, and constructive.

Add to Your Portfolio

Teamwork is one of the most essential skills for both students and teachers. Working in small groups, develop a handbook for effective teamwork. Sections should include, but are not limited to: characteristics of effective teams, qualities and skills of effective team leaders and members, and common problems with possible solutions. Incorporate your own experiences, interviews with others, and research on the topic. All group members must participate. Duplicate your finished product so a copy is available for each group member for inclusion in your portfolios.

11 PLANNING FOR INSTRUCTION

Key Terms

educational standards

course plan

instructional units

lesson plans

instructional objectives

learning activities

transitions

guided practice

independent practice

Objectives

After studying this chapter, you will be able to

- **analyze** the types of information included in the educational standards for a state.

- **compare** curricula for the same course or level from two different sources.

- **explain** the relationship between instructional units and course plans.

- **identify** and **describe** the key parts of a lesson plan.

- **write** an educational objective that includes all necessary components.

- **create** a lesson plan on a chosen topic.

W ho determines what teachers teach? The answer is much more complicated than it would seem. Teachers make many day-to-day decisions about what they teach, but there are many influences on those decisions. They do not simply decide what they would like to teach.

The quality of education is of great importance to every child's future, but also to the nation as a whole. Society, parents, and employers, as well as teachers, all have a stake in making the educational system work well. That does not mean that they all agree about how best to do so.

As at every other time in history, the educational system works better for some students than others. Currently, there is more emphasis on trying to make certain that all students learn well. The debate about how to improve education impacts how individual teachers function in the classroom, both directly and indirectly.

This chapter focuses on how teaching decisions are made and what influences those decisions. The process is somewhat like a funnel with the classroom at the bottom. Decisions about what will be taught and how it will be taught become more detailed and specific the closer they get to the classroom.

Standards: What Should Students Know?

Many people believe that choices about what should be taught in schools should begin with decisions about the desired end product. **Educational standards**, sometimes called *instructional goals,* are statements of what students are expected to know and be able to do at certain points in their education. Advocates of educational standards say that when you first decide what outcomes you want, you can plan what to teach to reach those goals, 11-1.

Various groups have created standards. As you read in Chapter 1, *national standards* have been developed by teacher organizations for different subject areas in conjunction with state departments of education. Many states have also written standards for the schools within their state. These *state standards* often draw on the national standards but differ in some ways. Some local school districts have also developed their own standards.

Standards are linked to the move for accountability in education. Published standards tell the public what students will be able to do when they complete this particular part of their education. Administrators and teachers are expected to make certain that students meet these goals at acceptable levels.

11-1
Teachers plan lessons to meet educational standards or instructional goals.

Standards tend to be fairly general statements. For example, one of the national standards for language arts for grades K-12 reads:

"Students adjust their use of spoken, written, and visual language (e.g., conventions, style, vocabulary) to communicate effectively with a variety of audiences and for different purposes."

As the example shows, standards do not include details about how the topic will be learned or how attainment of the standard will be proven. More of those details emerge at the next step—curriculum.

Curriculum: What Will Be Taught?

As you learned in Chapter 1, *curriculum* can refer to the courses taught in a school and what is to be taught in each course. (The plural of curriculum is *curricula*.) It is this second definition that most directly impacts what teachers teach.

While curriculum is linked to national, state, and sometimes local, standards, it is much more specific about the content that teachers are expected to teach. You may be surprised to learn that decisions about what is included and not included in curriculum can be the subject of intense debate. One current area of argument is whether both evolution and creationism (sometimes called *intelligent design*) should be taught in science courses. Issues exist in other subject areas as well.

Determining what to teach in each course and at each level is called curriculum development. States, local school districts, and individual schools may all develop curriculum.

The curriculum development process generally involves a team, including administrators, teachers, and others, 11-2. For example, if a curriculum is being written for a culinary program, representatives from industry may help the writing team determine the specific skills essential for entry into that field. National and state standards typically influence curriculum written at the local or school level, called *school-based curriculum*, but there

11-2
This curriculum development team is made up of a teacher, a parent, and an administrator.

is also room for local input. One reason for the influence of state standards is that most states test students at various grade levels to determine how well they know the content designated in the standards to be mastered by that grade.

While the format and content of curriculum varies considerably, it generally determines which topics and skills are most important to teach and how much emphasis each receives. The curriculum organizes the content in a logical way. For example, multiplication is learned before division, since students must be able to multiply in order to divide. When a subject is taught at more than one level, the curriculum identifies what to teach in the introductory course and the advanced course.

The role of organizing what will be taught in which class and at what level is a key element in making education an orderly, step-by-step process. Imagine that you are a fourth-grade teacher in a large school. Your new class of students came from several different third-grade classrooms. The third-grade teachers decided independently what they would teach during the year. Consequently, it would be difficult for you to know where to begin. In math, for example, some students learned their multiplication tables last year, but others did not. Should you spend a month teaching them again, divide the class up, or try some other strategy? A curriculum sets a plan for which main concepts and skills will be taught at each grade or course, regardless of the teacher.

Curriculum goes beyond a list of topics to be taught. Important skills and attitudes are included, as well. Many key skills, such as problem solving, are integrated into different parts of the curriculum at all levels. Students learn a skill over time and are able to apply it in various circumstances. Curricula also identify suggested teaching methods and ways to determine whether learning has occurred.

Course Planning: How Will Learning Be Organized?

As a teacher, even though your state or school district has a recommended curriculum, you still need to translate those guidelines into a plan that will work for you, your class, and your circumstances. A **course plan** is a detailed outline of what a particular teacher will teach throughout a course or year based on curriculum but adapted to the characteristics of the teacher, students, and teaching circumstances. A course plan typically includes as series of instructional units. Your course plan must incorporate any required content and skills to enable students to meet educational standards. However, you still must choose and organize what you will teach during the course or year. This plan provides a road map for your day-to-day teaching.

Putting together such a plan requires considering many influences and variables. Some of these include the following:

- *Class and school schedules.* How often does the class meet and for how long? This will tell you how much time you have for instruction during the entire course or semester, once you have subtracted holidays, assemblies, etc.

- *Characteristics of your students.* If you have taught the grade and class before, you will have had experience with similar groups. If not, you can make reasonable assumptions about them based on what you know about typical child development. First graders have a fairly short attention span and new learning needs frequent review. Test scores can be helpful. Previous evaluations may show a particular class, as a group, is behind grade level in reading. Whatever information you can gather can help you plan your course more effectively.

- *Instructional Units.* Teachers organize what they will teach in a logical order. Similar topics are grouped together into **instructional units**, and these units are placed on the schedule in an order that makes sense. A child development teacher might teach units on prenatal development, infants, toddlers, preschoolers, and school-age children, in that order. A kindergarten teacher might plan a unit around a particular theme, such as life on a farm, and identify specific related activities to teach math, reading, science, and other skills. Teachers often take into consideration the sequence of topics in the textbook they are using in planning the order of content in their course. For each unit, the teacher identifies the specific information and skills to be learned, often in outline form.

- *Opportunities for learning.* Teachers try to take advantage of special opportunities and incorporate those into their teaching. For example, a social studies or government teacher might plan to teach about elections while local, state, or national elections are in process. A physical education teacher may choose to highlight the Olympic games. That would mean scheduling certain learning topics from the curriculum at that time. Other factors also impact where topics are placed on the course plan. If teaching in a cold climate, a physical education teacher would schedule most outdoor activities to be taught during warmer weather.

- *Teacher characteristics.* Every teacher has different strengths, interests, and a personal teaching style. The teacher's course plan will reflect these characteristics.

Having a course plan helps a teacher make certain that everything that needs to be taught has a place on the schedule. Once everything is listed, the next step is to decide how much time will be allotted to various topics or sections of the plan. Without such designations, it is easy to spend more time on topics near the beginning of the semester or course and then have to rush through or skip topics at the end when time runs short. Even with a plan and good intentions, adjustments always have to be made as teachers move through the course. A teacher may have to spend an extra day on an essential topic or an unscheduled assembly may wipe out a class period. Having a course plan can help a teacher make minor adjustments and still stay on track.

Lesson Plans: How Will Learning Take Place?

As a teacher, once you have established a course plan, you must make specific decisions about how you will teach each part of it. Together, the individual lessons build the knowledge, skills, and attitudes designated for the course and allow students to meet the standards that have been set.

Lesson plans, sometimes called *instructional plans* or *teaching plans*, are detailed outlines of what will be taught, how it will be taught, why it is being taught, and how learning will be evaluated. Teachers develop lesson plans for individual topics or groups of related topics. One lesson plan may include what will be taught in a single lesson or over a number of days.

Lesson plans serve a number of important purposes. That is why most schools require that teachers prepare them. First, they document what is being taught and how that matches curriculum guidelines and standards. In addition, the process of developing a lesson plan helps teachers think through what and how they will teach. They come to class better prepared. Lesson plans also allow a substitute teacher to step in and continue the learning process.

Elements of a Lesson Plan

Lesson plans vary in format from place to place and person to person. Some schools have a standard format that all teachers must use. In other cases, teachers find a format that works best for them and use it for their personal plans.

The sample lesson plan in 11-3 includes various elements that help teachers plan their teaching carefully. Although this type of thorough format is helpful for all teachers, it is especially worthwhile for newer teachers. Experienced teachers may use a shortened version.

The three most basic parts of a lesson plan are the instructional objectives, the learning activities, and the assessment. Most of the other elements flow from these decisions.

Sample Lesson Plan	
Lesson Plan Title:	Topography: The Ups and Downs of States
Topic:	Map skills: Identify shape, topography, location of U.S. states
Standard(s) Addressed:	Understand how to use maps and other geographic representations, tools, and technologies to acquire, process, and report information from a spatial perspective. *(State Social Studies Standard 8B)*
Students/Participants:	Fifth grade social studies
Specific Objectives:	Students will use outline and topographic maps to create a 3-D topographic map of a state, correctly indicating the locations of at least four key water features and three major cities.
Time Period:	Two consecutive class periods
Introduction:	Students will draw slips of paper to determine their assigned state. Ask: *What does your state look like?* Using play dough, give students 3 minutes to make the shape of their assigned state without a reference map. Expect interesting interpretations. Transition: *Let's look at some maps and see what your state really looks like.* (Supplies: paper slips with state names, play dough, hand wipes)
Step-by-Step Procedures:	1. Give each student an outline map of his or her assigned state. Students will duplicate the shape of their state using salt dough on a cardboard base. (Supplies per student: handout with state outline, cardboard, salt dough, dowel for rolling, plastic knife for cutting) 2. Provide each student with a color topographic map of his or her state. Briefly review previous lesson on topographic maps. Using additional salt dough, student will construct a 3-D map of the topography of their state on the outline base (using coils or slabs of dough). Note that during the next class period, students will paint their dough maps to show elevation changes and the location of major waterways and cities. (Supplies per student: topographic maps of student's state, additional salt dough) 3. Provide a place for the dough maps to dry overnight. 4. During the next class period, students will paint maps, using colors to indicate elevation changes. Using classroom or textbook maps, they will use a marker to identify the locations of four major water features (rivers, lakes, coastlines) and three main cities. (Supplies per student: topographic map from last class, textbook, watercolor set and brush, cup of water, fine marker, hand wipes)
Guided/Independent Practice:	Teacher will interact with students as they work, asking them to explain what they are doing. Explanations will verbally reinforce their visual and kinesthetic learning. Teacher will provide feedback.

11-3   (Continued)

Lesson plans often include many of the elements shown in this sample lesson plan.

Sample Lesson Plan (Continued)	
Summary:	Students will form groups based on the location of their state (divisions from textbook: Pacific Northwest, West, Plains, South, Central, Southeast, Northeast). In groups, students will present their map, briefly describing the topography (flat, mountainous, etc.) and identifying their state's major water features and cities. Group members will use textbook maps to verify and students will correct their maps as needed. Students will note the location of their states within their region.
Assessment:	Students will present their completed map to the whole class, identifying the state, four major water features, and the names and locations of three major cities. They will give a verbal description of the topography of the state.
Materials and Equipment:	• Folded paper strips with names of states to be used (one per student) • Container for drawing state names • Play dough • Hand wipes • Outline maps of students' states • Corrugated cardboard bases for topographic maps • Salt dough clay *(See Notes)* • Pieces of wooden dowel for rolling (or clay rollers borrowed from art department) • Plastic knives • Topographic maps (color) for students' states • Watercolor sets with brushes • Plastic cups, half-filled with water on tray • Pitchers with water • Paper towels or newspaper • Fine-point markers, black • Textbooks for maps
Adaptations for Students with Special Needs:	One student with color blindness: label watercolor paints
Notes:	• For smaller classes, use states from a limited number of geographic regions. • Eliminate states with extreme topographical variation. Maps take too long to construct. • Recipe for salt dough in "Materials" file. Each batch sufficient for 5 students. Make one extra batch.

Instructional Objectives

Each lesson plan includes one or more instructional objectives. **Instructional objectives** are clear statements of what students will achieve as a result of a lesson that will be shown in an observable way. By starting with the objective, the teacher identifies the purpose of the lesson. The lesson is developed to allow students to meet that objective. As such, objectives provide a focus for teaching.

Instructional objectives translate educational standards into specific smaller segments. Together, these form the stepping-stones toward meeting the goals of a standard.

Instructional objectives are often called *performance objectives* because they focus on what students will do to demonstrate learning. A well-written objective includes these characteristics:

- *Specifies observable behavior.* The verb in the statement tells how the student will show learning in a way that can be seen. "*Sort into categories*" is observable. "*Understand similarities*" is not. When objectives are observable, teachers can judge whether or not they are met by viewing student behaviors. Some common verbs used in instructional objectives because they lead to observable evidence of learning are listed in 11-4.

11-4
When writing objectives, use verbs such as these to describe how the student will show what he or she has learned.

Examples of Verbs for Observable Objectives		
add	draw	prepare
analyze	estimate	present
apply	evaluate	produce
calculate	explain	rank
categorize	find out	rate
combine	identify	revise
compare	judge	rewrite
complete	label	select
compute	list	sort
construct	make	spell
create	match	suggest
debate	measure	summarize
define	operate	throw
demonstrate	organize	translate
describe	plan	write
design	predict	weigh

- *Identifies an action or product.* Students must do or produce something concrete to indicate learning. A kindergartener might *"assemble <u>a 20-piece puzzle</u>."* A high school student studying personal finance might *"make a <u>list of all personal expenses</u>."*

- *Describes any conditions.* An objective usually tells under what circumstances the student will demonstrate learning. Phrases such as *"<u>working independently</u>," "<u>without a calculator</u>,"* and *"<u>within a 10-minute period</u>,"* are examples of such conditions.

- *Indicates acceptable level of performance.* The objective should specify what determines successful performance. Students might be required to *"identify <u>three reasons</u>," "complete 30 problems with <u>80 percent accuracy</u>," "score at least <u>7 of 10 points</u>,"* or *"rewrite the sentence <u>with no errors</u>."*

Can you identify the four characteristics of a well-written objective in the following examples?

Students will be able to serve the tennis ball within bounds in 6 of 10 attempts.

Students will identify in writing four characteristics of each of the three major types of government: autocracy, oligarchy, democracy.

Learning Activities

Learning activities are the second major component of a lesson plan. These are the learning experiences used to help students learn the content and reach the instructional objectives. Possible types of activities range from discussions, labs, hands-on activities, debates, problem solving, and field trips to computer exercises, simulations, and experiments. Instructional activities are sometimes also called *instructional methods* or *learning experiences.*

There are many teaching options for every topic and objective. How do teachers choose? That is where their knowledge of their students, experience, and creativity come into play. Activities must match the abilities and interests of the students in the class. For example, high school students are better able to bring new ideas to a class discussion than first graders. Chapter 12 discusses the pros, cons, and best uses of various types of activities in more detail. An elementary teacher may want to alternate quiet activities with ones that are more physically active throughout the day. Available resources can impact teachers' decisions. For example, a teacher might decide a field trip to a museum would best teach a concept but substitute an online museum tour if no travel funds are available.

Assessment Strategies

Assessment strategies must link directly back to those identified in the instructional objectives. Assessment is how you will evaluate whether learning you specified has taken place. You must be able to observe in some concrete way that students have learned the important content of the lesson. Chapter 14 describes many different assessment techniques and their uses. Developing and implementing effective assessments takes time, creativity, and energy, but the ability to truly evaluate students' learning makes the effort worthwhile.

Other Lesson Plan Elements

Once you have decided on the activity or activities that will make up the lesson, several related portions of the lesson plan can be completed. These include the following:

- *Title.* Give your plan a clear, but descriptive, title.

- *Topic.* Identify what concept or skill is being taught in the lesson.

- *Standards.* List the educational standards (state or local) that the lesson plan helps achieve.

- *Students/Participants.* Identify the grade level and subject area.

- *Time Period.* Specify how long the lesson plan will take to complete, such as one or two class periods.

- *Introduction.* Finding a good way to introduce a lesson is important to its success. An effective introduction must meet three goals: capture students' attention and interest, convey your expectations during the lesson, and link what students will be learning to what they already know.

- *Step-by-Step Procedures.* Thinking through the sequence of what will take place during the lesson and identifying the specific steps will help the actual lesson go smoothly. This process allows you to visualize how things will happen and identify potential problems that may arise. You can note questions you will ask and plan **transitions**—smooth ways to move from one part of the lesson to the next. This section acts as your guide as you present the lesson.

- *Guided/Independent Practice.* A good lesson includes opportunities for students to practice what they have learned. **Guided practice** is an activity designed to reinforce and apply learning that includes feedback from other students or the teacher. For example, students might work in small groups to complete math problems related to the lesson. Other times, practice can be a personal activity outside of class, such as a homework assignment, that is designed to apply and reinforce recent learning that students complete on their own. This is called **independent practice**.

- *Summary.* A good summary not only reviews what was learned, but helps students apply it. Verbal summaries of a lesson are just one option. Students can summarize by performing a skill they have learned. They can apply knowledge to a different situation or solve a problem using information from the lesson. They can create something that tells someone else about what they learned.

- *Materials and Equipment.* When you prepare a complete list of everything needed to complete the lesson plan, it is easier to assemble everything when you are ready to teach.

- *Adaptations for Students with Special Needs.* Depending on the nature of the lesson, it may be necessary to modify some activities so that students with special learning needs can successfully complete them.

- *Notes.* Use this space for additional information, reminders, and ideas for improving the plan.

Thinking through all of the elements of a lesson plan and putting them in writing helps teachers be well prepared for teaching the lesson. They know what they need and how they will proceed. By keeping the instructional objectives in mind, they can make any necessary adaptations during the actual lesson, concentrating on the essence of what students need to learn.

Finding Ideas and Inspiration

How can you come up with interesting ideas for lesson plans? As you learn more about teaching, you will begin to see learning opportunities in many aspects of life. Good teachers are also known for jotting down notes about teaching ideas and accumulating materials that could be used to enliven future lessons.

Teachers also freely share ideas with one another, 11-5. This may happen formally with a mentor or informally, teacher to teacher. Professional conferences typically include sessions where teachers present ideas that work well for them. Teaching magazines and many Web sites can also be excellent sources. The teaching materials that go with textbooks suggest many different ways teachers can supplement, expand, and apply text topics.

Many schools use teams to develop teaching plans. Groups of teachers collaborate to design lessons for effective instructional units. Working in teams encourages creative thinking. Individual areas of expertise can be shared.

11-5
Teachers often collaborate to share ideas of lesson plans.

It can also be invigorating as one person's idea inspires another's. While each teacher may still personalize the plans somewhat, team planning allows teachers to share preparation tasks and resources.

If you are interested in becoming a teacher, it is not too early to start keeping track of ideas you might use or adapt in your own classroom. You might use a combination of electronic and paper files to organize your materials.

Making Plans Come Alive

A lesson plan may look good on paper, but how do you make it work in the classroom? How you present a lesson to students has an impact on how well your students learn.

The introduction is the first key element. By capturing students' interest and attention, you begin the process of engaging them in learning. There are endless possibilities. You might ask a question, show a video clip, tell a story, or have students perform a task. Also let students know what to expect in terms of what they will learn and, perhaps, how you want them to work. Finally, linking the learning to prior knowledge or experiences will help enhance their understanding.

Your choice of activities will affect the success of your lesson. You may have experienced a class in which the teacher depended heavily on worksheets instead of more variety and active learning. Worksheets can be useful at times, but a steady diet of them is not very motivating. Students need variety. Engaging activities usually involve manipulating information either physically or mentally.

Incorporating an unexpected element into an important lesson can make it memorable. A history teacher comes to class dressed as Thomas Jefferson. A first-grade teacher incorporates a colorful parachute into a physical exercise activity. A science teacher displays a covered tray of objects related to the lesson as students enter and then removes the cover. All are out of the ordinary and can help generate interest and boost learning.

Remember, too, that a class is a collection of individuals, each with different learning styles, abilities, and interests. Include opportunities for visual, auditory, and kinesthetic learners in presenting your activities. The more senses you activate, the more likely learning will occur.

Lesson plans often appear linear on paper, simply moving from one point to the next. In reality, effective teachers often take a few steps forward, then a step back, and then take a step forward again when teaching new concepts. They allow time to encourage students, provide feedback, and check on students' progress. They take breaks from new learning by reviewing and reinforcing what has been learned.

How you present activities is as important as which activities you choose. A teacher's excitement is contagious. Be enthusiastic about learning and the opportunities you have planned. Your enthusiasm can help even reluctant students become engaged in activities, 11-6.

11-6
An enthusiastic teacher is likely to actively engage students in planned activities.

While you are learning teaching skills, it is easy to become flustered when a lesson does not go as planned. Practicing your presentation and learning activities can help give you confidence. Being well prepared and having a step-by-step procedure in your lesson plan can keep you on track. If you have thought through potential problems in the planning process, you will have solutions in mind. If something unexpected occurs, experienced teachers' best advice is to stay calm. Often, students are not even aware something is not working out as planned. Even if they are, showing that you, like all good teachers, can be flexible and adaptable will keep the lesson moving forward. Keep a sense of humor. Not everything can be planned for. Good teachers simply keep their goals in mind and adjust their plans.

Evaluating the Lesson

Even at the end of a hectic day of teaching, teachers know it is worth the time to reflect on the day's lessons. They make notes about what worked well and how they might modify their lesson plan to make it better. Notes made while the experience is still fresh can be invaluable later. Teachers often reuse lesson plans that they have found to be successful. However, effective teachers continually make improvements and try new ideas.

Summary

There are many influences that impact what teachers teach in their classrooms. Education is important to society and many groups within it. Not all agree on educational matters, including what should be taught in schools.

Standards, statements of what students should know and be able to do at certain educational levels, can be very influential. Groups at the national, state, or local level develop them.

Curriculum development is the process of deciding, more specifically, what topics and skills should be taught and what attitudes should be developed in different subjects and grade levels. Standards often influence curricula. Curriculums provide suggested or required guidelines for classroom teachers.

Teachers translate the curriculum into a course plan showing how they will organize what needs to be taught for their particular situation. A plan usually includes a sequence of instructional units.

Lesson plans record teachers' decisions about how they will teach specific topics to produce desired learning. The format of lesson plans varies. Careful planning and enthusiastic presentation of lessons helps boost learning. Evaluating how well lessons worked can help teachers identify and improve those they may use again in the future.

Review

1. Why do many people believe that setting educational standards should be the first step in deciding what will be taught in schools?

2. Who might have been involved in developing a new state curriculum for this course for students interested in the teaching profession?

3. Why is it important for a state or local curriculum to determine what will be taught at each grade level?

4. If there is a curriculum, why does a teacher need a course plan?

5. What are instructional units?

6. Name the three most important parts of a lesson plan.

7. Identify the four key parts of an instructional objective and write an objective that includes all four.

8. What three goals should be achieved with the introduction to a lesson?

9. Explain the difference between guided practice and independent practice.

10. How do teachers evaluate a lesson?

Reflect

1. What would be the advantages and disadvantages of having required national standards and a national curriculum in the United States?

2. Some countries tightly control what is taught in schools as a way of restricting information and controlling the population. Why is education seen as such a powerful tool? Do you think this method is effective? Why or why not?

3. Think of an example of a memorable lesson you experienced as a student. What was the topic of the lesson? How was it taught? What made it so special that you still remember it?

4. Describe an incident in a class when things did not go as planned. Describe what happened to upset plans. How did the teacher handle the situation? What was the result? What might have been done to improve the outcome? (Do not use names in your description.)

Act

1. Analyze the educational standards for your state or another. Standards are generally available online. (Try searching educational standards and state name.) Prepare a report on your findings. Include information such as how the standards are organized and what subject areas and types of skills are included. Are they divided by grade level? Review the standards from one subject area and include three of these in your report. What types of information do they provide for curriculum writers? For teachers? In class, compare your findings with those of your classmates.

2. Examine two curriculum documents for the same subject area and level (such as two curricula for world history or sixth-grade science). Choose a topic common to both curricula and compare what is to be taught. How are the recommendations for teaching this topic similar and different? How do the two curricula match up in terms of format, level of detail, and types of information included (objectives, activity suggestions, etc.)? Which version do you think would be more helpful to a teacher?

3. Obtain permission to observe an elementary or middle school classroom teacher introducing and teaching a lesson. Using the lesson plan format provided by your teacher, identify as many parts of the teacher's plan as possible based on what you have observed.

4. Find three online sources of teaching ideas or lesson plans. Identify the URL (Web address) and evaluate each. How is each site organized? Who sponsors it? What types of information are provided? Would a teacher find the site easy to use? Does the information seem useful? Combine your list and evaluations with those of your classmates to develop a guide for future reference.

Add to Your Portfolio

Create a lesson plan on the topic and grade level of your choice using the lesson plan template provided by your teacher. Based on your teacher's evaluation, revise your plan and add it to your portfolio.

12 INSTRUCTIONAL METHODS

Key Terms

instructional methods

instructional strategies

teaching strategies

Bloom's Taxonomy

open-ended questions

wait time

pacing

closure

teacher-centered
  methods

learner-centered
  methods

panel discussions

moderator

simulations

skits

role playing

case studies

reflective responses

productive lab

experimental lab

cooperative learning

individual
  accountability

Objectives

After studying this chapter, you will be able to

- **explain** the role of all teachers in the development of critical thinking skills.

- **develop** questions appropriate for instruction based on Bloom's Taxonomy.

- **identify** the characteristics and uses of specific types of instructional strategies.

- **analyze** a lesson, identifying the teaching strategies and use of questioning, examples, and closure.

- **explain** teachers' primary considerations when deciding which teaching strategies to use.

Amy is finishing her first week as a student teacher in Mr. Sanchez' third-grade classroom. It has been a great experience so far. She has primarily been observing the class, getting to know the students, and working with individuals who need extra help. She is impressed with Mr. Sanchez' ability to channel the students' abundant energy into excitement toward learning.

Right now, though, ideas are swirling through Amy's brain. After school she met with Mr. Sanchez to go over the teaching plan for the next two weeks. In science, the students will be starting a new unit on weather. They will learn about seasons, clouds, forms of precipitation, tornadoes and hurricanes, and weather forecasting. Mr. Sanchez asked Amy to develop and teach a lesson to introduce the weather unit. Mr. Sanchez challenges Amy to get the students enthusiastic about the study of weather so they will be motivated to master the stated learning/performance objectives. This will be her first solo lesson with the class.

Since that discussion, possibilities keep popping into her head. Because this is an introductory lesson, she has much more flexibility in choosing a topic. That almost makes it more difficult! Her brainstorming list includes:

- Having students think about a particular weather-related memory. How did the weather make them feel? Was it exciting, scary, or relaxing? They could draw a picture of their weather memory and describe it to the class.

- Having students use thermometers to measure the temperature of different places and substances (cold water, warm water, dirt, near a window) and record their readings. As a class, they could record their readings on a giant chart and discuss them.

- Having students create a giant wall mural picturing different types of weather.

More ideas come to mind. None seem quite right, but several have potential. She wants this to be great! Just then the chart on activity planning from Ms. Neeley's teaching methods class last semester pops into her mind. It's a reminder that coming up with ideas is only one part of the process. She also needs to meet the objective, match the needs of her students and the topic, and make sure the activity is practical. Not all of her ideas will pass those tests. In the past, using the process has helped her with planning. Hopefully, it will again, because this is real and it needs to be right!

T eachers face a similar dilemma all the time. They know what they want students to learn. Next, they must decide how best to achieve it.

Chapter 11 explored the process that determines what will be taught. The end result, a lesson plan, is an individual teacher's strategy for teaching a particular topic. Learning activities form the heart of lesson plans. Teachers can create successful learning activities because of their knowledge of and experience with various instructional methods. **Instructional methods**, often called **instructional strategies** or **teaching strategies**, are the basic techniques used to promote learning. Teachers know the uses of these methods—such as discussions, skits, and demonstrations—and choose the best one for a particular learning objective, topic, and class situation. They then use that method as the basis for developing a specific learning activity.

This chapter looks at the characteristics of a variety of common instructional methods. There are certainly other strategies that you may want to add to your instructional repertoire. Often more than one strategy will be combined. You have the perspective of experiencing these as a student. Now, you will see how teachers view and utilize them. Before these specific teaching strategies are described, however, the chapter explores some essentials for success with any instructional method. Teachers build students' development of critical-thinking skills at every level and in all subjects. There are also some skills directly related to effective teaching that should be added to your tool kit. These skills are keys to making instructional methods work in the classroom. The end of the chapter includes some guidelines for choosing the most appropriate instructional method for a particular situation. Together, these topics will give you a better understanding of considerations involved in teaching decisions.

Engaging Learners in Critical Thinking

Too often, people think about education in terms of the amount of information learned. Knowledge is certainly important. However, in this age of swiftly changing information, well-developed thinking skills are even more essential. They prepare learners to deal with new situations and challenges far into the future.

What kinds of thinking skills do different tasks require? Benjamin Bloom considered that question. **Bloom's Taxonomy**, originally published in 1956, is still used as a basis for understanding and teaching various levels of thought.

(Because this original version is so well-known and widely used, switching to the dramatically different Revised Bloom's Taxonomy is moving very slowly. You will likely encounter use of the taxonomy in future college courses.) Bloom's six levels of thinking are shown in 12-1. The lower levels—Knowledge, Comprehension, and Application—are the most basic. The upper levels—Analysis, Synthesis, and Evaluation—are more difficult to learn but very important. These top three levels are often called *higher-order thinking skills*. Together, the complex combination of skills required at these upper levels are known as *critical thinking*. Critical thinking allows people to gather information, evaluate its quality, and use it effectively.

Building students' abilities to use progressively more complex thinking skills is a major goal of education. Younger children are not able to see problems with a perspective other than their own, a skill necessary for critical thinking. However, they can learn to think about different possibilities when presented with a problem. Young children also have a sense of curiosity, an important part of critical thinking. They can ask questions and learn to ask better ones. Teachers can use these abilities to begin to lay the framework for critical thinking in the elementary grades.

The ability to think abstractly comes in later childhood and adolescence. Students gradually develop the ability to take charge of their own thinking and learning. They learn to ask probing questions and find new solutions. They begin to rely on reason, not just emotion, in analyzing points of view. They can develop criteria and standards for evaluating their own thinking. As they enter adolescence, they can learn to examine problems closely and reject information that is incorrect, irrelevant, or biased. Skills such as these evolve through activities that incorporate critical-thinking skills.

In Chapter 11, you learned about the importance of setting clear learning goals that identify how students will demonstrate their learning. Bloom's Taxonomy helps teachers develop these objectives. Examples of verbs that can be used in writing objectives that match the desired level of thinking were listed in 11-4. (Note that the whole objective, not just the verb, must reflect a particular level.)

Because of their students' abilities, elementary teachers primarily use objectives at the lower end of the thinking scale. That proportion should gradually shift in middle and high school. High school teachers should include more objectives and learning activities at the analysis, synthesis, and evaluation levels to help students refine important critical-thinking skills.

Applying Bloom's Taxonomy
Level 1: KNOWLEDGE: *Acquiring and recalling information*
<u>Sample associated verbs</u>: define, describe, list, label, match, memorize, name, recognize, tell <u>Sample question</u>: Who were the main characters in the story? <u>Sample objective</u>: Students will match at least 20 of 25 words with their correct definition.
Level 2: COMPREHENSION: *Understanding and making use of information*
<u>Sample associated verbs</u>: describe, discuss, explain, outline, predict, summarize, translate <u>Sample question</u>: Describe the main characters in the story. <u>Sample objective</u>: Students will identify at least four statements that support the author's point of view.
Level 3: APPLICATION: *Using information learned in a new situation*
<u>Sample associated verbs</u>: apply, build, complete, demonstrate, develop, examine, illustrate, plan, show, solve, use <u>Sample question</u>: How would the rule apply if the angle were 90° instead of 45°? <u>Sample objective</u>: Students will use the guidelines to write a business letter requesting an interview that contains all key elements.
Level 4: ANALYSIS: *Examining the parts of a whole and their relationships*
<u>Sample associated verbs</u>: analyze, classify, compare, contrast, categorize, distinguish among, examine, investigate, separate, test <u>Sample question</u>: Which two of the three musical selections are in the same key? <u>Sample objective</u>: Students will analyze a photo of a room, correctly identifying an example of effective or ineffective use of each principle of design.
Level 5: SYNTHESIS: *Using parts in a new way to create something*
<u>Sample associated verbs</u>: adapt, combine, construct, create, design, develop, imagine, improve, invent, organize, plan, produce <u>Sample question</u>: How would you adapt the exercise guidelines to fit your personal situation? <u>Sample objective</u>: Students will develop a sketch and description of a new product that would be helpful for someone with limited hand strength.
Level 6: EVALUATION: *Assessing or judging value based on information*
<u>Sample associated verbs</u>: assess, choose, criticize, debate, decide, defend, evaluate, judge, prioritize, rank, rate, select <u>Sample question</u>: What choice would you have made if you were in Churchill's place, and what is your reasoning? <u>Sample objective</u>: Students will develop a rating scale to evaluate the posters submitted for the "Stamp Out Litter!" campaign.

12-1

You can apply Bloom's Taxonomy to help build students' abilities to use progressively more complex skills.

Key Instructional Skills

No matter which activities you devise to meet your learning objectives, there are basic teaching skills you will utilize constantly. Several are related directly to developing and presenting learning activities. These include developing effective questions and examples to stimulate learning. Teachers also must know how to judge timing within a lesson and help students reflect on their learning at the end of a lesson.

Teacher education students learn these skills and practice them in various situations. However, it is in student teaching and their first years as teachers that they truly understand their importance. That is why even experienced teachers continue to look for ways to enhance these key teaching skills.

Questioning

There is no skill more basic to teaching than the ability to use questions effectively. They are a key part of almost every learning activity. Teachers use questions for many purposes. They can generate interest, stimulate learning, check for comprehension, encourage participation, develop thinking skills, and evaluate learning.

Throughout your years as a student, you have answered thousands of questions, both oral and written. As a teacher, it will be your responsibility to decide when questions are appropriate, how to ask them, and how best to respond to students' answers. Begin now to pay more attention to the ways your teachers utilize questioning. As you practice developing questions of your own, keep these guidelines in mind:

- *Plan questions along with the lesson.* Preplanning questions allows time to make sure they match your learning objectives and are clearly worded. They provide a structure for the lesson. As the lesson progresses, questions can be added or modified, but having the original plan helps keep the lesson on track.

- *Ask questions of varying difficulty.* Look again at 12-1 to review Bloom's Taxonomy. Focus on the sample questions. Questions at different levels serve specific purposes. For example, simpler questions can check for understanding and comprehension. Just be sure to include questions from all levels appropriate for the abilities of the students.

- *Include open-ended questions.* Using **open-ended questions**, ones that require more than a few words as an answer, generally encourages higher-level thinking.

Encouraging Participation

What if you ask questions and no one answers? You have probably experienced a class where there was little student participation. There are ways to minimize this possibility.

Activities that include oral discussions depend on student participation. Most importantly, learners should feel comfortable participating. Teachers must create an atmosphere where everyone is respected. That means that neither the teacher nor other students tease or put down anyone for a wrong answer or a different opinion, 12-2.

Questions asked should be appropriate for students' level of knowledge and experience. Otherwise few will be willing to venture an answer.

Questions must generate interest. That means that they should be applicable to learners and varied in type. Questions can encourage students to classify, rank, or sort things. Others might focus on opinions or attitudes. Some questions direct learners to one right answer, while others help students find an appropriate answer for a given circumstance.

Students need time to think before responding. Allowing **wait time** between asking a question and calling on a student allows all students to mentally process the question and formulate their replies. Although it may feel awkward at first, this brief period of silence encourages more and better answers.

12-2
Teachers can encourage participation in class by making students feel comfortable.

Varying methods of asking for responses keeps students thinking. Sometimes a teacher might randomly call on students for a response. Other times, the same teacher might call on those who volunteer. With encouragement, shy students may be more willing to participate. However, it is important to remember and respect the fact that various cultures have different traditions regarding asking and answering questions.

Responding to Students' Answers

How should you respond to students' answers to your spoken questions? That depends on the answer and the situation. If an answer is inaccurate, an effective response helps lead students to the right answer. Saying, "No, that's wrong!" discourages further participation. Instead, a teacher may say, "Let's look at this again," or "Let me state the question in a different way." Some answers are partially correct. A teacher should acknowledge what is accurate first. For example, "Yes, using a virus protection program is one way of protecting personal information, but using an alias may not be appropriate. Who can suggest other steps to take?"

In responding to answers, teachers can help students process learning by posing follow-up questions to the class. These are usually developed on the spot and can lead to deeper understanding.

Responding to Students' Questions

Not all questions are teacher initiated. In an interactive learning environment, students feel free to ask questions. These deserve a thoughtful and respectful response. If the question furthers the discussion, the teacher can provide an answer or counter with another question.

What happens if you are teaching and are asked a question you cannot answer? It is fine to acknowledge that you don't have an answer. You can say that you will find one and get back to the student or class. You could also ask if anyone else has an answer or help the student figure out how to find an answer.

Many times questions are slightly off topic. In that case, it is best to give a brief answer to avoid distracting other learners from the lesson. A question may be interesting, but definitely off track. A good way to respond would be to say, "That is an interesting question but not what we are discussing right now. If you stay after class, we can talk about it."

Sometimes students' questions are inappropriate in their timing or their personal nature, but a reply is still needed. For example, a kindergartener may ask about your personal life in the middle of a lesson. Helping the student understand when a question is appropriate is an important part of education.

Using Examples

Sometimes when a teacher presents new information, it is difficult to grasp the concept. Often, however, when the teacher offers a concrete example, everything falls into place. Examples help bring information to life for learners.

The use of examples increases understanding and retention of subject matter. Examples can show how theory applies to the real world. Other times, as in math, they help make sense of a process. When learning is complex, using multiple examples can improve understanding for more students.

As a teacher, you will plan effective examples as you develop lessons. When choosing examples, start with simple and progress to more complex. Be sure they are relevant to what is being taught. Ask students to provide examples to check their level of learning.

Try to include different formats to match varied learning styles. A diagram, photo, or demonstration might serve as a visual example. Include verbal examples in oral explanations. Sometimes examples can involve student movement to help kinesthetic learners. For example, a teacher might have students physically show how chemical compounds are formed. Using sodium chloride as an example, one student might act as the electron in a sodium atom and others the electrons in a chlorine atom. The sodium electron joins the chlorine electrons, moving the atoms together as a sodium chloride ion.

Pacing

Pacing refers to the rate at which a teacher moves through the components of a lesson or the lessons throughout the day. If the pace is too slow, students become bored. If it is too fast, they cannot keep up and fail to learn all that they should.

The ability to pace a lesson appropriately is a learned skill. However, when you understand the various points to consider, it is easier to learn how, 12-3.

- *Know your natural style.* During your preparation to become a teacher, you will have many opportunities to develop and present activities. In most instances, a teacher or your peers will provide feedback and suggestions. This will help you find out whether your natural pace of presentation tends to be fast, slow, or on-target. If necessary, you can consciously adjust your style to better meet learners' needs.

- *Look for signs of understanding.* Students learn at different rates. Teachers watch students' reactions and use questions and activities to gauge when most students understand a lesson. Remember that the age of students and complexity of the information will affect pacing.

12-3
When a teacher paces a lesson appropriately, students are less likely to become bored or fall behind.

- *Alternate types of activities.* Using a variety of types of activities helps keep students involved, attentive, and learning. Particularly for younger students, quiet individual work needs to be balanced with activities that involve movement and talking. Even older students need a change of pace during the class period.

- *Plan for smooth transitions.* As you learned in Chapter 11, transitions are methods teachers use to move students from one activity to the next. Unless well planned, too much time can be lost changing activities. Inappropriate behaviors can occur. Effective teachers often alert students to finish up their work in preparation for a new activity. They set clear guidelines for transitions, including behavioral expectations.

Learning appropriate pacing in teaching takes practice. It requires a balance between having a lesson drag and having it speed along too quickly. Proper pacing requires knowledge of learners, both as a group and as individuals. Sometimes teachers must pace a lesson at different speeds for different students. As the school year progresses, an effective teacher will know the class well enough so that a "natural" pace will be achieved.

Achieving Closure

While participating in activities, students get caught up in the process. At the end of an activity, it is essential to help students reflect on what they have learned, its purpose, and meaning. This process is called closure. It is more than a quick summary. **Closure** helps students draw conclusions based on what they have learned. It helps them apply it. It lends a sense of achievement.

Closure can be handled in many ways. It is generally part of the *Summary* section in a lesson plan. For learning to be effective, students need to relate new knowledge to past knowledge and to future knowledge. In the end, students should be able to answer the question, "What did I learn and what does it mean to me today?"

Basic Teaching Strategies

Most specific learning activities that teachers plan in their lessons are based on common instructional methods or teaching strategies. There are dozens of strategies teachers can use. This section discusses the pros, cons, and uses of some that are used frequently.

Educators sometimes classify these strategies as either teacher-centered or learner-centered. In **teacher-centered methods**, the teacher's role is to present the information that is to be learned and to direct the learning process of students. Students then practice what they have learned. For example, with lectures, the teacher provides information, and students learn by listening. They may discuss the information in small groups after the lecture. **Learner-centered methods** are different. In these approaches, the teacher acts as a facilitator, or guide, for learning. Students are more actively involved in directing and achieving their own learning. Group projects are an example of learner-centered instructional activities.

There is no one perfect instructional method or activity. Teachers use multiple factors in deciding which to use. They also vary their methods to keep students interested and engaged in learning.

Lectures

In its most basic form, a lecture consists of a teacher presenting information orally and students learning through listening. Although the lecture is used frequently, especially in upper grades, it has drawbacks. Most students are stronger visual learners than auditory, so they find it more difficult to learn simply by listening. In addition, the lecture method puts students in the role of passive listeners. Although a lecture supplemented with visual aids would also reach a visual learner.

Still, lectures have benefits. They can be used with any content and are particularly suited for presenting factual information. They are a good way to present information to large groups of older students.

How can you improve the effectiveness of lectures? Keeping the lecture period short helps. Adding visual elements can increase interest and improve understanding. For example, some teachers use PowerPoint™ presentations along with their lectures. There are also ways to make lectures less passive. For example, you might insert a question-and-answer period within or after the lecture. Some teachers facilitate note taking by providing partial outlines for students to complete or written questions to be answered during a lecture.

Teachers who lecture must be especially effective presenters. That starts with preparing well-organized material. Main points must be clear and presented in a logical order. Examples help clarify information, especially ones that link new material to what students already know. Conveying enthusiasm is important, and teachers need to make eye contact with students around the room, not just read from notes. This also helps detect signs of restlessness, boredom, or misunderstanding. Asking a question, clarifying a point, or using another technique as a change of pace can help reinvolve students.

Reading

Your teacher has likely assigned you to read form this textbook. While not particularly creative, reading is one of the basic ways of learning a wealth of information. In addition to textbooks, students might read periodicals, Internet articles, and other researched material. You will continue to learn by reading. This is one reason so much emphasis is placed on literacy skills.

Discussions

Discussions may be teacher- or learner-centered, depending on the role the teacher plays. They help students explore options and ideas and develop key communication skills, 12-4.

A discussion begins with a stimulating question or problem based on a learning objective. It must be one without a simple answer. Discussions encourage, and provide practice in, thinking skills. In participating in a discussion, students draw on their own knowledge and experiences. A series of questions are used to guide the discussion toward the learning objective. At the end, a student or teacher summarizes or draws conclusions.

Participating effectively in discussions is a learned skill. Teachers must set the ground rules. Even young children can learn to take turns, be polite, and respect others' opinions. Teachers can encourage quieter students to participate and talkative students to listen. Seating arrangements in which students face each other promote discussion.

12-4
Teachers often play a key role in class discussions.

Discussions can take different forms. In a teacher-led discussion, the teacher keeps the discussion on task, moving forward with a logical progression of ideas. In small-group discussions, each group takes on this responsibility, so these are appropriate for older children and teens. Groups often must report their conclusions to the class. In **panel discussions**, a group of people present and discuss a topic. The teacher acts as a **moderator** (leader) by introducing the panel, summarizing the main points, and relaying students' questions to panel members. Panelists may be outside experts or students who have prepared for their roles. In a debate, participants try to persuade others to their opposing points of view. Sometimes students are divided into two groups and must argue for or against an issue.

Demonstrations

A demonstration is the best way to teach a process. Students see how to complete each step, helping visual and kinesthetic learners. At the same time, the accompanying verbal explanation helps auditory learners. This technique is particularly helpful when a process is complex, procedures are difficult to explain, or visual cues are important. For example, a teacher might show how to balance a checkbook or the steps in making a mask out of paper and plaster.

Demonstrations are usually teacher-centered, putting students in a passive learning role. However, there are ways to make them more interactive, 12-5. The teacher can have students make predictions about what will

12-5
When teachers make demonstrations interactive, students are more likely to learn a process.

happen or ask a student to perform a step or two of the procedure. For a science experiment, students might fill out a lab sheet as the demonstration progresses. Asking questions throughout the demonstration involves students. In other situations, such as a demonstration of how to use a computer program, students might perform the process at the same time as the teacher demonstrates it. Adding activity and involvement generates interest and aids learning.

A demonstration requires careful preparation, especially if the process being explained is complicated. What is the sequence of steps? How can they best be shown and clearly explained? Are there any safety precautions to be observed and emphasized? What equipment and materials must be gathered and ready to use? How can the room be arranged to make sure all students will have a clear view of the demonstration? What questions and examples will help students understand the process?

Sometimes teachers reverse roles and have students prepare and present demonstrations. This may be a learning activity with students researching the topic they will demonstrate. It can also be used as a way of checking students' mastery of a process they have learned.

Guest Speakers

Guest speakers can bring outside expertise into the classroom and generate interest. For example, for young children, having a firefighter talk about fire safety and show firefighting gear can be an exciting and memorable way to learn the topic.

Before inviting a speaker, be sure you understand your school's policy regarding outside guests. The guest may have to be approved and/or have to have a background check. These policies help ensure students' safety.

When using a guest speaker, it is essential to make sure the experience is a positive one for all involved. When inviting the speaker, be clear about the topic, the objectives, and the time frame. Agree on the format the speaker will use and identify any special arrangements, such as equipment needed. You might have students prepare questions for the speaker ahead of time. When you, as a teacher, have a community member in your classroom, you and your students represent your school. If students are attentive and polite, the speaker will leave with a positive impression. Be sure to follow up with a personal note or notes from students thanking the speaker for sharing his or her time and knowledge.

Simulations

Simulations are used to put students in situations that feel real, even though they are not. This means that risks are eliminated. Simulations give students opportunities to experience certain aspects of a situation as if they are in them, including making decisions and solving problems.

Simulations come in many forms. High school students may hold a mock trial. A group of fourth-graders might spend a morning as students at a pioneer school, learning as children did then. Computer-based simulations are very common today. For example, instead of providing real frogs for dissection, frogs can be virtually dissected using computers, 12-6.

While simulations are most common in social studies and science, they can be used in other areas when student involvement is needed. Simulations work well when students are learning new skills or exploring feelings and attitudes. Skits, role playing, and case studies are variations of simulations.

Skits

Skits involve acting out stories. They are miniplays based on scripts written by the teacher or students. Students play the various parts.

Skits actively involve students in learning. Performing a skit involves auditory, kinesthetic, and visual learning. Students speak, listen, perform, and watch the skit. Adding costumes and props helps make situations more real, increasing student involvement. Interacting with the content provides more understanding than simply reading or watching media.

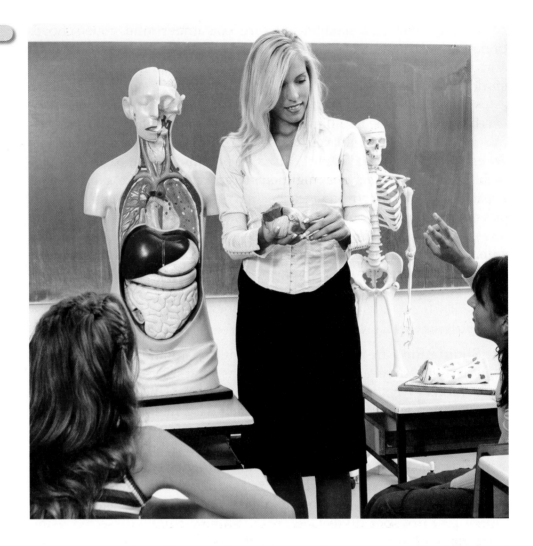

12-6
Simulations are often used in science classes to represent real concepts.

Skits are adaptable to different ages, subject areas, and educational objectives. For example, a first-grade teacher might develop a simple skit to help young students learn addition and subtraction. After arranging chairs to represent seats in a bus, the teacher could use a simple story line about people getting on and off the imaginary bus to help students practice the concepts of addition and subtraction. Older children might write and perform skits about the Revolutionary War. The process of writing would require review of previous learning and additional research. What additional skills would be built through editing the script, gathering props and costumes, and practicing and presenting the skit?

Role Playing

Role playing is like a skit without a script. The teacher clearly describes a situation that includes an issue or problem. Students act out the role of the people in the situation, basing their actions and conversations on how the person they represent would likely react. Playing their roles, students work through the situation or solve the problem. After the role play ends, students discuss what happened. They explore why the various characters acted as they did and how the people playing the parts felt in those roles. The teacher helps summarize how the experience relates to the instructional objective.

Teachers can use role-playing situations for a variety of purposes. It can help students understand feelings and behavior. For example, it could be used with young children learning about the danger of interacting with strangers. The teacher might create a simulated situation in which a child can role play an interaction with a stranger, without risks. Role plays can provide practice. In a French class, students could take various roles, simulating buying tickets and boarding a train in France, using the French vocabulary terms they have just learned. Role playing can also be used to check and strengthen students' understanding of information. For example, a teacher might have students represent the positions of various nations on a topic of disagreement. Follow-up discussions could focus both on understanding points of view and reactions to conflict.

Case Studies

Case studies involve groups of students working together to analyze a situation, called a "case." A case is a description of a realistic problematic situation that requires a solution. Case studies allow teachers to direct learning by using a case that focuses on the exact issues that meet the learning objective. For example, in a lesson on ethics, a business teacher might present students with a case in which an employee is directed by a supervisor to do something contrary to company policies.

Case studies allow students to apply new knowledge and skills for solving complex, real-life issues. Students work in small groups to consider the case, come up with possible solutions, and agree on one. Part of the learning experience comes from listening to the different solutions group members propose and their reasoning behind them. Coming to a consensus requires analysis and negotiation. Individual groups then present and explain their solution to the class, leading to a larger discussion debating the merits of different options.

Teachers can use case studies to actively involve students in dealing with real issues. The case must be well written. Sometimes teachers start with a current news story, adding or subtracting information to make it fit the learning situation. They clearly outline what students are to accomplish in their groups, set time limits, and move from group to group listening and helping students move forward. They use the large-group discussion at the end to help students identify the issues and principles involved. As with other learner-centered methods, the teacher starts with a clear plan. However, as the lesson plays out, the teacher decides how best to guide students toward the desired learning goal.

Reflective Responses

When teachers use **reflective responses**, students think deeply about an issue or something they have learned. When using reflective responses, they ask students to think about thinking (cognition). For example, a teacher may ask students to take out a piece of paper and write about what they have just learned in their own words. Reflective responses can also be used at the beginning of a lesson to capture a learner's attention. Used in this way, reflective responses can give a teacher a sense of where the students are in their learning. They can then build on what is already known. Reflective responses offer students the opportunity to be thoughtful and insightful. Reflective responses can be either written or verbal.

Labs

Labs offer students the opportunity to work with materials, ideas, people, or processes to solve a given problem. For example, kindergartners may plant seeds to experiment with the effects of sunlight and water—or the lack of them—on growth. Middle school students may experiment with the effects of discrimination through a controlled environment that takes away privileges of some members.

Basically, there are two types of labs used by teachers. A **productive lab** focuses on producing an end product. For example, a middle school student may produce a children's book written in elementary Spanish. A third grader may produce a replica of the solar system. A high school student in a culinary program may produce three kinds of appetizers.

Another type of lab, the **experimental lab**, uses a formal process to research a problem. This type of lab is common in scientific experiments. Students are given a problem and they must find an answer through experimentation. Because they are experimenting, specific results are not always assured. The question, "What will happen if…" motivates learners in experimental labs.

Labs require careful planning. Teachers act as planners and organizers, as well as managers, during the lab activity. Clear instructions are essential. It takes practice to accurately estimate the amount of time students will need to complete a lab activity. In experimental labs, safety may be a concern, 12-7. Students, equipment, and facilities must be considered and rules established. Although labs can be expensive in terms of time, materials, and resources, they can provide excellent opportunities for learning.

Cooperative Learning

Cooperative learning is a form of small-group learning in which everyone works together to achieve a common goal. The group is

12-7
Safety is an important consideration when conducting labs.

responsible for making sure all members participate, contribute, and learn. When used well, cooperative learning has been shown to be a highly effective learning technique.

Cooperative learning takes many different formats and is adaptable to most subject areas and age groups. The specific assignment must be carefully planned. The teacher divides students into groups, usually of two to six students with diverse characteristics. The learning task is structured to encourage students to work together and to be responsible for each other's learning. At the same time, **individual accountability**, or a way to assess each student's participation and learning, is built in. Group members share ideas and propose solutions. The group must resolve differences and work together to complete the assignment. The teacher acts as a facilitator, monitoring the groups to keep them on track, but not offering solutions.

Cooperative learning offers many advantages. The ability to work together in a group is an important life skill. Opportunities to work together build students' willingness to contribute, listen to and respect others' opinions, help one another, and negotiate differences. Self-esteem and responsibility improve, as well. Most students enjoy learning more when working with their peers.

Student Presentations

Student presentations are common in all grades. They give learners the opportunity to share what they have learned. Depending on the assignment, presentations may be oral, visual, or use both formats. Presentations help students build communication skills. Learners must think about how to best relay the information they are attempting to communicate to their audience. This helps them achieve a higher level of understanding. Sometimes teachers use group presentations. These add practice with cooperation and organizational skills.

Games

Remember the sense of accomplishment you felt when you mastered a new game? Games can be fun and challenging. They can also be used to reinforce learning, build skills, and provoke thought. These attributes make games effective instructional activities to meet many learning objectives.

Paper-and-pencil games include hidden-clue puzzles, word searches, crossword puzzles, or other word games. Word games give students a chance to practice spelling and other language skills. Students can complete them independently or work together in groups.

Card games are effective for reviewing factual information. They are often based on traditional games such as *Go Fish* or *Memory*. Rules can be simple or complex and may be changed once the game is learned. Students often create their own rules for card games as they become more familiar.

Board games are typically played in small groups. Sometimes teachers adapt well-known board games to meet their learning objectives. Commercial board games designed to teach various topics are available, and teachers often share ideas for making their own. Games that use dice or play money can be effective ways to practice simple math skills.

Active games offer opportunities for students to be physically involved in learning. This appeals to young children who learn through play and movement and to kinesthetic learners. Such games also offer a change of pace in learning.

Many educational games are available for the computer, 12-8. They can be used with individual students and targeted to meet specific learning needs. Sometimes, the student competes against the clock, trying to complete a game within a given time period. Computer games often have more than one level, allowing students to progress to more difficult knowledge or skills.

When used appropriately, games can generate enthusiasm and increase learning. In choosing or constructing games, it is important to evaluate the type of learning involved, student appeal, initial cost or effort, and whether the time involved produces sufficient learning.

Choosing Appropriate Teaching Strategies

Where do you start in choosing an appropriate teaching approach? Once again, it begins with your learning objectives. Your learning activities

12-8
Games can be used to meet and reinforce learning objectives.

must lead students toward meeting the objectives. Keeping this in mind, see how various teaching strategies fit your situation. Then develop your activity based on the teaching strategy that is the best match. Be sure to consider the following:

- *Student characteristics.* A strategy must match the ages and developmental abilities of your students. For example, you would not choose a lecture format for first graders. If this is a whole-class activity, make certain it is a strategy all students can participate in. Keep in mind students preferred learning styles and variety.

- *Subject matter.* The subject you are teaching and topic of the lesson play a large part in narrowing your choice of appropriate strategies. Some subjects require teaching methods that involve a lot of content repetition. Perhaps facts must be learned. Other subject areas require more creativity and exploration. Sometimes you may need to reinforce other skills while teaching the subject content. For example, students may need to develop interpersonal skills along with content skills.

- *Teaching situation.* The strategy you choose must work from a practical standpoint. Time, materials and equipment availability, space, and any additional cost are all considerations. If taking the class on a field trip to a symphony performance an hour away is not an option, how else could you meet your learning objective?

All of these options and considerations may seem overwhelming. In fact, having options is a great part of teaching. It allows you to pair your creativity with your learning objectives to develop unique activities for your students. When you spend time with a group of students, as you will as a teacher, you become attuned to their needs and preferences. You quickly develop an instinct for what will work well and what will not. (Of course, there are always surprises!) In the meantime, as you gain experience, you can use tools like those outlined in 12-9 to help you make appropriate choices.

12-9

A checklist, such as this, is helpful when choosing teaching strategies.

	Checklist for Choosing a Teaching Strategy
✓	Meets objective(s)
✓	Age and developmentally appropriate
✓	Meets varying learning style needs
✓	Includes all students in learning process
✓	Will engage students' interest
✓	Respects cultural differences
✓	Appropriate for the subject matter and topic
✓	Allows for active involvement in learning
✓	Promotes thinking skills
✓	Allows appropriate reinforcement of content
✓	Can be completed within available time
✓	Will work in available space
✓	Uses available resources/materials
✓	Matches teacher's experience and skills

Summary

Teachers know what they want students to learn and have plans for how to measure their learning. They use instructional methods, also called teaching strategies or instructional strategies, to meet their objectives.

Students need to learn the complex skills required for critical thinking. Teachers at every level and in every subject area must provide opportunities to practice these skills.

Teachers rely on key teaching skills for the success of learning. Effective questions and examples are essential to most teaching strategies. The use of appropriate pacing and providing closure help maximize learning.

There are many basic teaching strategies, ranging from lectures to lab activities. Some are more teacher-centered, while others are more learner-centered. Each type of strategy has certain characteristics. Understanding these helps teachers identify appropriate options for developing learning activities for specific lessons.

Teaching strategies, and activities based on them, must lead students to meeting the lesson's objectives. In addition to matching the topic with an appropriate strategy, in planning lessons, teachers must consider the specific characteristics of their students and other aspects of the teaching situation.

Review

1. Explain why well-developed thinking skills are even more essential than knowledge.

2. Give an example of an open-ended question, and identify the level of thinking it requires based on Bloom's Taxonomy.

3. What is wait time? What is the reasoning behind its use?

4. If you were teaching a second-grade class about cause and effect, identify an appropriate example that you might use to clarify the concept.

5. How are learning activities and basic teaching strategies related?

6. How do teacher-centered and learner-centered instructional methods differ?

7. What are two ways skits and role playing are similar? Identify at least one way in which they differ.

8. What is the difference between productive and experimental labs?

9. What would be an appropriate situation to use each of the following as a learning tool—crossword puzzle, card game, board game? Identify the topic, grade level, and learning to be achieved.

10. What is the starting point for determining an appropriate teaching strategy for a lesson? What other general areas must be considered as part of the decision?

Reflect

1. Some students purposely ask off-track questions to disrupt the flow of lessons. In your experience, how do teachers handle these most effectively?

2. Considering the characteristics of the various teaching strategies described in this chapter, identify three that might pose particular pacing problems for teachers. Explain your choices.

3. Explain in your own words why closure is so important to learning.

4. Why is individual accountability a concern in cooperative learning activities? Come up with two ways this might be accomplished.

Act

1. Choose a topic that you are studying in one of your classes. Write an original question, based on that topic, at each level of Bloom's Taxonomy.

2. Based on your experiences taking part in discussions, develop a list of guidelines you would use as a teacher to make sure students felt comfortable participating. Identify whether your guidelines are for elementary, middle school, or high school students.

3. Watch a how-to television program such as one on cooking, home improvement, or some similar topic. Evaluate the strengths and weaknesses of the way techniques are demonstrated. How would a similar demonstration in a classroom differ from the one you watched?

4. Arrange to visit a classroom to observe a teacher conducting a learning activity. Report on your experience from an instructional viewpoint. What is the topic and level of the lesson? Describe the learning activities and identify the basic teaching strategies on which they are based. How did the teacher use questioning and examples in the lesson? How did the teacher achieve closure?

Add to Your Portfolio

Review the lesson plan you created in Chapter 11. Based on the information in this chapter, develop an alternative or additional learning activity using a different teaching strategy. Write a rationale for your new choice. Formulate at least eight questions, using various appropriate levels of thinking, you would use as part of the activity. Add the possible alterations to your lesson plan to your portfolio.

13 TECHNOLOGY FOR TEACHING AND LEARNING

Key Terms

instructional technology

distance education

online learning

accredited

interactive whiteboard

model

acceptable use policy

plagiarism

WebQuest

Objectives

After studying this chapter, you will be able to

- **describe** the current status of technology use in education.

- **assess** personal interest in and readiness for taking an online course.

- **evaluate** online Web sites for teaching and learning.

- **link** a plan for integrating technology into a lesson plan to the plan's learning objectives.

In the last decades, technology has changed virtually all aspects of society and continues to do so. Education is no exception. While computers were originally developed for use by business and government, their application to other areas, including education, quickly became apparent. Other related forms of technology soon followed. The term **instructional technology** was coined to describe the application of technology to enhance teaching, learning, and assessment. Everything from computers in the classroom to the use of multimedia for educational presentations can be considered instructional technology.

Teaching and Learning in the Digital Age

Today, technology of various types is used at every level of education, 13-1. For example, kindergarteners play simple computer games that help build reading skills. Elementary students create data bar graphs comparing the daily high and low temperatures of their city with others across the country by entering the information on a spreadsheet program. Middle school students studying the Louisiana Purchase read excerpts from the journals of Lewis and Clark and view artifacts from the journey through the Smithsonian Institution's Web site. A high school sociology class has a live discussion with a similar class in Canada via the Internet using a Web link.

In each of these cases, the teacher created the activity to help students reach course learning objectives. Developing knowledge and skills for using technology in everyday life and work is a useful byproduct, but it is normally not the main goal. Technology should be chosen as a tool only when it is effective for the situation.

13-1
From simple art pictures to complex design projects, computer technology is used at all levels of education.

As technology continues to evolve, new classroom applications will emerge. As part of your teacher education, you will learn how to evaluate, select, and use technology appropriately in the classroom. You will also have opportunities to see how it can help with many of the other tasks teachers perform. The International Society for Technology in Education (ISTE) has developed a set of educational technology standards for teachers. These are helping teacher education programs make certain that new teachers feel prepared to use instructional technology. They identify specific skills teachers need in order to incorporate technology into their teaching and model appropriate use of technology for work and professional growth.

Assessing Current Practice

Technology offers countless options for enhancing learning, inspiring teachers, and speeding routine tasks. At the same time, there are vast differences in its use in schools. In some schools, each student has a laptop, or similar device, they use at school and take home to complete assignments. Other schools are not yet connected to the Internet. Most fall in the broad spectrum between those extremes.

Why is there such wide variation? The primary reason is cost. Computers and other technology are expensive, especially when multiplied by the number of teachers and students in a school district who would like to use them. Add on related expenses such as software, Internet access, and technical support. In addition, equipment and software need frequent updates or replacement.

As you learned in Chapter 8, school funding methods vary from state to state. In many states, some school districts have much less to spend per pupil than in other districts. One way this shows up is that less wealthy districts tend to have significantly fewer technology resources. Federal and state government programs, grants, even local fundraising efforts have helped some schools, but real inequities exist.

Even in schools where technology is available, its use varies from teacher to teacher. This may be due to differences in technology skills, teaching style, or even subject area. As a group, younger teachers are more likely to embrace technology. Most grew up using a computer and acquired new skills gradually along the way. Some teachers find new technology intimidating and do not want to base lessons on something that may or may not work when they need it. Other teachers use more traditional techniques very effectively. Technology is also more applicable and important to some subject areas and grade levels than to others.

Adapting to the Situation

What happens if you believe in integrating technology in teaching, become prepared to do so, and end up in a school with little available technology? You can use what is available as effectively as possible. If you have one computer in your classroom, design activities that allow students to use it in small groups or individually. If there are computers available in the library or a computer lab, make use of those. If you have a computer at home, use it for research and planning. You may have other personal technology, such as a digital camera, that you could use to enhance lesson material. Look into the possibility of grants or community support to improve the situation.

You might find yourself in a situation where the school has many technology resources, including ones new to you. You can ask the technology coordinator or another teacher to help you learn new skills. Look online for ideas about successful applications. Practice on your own. Then try using the technology in a small way. As your confidence increases, take advantage of professional development opportunities to expand your skills.

You may also be able to share your technology successes with other teachers. Think about ways that you could approach this so that teachers feel comfortable. You might form a study group, with teachers volunteering to show how equipment or software might be used in various classes. If a teacher seems to need one-on-one support, ask the teacher to teach you something in return. Everyone has different knowledge and strengths. Being part of a committed faculty means sharing these with one another. Most schools have a technology resource person that staff can utilize for assistance and to build skills.

Technology: Making Learning More Accessible

While the American educational system is open to all, some students face real barriers to learning. Technology now offers very practical ways to overcome some of those obstacles. Students and teachers no longer need to be physically in the same classroom in order for quality learning to take place. In addition, technology now allows many students with disabilities or other impediments to learning to participate more fully in their education.

Expanding Classroom Walls

Technology allows teachers to go beyond traditional classrooms to meet the needs of students. **Distance education**—a learning situation in which the teacher and student are not in the same location—is not a new concept. However, technology has made it much more widely available. In addition, there are now options that make the experience more similar to classroom learning, 13-2.

These arrangements use various technologies. Most commonly, lessons are available to students through the Internet, often called **online learning** or virtual education. Students complete assignments, participate in discussion boards, and may even take exams online.

Distance education first gained popularity at the college and university level. Students could take some, or even all, classes with few trips to campus. Now, online courses and even virtual schools are available for students at the secondary level and even below. Students may take individual classes or even complete all their graduation requirements via computer. Traditional schools may offer some online courses. Virtual schools—those that exist only online—are another option, but students need to make sure that they are accredited. An **accredited** school has passed a quality assessment and credits earned generally qualify for graduation at traditional schools.

In online courses, students submit their work to the teacher electronically. They usually interact with the teacher and other students on a regular basis. Sometimes classes take place in *real time*, meaning all students are online for class at the same time and function more like a traditional classroom. Most often, however, students complete lessons at times convenient to them but must meet assignment deadlines just as in a regular class.

One of the greatest advantages of distance learning is its accessibility. It can make educational opportunities available to those who cannot

13-2

Distance education can connect teachers and students around the world.

physically attend a regular course. It can give three high school seniors in a small rural high school access to an advanced physics class their school cannot provide. It gives options to a student unable to attend school because of a medical condition. It also appeals to students for whom school schedules are a problem. Distance learning makes learning more available by overcoming barriers to traditional classroom attendance.

This type of education is not right for all learners or teachers. Students need to have access to a computer and need basic computer skills. They must be motivated and self-disciplined to keep up with course assignments. One characteristic of high-quality classes is that teachers and students communicate frequently. In fact, some students who might be shy about expressing their ideas in a regular classroom are more willing to do so online. Teaching virtual classes requires technology skills, an emphasis on learning through projects, and a commitment to be available to students. Successful teachers also make use of the many technology tools to make learning as rich and interactive as possible.

Assistive Technology

Technology can assist students with a range of disabilities and characteristics that affect the learning process. These include students with some physical or learning impairments and English Language Learners (ELL).

The ability to utilize a computer can open up learning opportunities for students with a variety of disabling conditions. However, some have difficulty using a normal keyboard. Modified keyboards help many, but some use other devices such as trackballs or joysticks. These require less mobility to maneuver. Voice recognition software is also improving, translating spoken words into writing on the computer screen. For students who have difficulty with speech, text-to-speech software can "read" words typed into the computer using a synthesized voice. Students with limited sight can use programs that magnify computer type on the computer screen. Handheld magnifier technology can make books more readable. These and other uses of technology help many students function more easily in the classroom.

Technology can also aid students in coping with various types of learning disabilities, 13-3. While the adaptations must be learner specific, these examples can help you see the possibilities. An increasing number of books, including some textbooks, are available in electronic format. Using computer functions, the text (words) in these books can be changed in appearance. Many students who find reading difficult do better when the words are larger, there is more space between the lines, and the text is very dark on a white background. Devices such as a spell-checking dictionary, grammar checker, or a speaking dictionary can help students with the details of writing and allow them to focus on self-expression. Calculators

13-3
Assistive technology can enhance the learning of students with a wide range of disabilities.

can improve math skills. Electronic organizers can help students remember due dates and tasks to be done.

English Language Learners (ELL) can benefit from some of the same technology. In addition, computer programs that build English skills are sometimes used to specifically help students learn English. However, classroom teachers often use technology in other ways to help students. Online picture dictionaries can help students with vocabulary. Some students use handheld translator devices. Video presentations and visual demonstrations aid ELL students' understanding.

New technology will undoubtedly bring additional options. Finding ways to boost learning can make a real difference in students' lives.

Technology: Providing Tools for Teachers

Technology offers tremendous tools for teachers. Most types of technology have multiple uses within education. That makes it worthwhile to learn to use new types and explore additional applications for technology you already use. Existing technology can aid in planning, teaching, communicating, and managing tasks. It can also serve as a great source of inspiration for teaching.

Planning

Technology has brought real changes to the way teachers plan for learning. The Internet and Web offer easy options for discussing and sharing ideas with other teachers and for finding information and resources for teaching. Many teachers find that using these technologies in producing lesson plans has many benefits.

The Internet gives teachers easy access to colleagues worldwide. There are countless Web sites and other forums for sharing ideas and concerns. For example, a science teacher might seek advice on how to adapt science labs for a student with cerebral palsy who has limited mobility. Other teachers can respond, sharing their experiences and advice. Online discussions can help teachers explore the pros, cons, and uses of new teaching trends.

Many teachers post activity ideas online that spark others' creativity. These range from brief descriptions to full lesson plans. While teachers must adapt these to their own teaching situations, they can help stimulate creative new ways to help students learn.

The Internet is an unparalleled information and research tool. Teachers can easily search for information on any topic to expand their knowledge and enrich their lessons. Information from experts, government, business, and industry is available in an instant. In addition to regular Internet searches, it is helpful to check links from sites for teachers. These can lead to new sources of information on teaching topics that other teachers have found to be useful. However, all information on the Internet is not always correct. Teachers, as well as students, must be aware of the credibility of Internet sources.

Textbook publishers routinely make electronic teaching aids available to supplement students' textbooks. These typically include materials keyed to topics in the book that can be incorporated into lessons.

Technology can also help speed the process of creating written lesson plans. Many software programs are now available that assist teachers in lesson plan development. Some school districts provide their own versions for teachers to use. Using electronic lesson plans makes it easier to store copies of plans and related resources for future reference and possible use. It also simplifies the task of meeting administrative requirements to turn in lesson plans. Additionally, such plans—or parts of them—as well as assignments may be shared with students and parents to assist with make-up work for absent students or as home tutorials.

Teaching

Technology offers teachers exciting options for presenting information in diverse ways that can bring learning to life. It takes effort, imagination, and a willingness to learn new skills. Some options require more sophisticated technology than others, but even with limited equipment, teachers can add variety to lessons.

In this section, "teaching" refers to providing information and instruction to students. Another aspect of the teaching process, developing learning activities, is discussed later in this chapter. Assessment is the topic of the next chapter.

Because of differences in learning styles, teaching that integrates as many of the senses as possible helps to maximize learning, 13-4. Technology provides additional ways to do so. It also provides teachers with resources to more easily provide differentiated instruction.

13-4
Technology offers teachers many options to maximize the learning of students.

Most of the technology options discussed in this section can also be utilized in learning activities. Similarly, those highlighted in the activities section can be adapted for instruction.

Interactive Whiteboards

One of the most versatile types of teaching equipment is the **interactive whiteboard**. This can function like a traditional dry-erase board but is connected to a computer and projector to allow the board to become an extended computer screen. Teachers and students can access the computer functions at the board or the computer. An interactive whiteboard can significantly expand the usefulness of a single computer in a classroom.

Notes placed on the board can be captured and saved as electronic files. These might be e-mailed to an absent student, made available to a student who learns best through repetition, or stored as a record of the lesson.

Interactive whiteboards come with useful tools. A math teacher may use the graph paper background for students to plot points on a graph. Students can add those points with a special pen or even their finger. An English teacher might project a paragraph and have students use highlighting tools to identify the thesis, supporting statements, and conclusion. Even routine tasks are more interesting with interactivity and whole-class participation.

Teachers can utilize the functions of the computer's software during presentations and activities, projecting them on the whiteboard. A lesson on earth science might include a live shot of lava flow from a volcano in Hawaii projected on the board. If a student asks a question, the teacher could link to a relevant Web site, such as National Geographic, to find an answer or a relevant picture. Students can follow the teacher's search on the whiteboard "screen." Its large surface makes it easy for the whole class to easily see all aspects of a teaching presentation or interactive class activity.

Sight, Motion, and Sound

Technology has revolutionized the visual aspects of teaching, helping information come alive for students. In the past, a teacher might go through magazines hoping to find a relevant picture to post on a bulletin board. Today, teachers can search the entire Internet and easily find visual images—photos, drawings, diagrams, video segments, and more—that can enhance lessons. These can be saved electronically and called up in an instant, ready to be printed or inserted in a document or presentation.

Many sites contain excellent pictures, videos, television programs, or other materials that they allow teachers to use in class presentations. A 3-D animation segment might help students understand the process of division. A video clip from a Shakespeare play can help set the stage for studying it. A first-person account of life in the trenches in World War II might make the lesson's factual information come alive. Searching out such resources is worth the effort.

Teacher-developed visuals can also be effective teaching tools. When teaching tennis skills, a physical education teacher might play a video of a student game, projecting it on an interactive whiteboard. The teacher could use the whiteboard tools to show how players could better position themselves for shots. The teacher might also use a second video to show students how their serves and strokes compare with ideal ones.

Audio files, although often overlooked, can also be useful teaching tools. When talking about the heart, a teacher might play audio files of the heartbeats of a healthy and an obstructed heart. Many free audio files are available. *Podcasts*—audio broadcasts available on the Web—can also provide relevant material. They can be downloaded to a computer or digital audio player and played or saved and played later. Teachers might prepare podcasts of key information for students with learning disabilities or English language learners (ELL) students to use as study aids.

Simulated Experiences

It is not always possible to give students hands-on experiences, even when these experiences can improve understanding. Time, money, and lack of equipment may all be barriers. Technology offers opportunities to bring some of that realism to the classroom. Sometimes the virtual version is more accurate and clearly presented than if it occurred live in class.

Simulations can show how things happen. They may employ actual video, art, animation, or a combination. For example, a video clip might clearly show what happens when two different liquids are combined and a new mixture is formed. Math and science are typical areas for simulations, but they work in other subject areas as well. A foreign language teacher might take students down the aisles of an open-air market in Germany. These experiences are known as *virtual field trips*. (Administrators find them very cost-effective.) A child development or parenting teacher might send a baby simulator home with students to give them an idea what it is like to care for a newborn. Interactivity possibilities vary, but simulations can bring students' learning closer to the real world. Computer simulation games, which utilize similar technology, are discussed in the section on learning activities.

Virtual Field Trips

Many historic and cultural sites offer virtual educational tours, often with related activities. Teachers can show students eggs hatching into chicks, experience life in Colonial Williamsburg, or follow scientists as they work in Antarctica, 13-5. Other virtual field trips may highlight more

13-5
Students can take a virtual field trip to a jungle from the safety of their classroom.

everyday places and activities. They vary in quality. Some have related student activities or allow students to ask questions.

When teachers consider virtual field trips, they need to choose carefully to fulfill course objectives. They need to view the experience and make sure it is worthwhile and that the technology will work smoothly. When teachers set appropriate related learning tasks for students as they take the "tour," students stay on task. A follow-up discussion or other activity is important to solidify learning.

Communicating

Technology gives teachers options for enhancing communication. In fact, today's teachers have more avenues for connecting with students, parents, coworkers, administrators, and the public than at any time in history. Choosing an appropriate method and using good communication skills, discussed in Chapter 10, are keys to effectively sharing information and ideas.

As part of a school district or school Web site, teachers often have individual or class Web sites. These enhance communication with students, parents, and others. Teachers often post homework assignments, links to helpful online resources, announcements, calendars, and other useful information. Some have blogs, and there is usually an e-mail link.

There are many communication options, including e-mail, text messaging, online posting, as well as phone calls. Each can be appropriate in certain circumstances to get the needed information to the right people. While such forms of technology can make communication more accessible, there are situations in which direct face-to-face contact is what is needed.

Managing Information

Teaching involves keeping track of and using numerous types of factual information, or data, for future use. Computers are particularly suited to simplifying those tasks.

Keeping accurate grades is essential for teachers. Each time a teacher grades an assignment, the information must be recorded and saved for future use. At the end of a grading period, teachers must calculate students' many individual grades to determine grades for report cards. Electronic gradebook programs, chosen by the teacher or school, can simplify this process greatly. Any files that include confidential information should be password protected.

Electronic spreadsheet programs, such as Excel™, allow information to be adapted for different uses. For example, a teacher might set up a basic spreadsheet with a list of students in a class. This could be made into an attendance log. It could also be adapted to keep track of each student's progress toward meeting specific class goals or any other need. Various types of reports could be generated, based on the data in a particular spreadsheet.

There are countless other ways that teachers can use technology to boost their productivity. For example, a teacher might send out a newsletter to parents weekly or monthly. Once the template for the newsletter has been developed, new information can simply be added monthly. If the teacher has an electronic contact list of parents and guardians, this could speed the process of sending the newsletter electronically or printing labels for mailing. Many school districts encourage teachers to have their own classroom Web sites. As long as the Web site is updated often, this tool will keep students and parents constantly informed.

Technology: Enhancing Learning Opportunities

This section explores many types of technology used by teachers to strengthen learning activities. This discussion is certainly not complete. In fact, by the time you read this, new technology will be available, perhaps replacing some of these options. Teachers must stay current with technology and how to use it effectively in the classroom. When examining various uses of technology in learning, it is important to consider how teachers can plan and manage these successfully.

Planning Technology-Based Activities

The considerations teachers take into account in choosing and planning any activity also apply to those that incorporate technology. (You may want to review the *Checklist for Choosing a Teaching Strategy*, Figure 12-9, in the previous chapter.) Technology-based activities are not automatically better, more appropriate, or more interesting than those without the use of technology. It all depends on the situation, the activity, and the skill with which it is presented.

Activities that include technology require particularly careful planning. Classroom teachers who use technology successfully suggest starting with easy applications and working toward more complicated uses. This will help you gain confidence while you learn about what works best, how long things take, and students' abilities.

Experienced teachers make certain that students know:

- *The goals of the lesson.* Sometimes with technology, it is easy for students to get sidetracked.

- *The procedures they are to follow.* Step-by-step directions can help students succeed. This is particularly important when new technology skills are involved.

- *How much time they have.* For younger students and complex activities, consider setting time limits for various sections of the activity. Most activities that utilize technology require more time than those without. Timing is not always easy to predict, so be prepared to adapt as you go.

- *What they are to achieve.* Each activity must produce something that shows that the desired learning has occurred.

- *How they will be evaluated.* When students know how they will be rated or graded, they are more likely to achieve acceptable results. Having a **model**, a real example that shows the characteristics of excellence, helps students know what constitutes quality. Some teachers keep electronic files of exceptional student work from previous classes to use as models for future ones.

For group activities, each participant should have a specific role and be held accountable for his or her contribution as in cooperative learning. For complex activities, teachers often divide the class into groups and assign each group a different segment of the activity. This can allow better utilization of equipment and time. Each group then contributes its piece to the final product.

Assessing Students' Skills

Just as teachers vary in their technology skills, so do students. Even at the same grade level, classmates may have widely varying knowledge and skills related to computer and other technology use. This is usually due to differences in opportunities to use technology in and out of school. Some students also have more natural ability and interest than others.

It is critical that teachers evaluate students' knowledge, as a group and as individuals. Depending on the level of the students, this can be accomplished with simple activities, questionnaires, or a combination of the two.

Strategies for dealing with differences can take various approaches. Sometimes teachers explain and demonstrate the basics of the program or equipment to be used in an activity, and then they supply detailed instructions as a guide. They may divide students by level and provide more support for those just learning a program or technology. Sometimes dividing students into pairs or small groups with mixed experience allows them to teach one another.

Dealing with Technology Problems

Just as they make back-up plans for technology problems as they present information, teachers must do the same for activities, 13-6. They need to

13-6
Although technology has many advantages, teachers must be prepared for any problems that arise.

consider how they might cope if a problem arises with the technology planned for an activity. Technology glitches are inevitable. It pays to be prepared.

As you develop lesson plans, think about the possibilities. What if one group cannot access the Internet? What if three teams are all at a standstill because they cannot figure out how to make the program work?

Sometimes having backup paper copies of important information can save the day. If a computer goes down, you might regroup students so that you have fewer groups with more members. Perhaps you could switch the order of activities and substitute tomorrow's lesson that is not technology dependent.

Learn as much as possible about how to solve common problems. You may also have students in class who have more expertise with certain types of equipment or software and can help out when difficulties arise. (Sometimes teachers appoint such students as official "technology assistants.") For group projects, including a student familiar with the technology in each group can help keep everyone moving ahead. Also, the physical setup of the classroom must be considered. Are there enough outlets? Can the teacher "cruise" the room and see everyone's screen?

Guidelines for Student Use of Computers

For all of the learning opportunities that computers bring to the classroom, there are also potential problems and issues. As a student, you are probably already aware of many of these. As you begin to think like a teacher, you must shift your focus to how to minimize and deal with them. Often, these issues are equally applicable to other types of technology.

Safety and Security

The school and the individual teacher share responsibility for the safety and security of computers and their use. The school usually sets policies. Teachers are responsible for the equipment in their classroom and its appropriate use.

- *Equipment.* In many schools, computers and related equipment are distributed among classrooms. Teachers need to make frequent checks to be certain all unsecured equipment is in place and report any problems immediately.

- *Acceptable use.* Schools usually have specific policies in place regarding use of computers by students. Computer use is considered a privilege, not a right. Students are often required to sign a form stating that they know, understand, and will follow these rules. This is sometimes called an **acceptable use policy** or presented to students as a "computer code of conduct." Those who violate the rules can be banned from using the computer temporarily or permanently or face other disciplinary action. Rules include topics such as not damaging equipment and only visiting Web sites related to classroom projects.

- *Internet safety.* Since the Internet is not censored, many sites contain material unsuitable for students. Schools attempt to shield students from these sites by installing filters or blocking software. These attempt to screen out sites that may contain offensive material. However, they are not perfect. Unwanted sites may get through, and sites with legitimate educational use may be blocked. Computer screens should always face toward the classroom, and teachers must monitor students using computers. Student safety is a related issue. Students must never give out personal information, including their last names. Some schools do not permit students to access e-mail, chat rooms, and similar sites as a safety precaution.

Plagiarism and Copyright Issues

With seemingly endless information available on the Internet, it is understandable that students may be confused about how they can use that information. Not all adults know what they should about fair use.

From the time that students start using the Internet (and print resources) to gather information for projects or reports, teachers need to clearly explain the "rules" of research. The main issue is **plagiarism**. This is the use of someone else's original words or ideas without giving that person credit. Well-known facts, such as the date a state was founded or the categories of trees, are considered common knowledge. They can be found in many resources and can be used freely. On the other hand, copying paragraphs from various resources without acknowledgment and piecing them together with some original writing is plagiarism. Basing a paper analyzing the characters in *Huckleberry Finn* on someone else's analysis as if it is a writer's own is plagiarism. Turning in a paper that someone else wrote as your own goes beyond plagiarism. At the college level, plagiarism is often grounds for dismissal from school.

A paper can include other people's ideas and words if it is clear they are not the writer's own and if the original sources are credited. For example, a paper on the first English colony at Roanoke Island might contain some brief descriptions from the writings of Thomas Harriot, one of the early colonists. The paper must acknowledge the source of descriptions. Teachers need to explain how to give credit (within the paper, in a source list, in a footnote), depending on what is appropriate for the students' level.

Books, movies, music, and much online material are covered by copyright, 13-7. This means that the work's ownership and right to its use is protected by copyright law. The copyright symbol, ©, is generally shown

13-7

Before using or duplicating copyrighted material, follow copyright law.

as part of the copyright statement. Copyrighted material can be used only in limited ways unless the copyright owner grants permission for use.

Teachers, as well as students, must follow copyright law. The *TEACH Act of 2002* allows some use of copyrighted material for educational purposes. However, teachers must obtain permission from the copyright owner to make copies of copyrighted material semester after semester to give to students. Many teaching materials available online, even if they are copyrighted, specifically say that teachers may copy and use them in their classroom. The *TEACH Act* does allow a teacher to make a copy of a copyrighted work and display it, such as in a teaching presentation or posted on a bulletin board. Many Web sites have more information on acceptable use of copyrighted material for teaching.

Research Activities

Learning how to find, evaluate, and use information is certainly not a new educational goal. In today's digital environment, however, these skills have become much more important. One reason is that the rate at which new knowledge and information is being developed continues to increase. Students will need to learn throughout life at a pace far greater than their parents did, just to keep up with the demands of everyday life and work.

Graduation cannot be the end of learning. A second reason is that the Internet and other technology have caused an explosion in the amount of information available to the average person. No longer must information be published in a newspaper, magazine, or book. Anyone can "publish" on the Web. The downside is that there are few controls on the accuracy of much of that information. It is up to the reader to determine what is true, accurate, and worthwhile. Schools must teach these skills.

Many learning activities incorporate some form of research. Teachers need to structure such activities so they are appropriate for the grade level and skills of students. Besides helping students use research to gain and use information on specific topics, such activities must also actively teach research skills using print and electronic sources.

This is a gradual process. For young students, a teacher might limit research to a single reputable site. For example, the White House Web site for education includes information on a variety of topics at different levels of difficulty. Students can learn about the presidents, the White House, the functions of various branches of government, or the latest government initiatives. They can learn online information-gathering skills within a limited secure environment.

For students at the next step, a teacher might review and select several Web sites for students to use for a research assignment. By saving these as bookmarks in a file copied to class computers, the teacher allows students more exploration under controlled conditions. There are also search tools designed specifically for students that bring up student-appropriate sites for topics.

WebQuests are a popular form of Web-based learning. A **WebQuest** is an inquiry-based learning project utilizing information from preselected Web sites. They emphasize higher-order thinking skills. WebQuests are usually group activities with each group member taking on a particular role or responsibility to complete the group task. For example, a WebQuest might have students identify the causes and a possible remedy for depletion of fish populations in an area, using provided Web links. Individual teachers can develop WebQuests, but many are also available on the Web.

Older students can learn the skills needed to search effectively on the Web. This includes how to "word" search requests and identify which sites are most likely to yield appropriate information.

The process of learning to evaluate sites can start early. Even young students can learn how to identify sites from government, educational institutions, and other fairly reliable places. Students need to check for datedness, source of authority, bias, and similar issues that can help determine the reliability of information.

Online research is not limited to information on Web sites. There are also online library sites. In addition, many local libraries allow members to search online to find out what books and other resources are available.

Data Collection and Analysis

Many math and science activities involve gathering facts and statistics, exploring their relationships, and drawing conclusions. However, activities that analyze data can be useful in many subject areas, from social studies and art to physical education and music. Technology makes it easier for students to practice data-related skills.

Younger children can collect data (measuring the heights of students in their class or finding the seating capacity of ballparks) and turn the information into simple computer graphs. Middle school students might find the fat and calorie content of burgers or fries at various fast-food chains and use spreadsheet software to calculate the differences and determine pounds gained if eaten daily for a year. High school students can participate in real science experiments along with teams of scientists using data available online. Students can develop a realistic budget for living life on their own. Many government Web sites, such as the National Aeronautics and Space Administration (NASA), the National Oceanic and Atmospheric Administration (NOAA), the National Geological Survey, and the United States Department of Agriculture are rich sources of real data.

Spreadsheet software has other capabilities. It can be used to translate data into many kinds of graphs and charts, generate timelines, or even turn a spreadsheet into a poster-size print version.

Using Visuals and Sound

Activities that incorporate technology often take advantage of the visual and audio capabilities readily available today. These may be part of the material provided for student learning, or students may choose or make visual or audio material to enhance the projects and products they produce. Students are accustomed to multimedia (using more than one form) in so much of everyday life that they respond to it in learning, as well.

Visual capabilities range from the simple to the complex. Young students can learn to print pictures from free online sources and to copy them into documents. Middle school students might distill the content they have learned into an electronic slide show presentation. This would involve writing the copy, choosing the backgrounds and size and style of type, and perhaps adding graphics. High school students might develop a multimedia public service announcement. Some common technologies, in addition to those mentioned in the teaching section, include:

- *Digital cameras and Webcams.* With digital cameras, students can take photos, download them to a computer, and print them or use them in reports or electronic presentations. *Webcams* are digital video cameras that capture footage that is saved online. Many Webcam feeds are available on the Internet and may show everything from weather to ships in the harbor, animals at the zoo, or a falcon's nest with young birds hatching. These can be used for activities, or students can shoot their own footage. Using software, students can create visual projects. In doing so, they learn to plan, script, present, edit, and publish.

- *Graphics programs.* The capabilities of computer graphics programs vary. The most basic allow students to draw and paint. Most sophisticated and specialized programs allow animation, 3-D designs, Web page development, graphic design and page layout, and presentation development. Some even give CAD (computer-aided design) capabilities.

- *Audio files.* In many cases, audio files, without accompanying video, can be an appropriate choice for learning activities. They require less equipment and skill to develop and play. Students might record their spelling words for practice, conduct interviews, develop radio commercials, or put together a presentation on orchestra instruments.

Communication Activities

As with other forms of technology, educators have found uses for electronic communication as learning tools. A teacher could arrange for students to have keypals (electronic pen pals) with a class in another city anywhere in the world using simple e-mail exchanges, 13-8. For example,

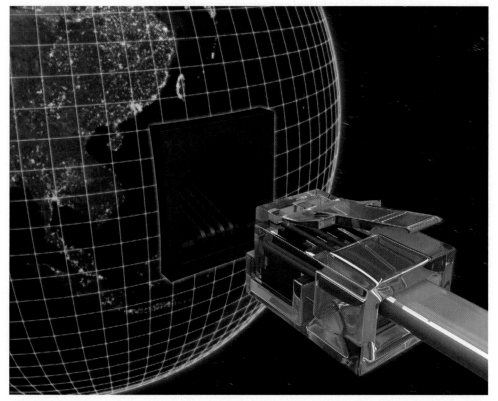

13-8
Electronic communication makes it possible to form global connections.

students studying Spanish could pair up with an English class in South America. Discussion boards or forums can allow students to discuss topics or post information (such as essays) and get feedback from others. Online conferencing allows communicating directly. Chat rooms are one example, but *VoIP* (voice over Internet protocol) allows direct audio (and video links with a Webcam) through the computer instead of using a phone. This could be used for direct communication between classes in different places or collaboration between classes in distant schools on a single project. Communication technology options are applicable to all levels and subject areas.

Games and Simulations

As you learned in Chapter 12, games can provide diverse auditory, visual, and kinesthetic ways to learn. Computers have revolutionized the world of games. Simple games, such as crosswords and word searches, can be made with easy-to-use software. When students develop such games, it reinforces factual information or vocabulary. Many other learning games are available online. Some are interactive, and computers can serve as an electronic opponent.

Computer simulation games use the power of computers to offer a virtual representation of a situation. In a fantasy or real-world environment, students perform specific tasks involving problem solving and decision making and then justify their reasons for certain decisions. They give the user the opportunity to build a city, family, or even to be a zookeeper. Computer simulations imitate the stock market, a historical war battle, or pioneer life. They can help students develop strategic thinking and planning skills.

Other simulations mimic real-life experiences. They may replicate what it is like to fly an airplane or bat a baseball, for example. Science simulations offer experiences such as virtual dissection, virtual microscope experiences, or a trip through the human body. They can give the experience of being in an earthquake or various types of weather. Simulations allow alternatives to hands-on experiences.

Summary

Innovations in technology have changed how teaching and learning take place and will continue to do so. Schools still vary considerably in the availability of educational technology, and some teachers use it more than others.

One very real benefit of technology is its role in making education more available and accessible. Many courses and even schools are now available online. Technology also helps improve learning opportunities for many students with disabilities or other impairments that affect learning.

Teachers can take advantage of technology for planning, teaching, communication, and information management. Most forms of technology have multiple uses, so once learned, they can be used in a variety of ways. The choice to use technology must always support the learning objectives for a lesson.

Well-planned technology-based activities can stimulate learning. A related benefit is that students learn important technology skills they will need for everyday life and work. To use such activities successfully, a teacher must acquire the skills to utilize technology, assess students' skills, plan carefully, and stay flexible to deal with any problems that arise.

Review

1. What is the goal of instructional technology? Give examples of technology currently being used in education.

2. What is the primary reason schools vary significantly in the amount of technology they have available for teachers and students? Would you predict that situation is likely to change in the near future? Give a rationale for your answer.

3. Why would it be important to choose a class from an accredited school if you wanted to try online learning?

4. Give a specific example how use of the Internet might help teachers in each of these areas: planning, teaching, communicating, and managing information.

5. Based on the chapter and any experience, briefly describe how you might use an interactive whiteboard in teaching a lesson (any subject and level).

6. Identify two possible advantages and two disadvantages of a simulated educational experience compared to a real one.

7. Explain why both careful planning and flexibility are needed when activities include technology.

8. What is plagiarism?

9. Why does teaching Internet search skills need to be a gradual process?

10. Give an example of a technology-based learning activity that would help prepare students for a real-world work assignment.

Reflect

1. What are the potential consequences for students from the great differences in available technology among schools? Consider both the short-term and long-term impact.

2. Think about whether or not you would be a good candidate for taking online classes. What would be the benefits and drawbacks for you?

3. Some experts have expressed concern that many of today's students are failing to develop essential interpersonal skills because they spend so much more time interacting with technology (such as video games or cell phones) than with people. Do you agree with this concern? What other potential effects—positive or negative—might growing up with technology have on students' learning or school experiences?

4. What about integrating technology into teaching and learning excites you the most? What concerns you the most? Explain your choices.

Act

1. Interview a teacher regarding his or her attitudes toward and use of educational technology. Develop a list of questions you will use for the interview. Prepare a summary of the interview to share with the class.

2. Find at least two Web sites that include helpful information for teachers regarding the use of technology in the classroom. In addition, find at least two sites with educational material that could be used by students. Write a review of each site for future reference, including the URL (Web address), sponsor or source of the site, types of information available, and an evaluation of its usefulness. Combine your information with that of your classmates in a single resource list.

3. For at least four days, keep lists of how your teachers use technology for teaching and how they include it in learning activities. From each list, choose the use that you think incorporated technology most effectively. Write a description of how technology was used and why it was effective.

4. Develop a computer code of conduct for elementary, middle school, or high school students. Keep the language, rules, and length appropriate for the age group. Format your list as a poster or a form that students would sign.

Add to Your Portfolio

Using the lesson plan you created in Chapter 11, identify one or more specific ways that you could utilize technology in teaching content or in an activity within the lesson. Describe what technology would be used, how it would support the lesson objectives, benefits of its use, and whether you currently have the necessary technology skills or would need to learn them. Add this alternative plan to your portfolio.

14 THE ROLE OF ASSESSMENT

Key Terms

formative assessment

summative assessment

mentor teachers

alternative assessment

student portfolio

rubric

checklist

scorecard

self-evaluation

peer evaluation

validity

reliability

course evaluation

Objectives

After studying this chapter, you will be able to

- **distinguish** between formative and summative assessment.
- **identify** the source of standards evaluated by assessments.
- **write** examples of appropriate and effective test questions.
- **develop** a rubric to be used for alternative assessment.
- **describe** the reasoning teachers use in choosing appropriate assessment strategies.
- **analyze** a grading policy.
- **develop** questions a teacher might use for course evaluation.

*A*ssessment, the methods used to gain information about students' learning, is central to the educational process. The term may bring to mind tests and grades. However, there are other ways to assess learning. The information gained from assessments may be used for determining grades, but it has other uses, as well.

Assessment completes the cycle of instruction. In Chapter 11, you learned that a lesson plan begins with formulating the objectives you expect students to achieve. In Chapters 12 and 13, you learned more about activities that guide learners toward achieving these objectives. This chapter focuses on ways to determine whether that learning results in accomplishing the objectives. You will also explore some of the other uses of assessments in improving learning and teaching.

The Purposes of Assessment

Assessment strategies are tools for evaluating and maximizing student learning. Through analyzing what students know, teachers, administrators, and others can make decisions about how to improve the education students receive. Assessment is generally divided into two types, formative and summative. They differ in their purposes and use.

Formative assessment is an ongoing part of instruction designed to provide feedback about students' learning as it is occurring. It takes place *during* instruction. The results allow teachers to adjust their teaching during a lesson to help improve learning. Because the purpose of formative assessment is to make instructional decisions, such assessments are not used as part of students' grades.

Teachers use many different methods to check on students' learning as they are teaching. For example, a teacher may give an ungraded quiz to help gauge how well students understand the roles of key nutrients in overall health. If the quiz shows students are meeting the learning objective, the teacher can move on to the next topic. However, if students seem confused about water- and fat-soluble vitamins, for example, the teacher may spend additional time clarifying that topic. Informal assessment occurs when teachers ask questions in class and monitor how well students complete learning activities to assess understanding. In summary, they may ask students to identify the most confusing point in the subject's lesson. As you become a more seasoned teacher, you will be able to "read" your classes so you will know when learning is taking place. Are hands raised? Are students engaged in an activity?

Summative assessment is an evaluation of students' learning *after* instruction has taken place. It measures results, assessing whether learning objectives have been met. (Those objectives may be ones identified by the teacher, a district or state curriculum, or some other source.) Summative assessments are often scored or graded. Summative assessments allow students' progress to be tracked over time. They can also be used to judge the success of educational programs.

Tests are commonly used for summative assessment, 14-1. These include chapter or unit tests, state tests, and other types of achievement tests. However, summative assessments can take many other forms, as well.

Both formative and summative assessments are used to evaluate learning and teaching. As you read through this chapter, think about how the assessment tools described could be used for these assessment purposes.

What Can Be Measured?

What exactly can assessments measure? There are three main ways assessment can be useful in improving education. It can measure students' achievement of learning objectives and also their growth and progress over time. In addition, assessment can measure teaching effectiveness. Some forms of assessment give information on all three.

Measuring Student Achievement of Objectives

Assessment of learning occurs at various levels. Classroom teachers constantly monitor whether students are reaching the goals set out in their learning objectives. This happens during the lesson (formative assessment)

14-1
A test grade can let both the student and teacher know whether learning objectives have been met.

and at the completion of a lesson (summative assessment). In addition, students, classes, and schools are periodically measured against district, state, or national standards. These assessments are often in the form of achievement tests.

In their classrooms, teachers usually use tests for some assessments. They also evaluate students' learning in other ways, such as through projects. District, state, and national tests are usually *standardized tests*. These are administered to large numbers of students and are scored in a consistent manner. Most scoring is computerized.

Measuring Learner Growth and Progress

Over time, students' growth and progress can be assessed. For example, a child's expanding vocabulary and reading ability can be documented. Changes in classroom behavior can be tracked. Improvements in math computation skills, the ability to express ideas, or cooperative group behavior can all be measured.

By keeping track of students' growth and progress, teachers can report it to learners and parents. Teachers can also monitor what topics and skills need to be reviewed or reinforced. Assessment gives feedback that can offer encouragement or highlight issues of concern. It can also provide necessary information for diagnosing learning difficulties or giftedness so that students can receive appropriate learning support.

Measuring Teaching Effectiveness

The assessment process extends to teachers, as well as students. Part of being a good teacher is continual self-improvement. In addition, schools use more formal methods to evaluate teachers and help them become more effective.

Personal assessment needs to be a part of everyday teaching. Low student scores on a quiz can cause a teacher to analyze why a lesson did not bring the desired results. Was the explanation unclear? Did the activity fail to teach the desired skill? Was more practice needed? Being attuned to learning helps teachers modify their teaching to maximize student achievement.

Sometimes teachers use other techniques to evaluate their teaching. They may make a video of a lesson for later review and analysis. They may ask another teacher for feedback and suggestions. They may network to learn about and try new teaching techniques.

Analyzing how well the students meet learning objectives is one way to measure teaching effectiveness. However, many factors influence individual students' learning. Even with excellent teaching, there are a variety of reasons students may not completely meet all learning objectives.

Schools have a responsibility to make certain their teachers are effective. Review and evaluation of teachers can be based on a number of factors. These may include observing the teacher in teaching situations, test scores of students on standardized tests, and parental feedback. Beginning teachers are often assigned **mentor teachers** who are experienced and skilled. Mentor teachers help new teachers assess and improve their skills, solve problems, and become comfortable in their new positions.

Using Tests to Assess Learning

Tests have long been the accepted way to check students' learning. While other methods have gained popularity, tests remain the most widely used assessment tools. Learning how and when to use them effectively is part of understanding a teacher's role.

Standardized Tests

Standardized tests assess students' learning (summative assessment), but they usually have other objectives as well. Thousands of students take the exact same test. Consequently, test scores can be used in a variety of ways. The results can show the achievement of individual students, schools, or even teachers, 14-2.

14-2
Standardized tests are often scored by a computer.

State achievement tests are meant to assess the learning of students in an entire state. They may be given every year or at certain grade levels. The scores from these tests are carefully monitored and analyzed. States may hold underperforming schools accountable for raising test scores. School funding is sometimes tied to test scores.

School districts also utilize information from these tests. A district might note that its middle school science scores are below the state average. Administrators and teachers might work together to identify possible reasons and devise a strategy for improvement. If students' scores improve over time, it may indicate that the changes were successful.

Tests such as the SAT and ACT are standardized tests of students' knowledge. They are generally used in the college admission process. However, schools also evaluate how their students score on these tests. It provides feedback on how well their students compare with other students across the nation. Schools use high college-entrance test scores as evidence that their schools provide quality education.

Teacher-Developed Tests

As a student, you have taken hundreds of tests developed by your teachers. You may think of them primarily in terms of the grades you received. Teachers, however, develop tests to assess students' achievement of the lesson objectives they have set. For example, if your geometry teacher wants you to be able to calculate the area of a random shape on a grid, a test could measure your understanding and ability to perform this task. From the scores on the test, your teacher will not only know if you have met the learning objective, but also how well all of your classmates understood this concept. The results of teacher-made tests can also give teachers feedback on the effectiveness of their teaching.

Well-written tests can check students' knowledge and understanding, particularly of factual information. Teachers usually write their own tests, basing them on learning objectives, what they have taught, and knowledge of their students.

Teacher-developed tests are sometimes called "paper-and-pencil" tests because that is traditionally all that is needed to complete them. However, as schools utilize technology to a greater degree, more tests are taken electronically, in the classroom or as part of an online course. The questions may be the same as if written on paper, but the method of completion is different. Some online tests take advantage of available technology in the types of questions posed and their format.

Types of Test Questions

Traditional tests generally use a limited number of question types. These include the following:

- *True-false questions.* A true-false question requires students to distinguish whether a statement is true or false. Such questions usually test recall of information, but not higher level thinking. A test should include about the same number of questions with true answers as false answers.

- *Multiple-choice questions.* Students must choose the best answer from among a list of alternatives. Multiple-choice questions are constructed so that there is an introductory statement or question (called the *stem*) followed by a series of possible alternatives. Experts advise avoiding use of "All of the above" or "None of the above" as alternatives or at least limiting their use. Multiple-choice questions can be written to test higher-level thinking.

- *Matching questions.* With matching questions, students must identify the relationship or association between two items. For example, on a test on the Civil War, learners may be asked to match specific dates with events that occurred. On another test, students may be asked to match important terms with their meaning. When writing matching questions, give each column a descriptive title, such as "Terms" and "Definitions."

- *Fill-in-the-blank or short-answer questions.* In fill-in-the-blank questions, students must complete a sentence by inserting the correct word or words (usually no more than two). Sentences must be carefully constructed so that there is one correct answer. Short-answer questions are similar. They pose a question that requires a very brief answer.

- *Identification questions.* Identification questions require the learner to label or locate the parts on a diagram or drawing. For example, students in biology may be asked to label the parts on a diagram of a cell. Students studying English grammar may be asked to label the verb, noun, and adjective in a sentence.

- *Essay questions.* With essay questions, students must compose a more extended written answer to a question. Essay questions can measure not only knowledge, but also the ability to think clearly, organize information, and express one's thoughts. Essay questions can challenge learners to make connections, see relationships, and make comparisons. They often require higher-level thinking and are generally appropriate for older students. Teachers find essay questions easy to write, but they take time and effort to grade. When writing essay questions, teachers need to identify the ideas they expect students to include in the answers. This can serve as a model during the grading process.

Constructing Tests

A well-constructed test fairly evaluates students' learning. However, not all tests meet this standard. Following these guidelines can help achieve that goal.

- *Write questions that match the levels of the objectives.* A true-false question can check for understanding, but not the ability to apply information. Use questions that evaluate whether students' learning matches that of the learning objectives.

- *Match the proportion of questions to the emphasis placed on various objectives.* Major objectives deserve more questions than those that are of lesser importance.

- *Limit the number of different types of questions to three or four.* Having too many types of questions is confusing and puts the emphasis on students' ability to follow test instructions, rather than on assessing content learning.

- *Group questions of the same type together.* Put all multiple-choice questions together, for example. Within each type, group questions about similar content together.

- *Be sure that questions do not give answers or clues to other questions.* This can easily happen when content is related. Each question should stand on its own.

- *Provide clear directions for each section of the test.* Even with familiar types of questions, specify in writing how students should indicate their answers. For example, writing out the words "True" or "False" avoids the problem of distinguishing between a handwritten "T" and "F" that may look similar.

- *Evaluate existing tests or questions carefully before use.* Teachers often save tests for possible reuse when they teach the same lesson or class again. In addition, many textbooks come with ready-to-use tests. In both cases, teachers must review such tests to make certain they reflect what has been taught and how it was taught, making modifications as needed. Sometimes individual questions may be suitable for use, but not the whole test.

- *Format the test for ease of use.* Make answer lines long enough for handwritten answers. Always begin a page with a new question, never starting a question on one page and finishing it on another. Avoid using negative statements. These can be confusing, evaluating understanding of the question, rather than knowledge of the answer.

- *Format the test for ease of grading.* The way you arrange questions and spaces for answers on a page can make a difference in how difficult it is to grade students' papers. Teachers often find that placing the answer options or lines for writing answers to the left of the questions makes it easier to grade quickly and accurately. Number questions consecutively through all sections. (There will be only one question #1.) For older students, indicate the point value of each question. Include a line for the student's name on each page of the test in case pages become separated.

Be sure to proofread tests carefully. In addition to factual accuracy, correct grammar and spelling are essential. Make and double-check an answer key for the test to speed correction later.

Using Alternative Assessment Strategies

Giving a test is not the only way to assess student learning. Educators also use a variety of methods other than tests. Collectively, these are known as **alternative assessments.** Alternative assessments range from written papers and multimedia presentations to real-life tasks and student portfolios, 14-3.

Sometimes the difference between tests and alternative assessment is explained by how they ask students to show what they have learned. With most tests, students *choose* an answer to show what they know. With an alternative assessment strategy, students *create* something that shows what they know.

14-3
A project such as this is an example of an alternative assessment.

Alternative assessments encourage teachers' creativity, as well as students'. That is because they can take so many forms. Teachers devise innovative assessments that allow students to demonstrate their knowledge and skills in ways linked to real life. An elementary teacher might have students demonstrate their math skills by measuring their classroom or playground. A middle school teacher might have students write and perform a play based on their study of a period in history. An automotive teacher might have students complete an oil change to verify mastery of that skill. A child care teacher might have students create games appropriate for preschoolers. Health students might choose appropriate media to develop an antismoking campaign. Reports, projects, posters, and presentations can all be used as forms of alternative assessment. In each case, students demonstrate their learning.

Some types of alternative assessment are meant to evaluate students' improvement over time, rather than achievement of a specific learning objective. As such, they may or may not be graded, depending on the purpose and situation.

Student portfolios are one type of alternative assessment that may be graded or not, depending on their purpose. A **student portfolio** is a collection of a student's work selected to show growth over time, highlight skills and achievements, or to show how well the student meets standards. The student is usually involved in selecting the material for the portfolio, often including reflections about his or her work and learning. Portfolios can provide important information about a student's attitude, level of development, and growth over a given period of time.

Giving Clear Directions

The ability to develop clear directions is a critical skill for teachers. They can affect the success of learning activities, impacting how well students learn. Similarly, clear directions in assessments make certain that students are able to show what they have learned. Confusing directions can actually prevent accurate assessment of learning.

Directions tell a person how to complete a task. You may have a natural ability to develop good instructions. Writing directions requires thinking in a logical, step-by-step way. If this does not come easily for you, take time to practice this essential skill.

When creating directions for students, begin by identifying the goal or objective. What do you want your students to achieve? This will be the introduction to your directions. Then break the process of reaching that goal into steps. Make sure the steps are placed in sequential order.

Use precise, descriptive language when giving written or spoken instructions. Directions need to be appropriate for the level of students. However, for all levels, sentences should not be overly complicated. Anticipate possible problems or misunderstandings and address them in the directions. Taking the time to think through directions is well worth the effort.

Evaluating Alternative Assessments

With traditional tests, it is the teacher who checks students' answers, determines their scores, and returns the tests to students. It is best for students to see which questions they answered incorrectly and learn from their mistakes. With alternative assessments, the teacher may play a similar role, but students are usually involved in the process.

Rubrics

Traditional tests typically contain questions that have specific correct answers. If you answer "True" to a question when the correct answer is "False," your answer is wrong. Evaluating and scoring many other types of assessments can be considerably more complicated. What is the difference between an excellent project, paper, or presentation and an average one? When students know specifically what "excellent" means, they can produce better work. To be fair, teachers need to judge every student's work by the same criteria.

In many situations, teachers use rubrics to solve these problems. A **rubric** is a scoring tool that lists the criteria for judging a particular type of work. A good rubric also describes levels of quality for each of the criteria. A rubric is often organized as a chart, with the *criteria* (characteristics that count for scoring) on the left, followed by columns that describe different levels of quality for each characteristic. (*Criteria* is plural. The singular form is *criterion*.) Quality ratings can be ranked using numbers and/or adjectives. A rubric for writing a letter of complaint is shown in 14-4.

A well-designed rubric provides clear grading criteria for both students and the teacher. In that sense, rubrics serve to communicate expectations and standards. They also help to communicate how student work did or did not meet expectations or standards.

When students are given grading rubrics before they begin their work, they can think critically about their work. They know what characteristics are identified with quality and can base their efforts on established criteria. As a result, they begin to accept more responsibility for their work and feel less like a victim of subjective grading. Rubrics also help students know when they have met the learning objectives or if their work has met established criteria.

Many rubrics are available from teacher resources. However, it is not always possible to find an appropriate existing rubric to use or modify. Rubrics are not difficult to create, but they do take time. The following are the steps for creating a rubric:

14-4
This well-designed rubric lists the criteria and different levels of quality.

Rubric for Letter of Complaint			
Criteria	**5–4 Points**	**3–2 Points**	**1–0 Points**
Contact Information	Addressed to appropriate contact and sender's contact information is provided.	Contact information incomplete for receiver <u>or</u> sender.	Contact information for receiver <u>and</u> sender is incomplete or missing.
Purchase Information	Includes all required information (product, item #, date and place of purchase, attempts to resolve).	Missing one key piece of purchase information.	Missing more than one key piece of purchase information.
Problem	Problem clearly explained.	Problem explained, but is somewhat unclear.	Problem inadequately explained.
Action Requested	Specific, reasonable action clearly requested.	Request for action is vague or timeline is unrealistic.	No specific action requested or request is unreasonable.
Format	Utilizes business letter format, no grammar or spelling errors, neat, signed.	Missing one part of business letter <u>or</u> contains one or two errors.	Letter lacks more than one key part <u>or</u> more than two errors.

1. *Identify the criteria that will be used in assessing performance.* The criteria should be based on the intended outcomes of the learning objective. For example, the criteria for a book report might include descriptions of the main characters, setting, plot, and outcome, plus an appropriate format, grammar, and clarity of writing. Place the criteria down the left-hand column of the rubric.

2. *Determine the possible performance levels.* There should be a rating scale for performance. Levels can be described (such as *Excellent, Good, Poor*) and/or based on point ranges that directly correlate to a grade. List the performance levels at the top of the columns across the top row of the rubric.

3. *Write a description for each performance level and criterion.* These will fill in the blank squares on the rubric chart. Clearly describing the different levels of performance that match each criterion provides guidance for students. It usually works best to start with the highest level of performance achievement for each criterion. Next, describe the lowest level of quality. Fill in the middle levels based on your knowledge of common problems that students have in meeting the highest performance levels.

4. *Proofread.* As with traditional tests, it is important to proofread rubrics carefully before use.

After using a rubric, you can refine your descriptions of what constitutes each performance level based on students' actual work and any difficulties they had understanding the rubric.

Checklists and Scorecards

A **checklist** is a simple list of items to be noted, checked, or remembered when evaluating learning. It can be an instrument that consists of a list of qualities that are checked off or questions to answer with a "Yes" or "No" response. There may be a space for teacher notes and, if it is to be scored, a place to calculate this. A kindergarten teacher might use a checklist to keep track of which letters a child knows and can print. While not used for a grade, the checklist can show the child's progress over time, 14-5.

Scorecards are somewhat different. Like a rubric, a **scorecard** lists the characteristics or factors to use when evaluating learning. Scorecards typically identify a maximum point value for each criterion but do not describe levels of quality. The automotive teacher evaluating students' ability to perform an oil change might use a scorecard. The teacher would identify the steps to be completed and assign possible point values to each. The number of points would depend on the importance and complexity of each step.

14-5
A checklist is a simple way to keep track of a student's progress.

(Greeting the customer politely may be worth fewer possible points than draining the old oil completely without spillage.) While evaluating a student, the teacher would determine the number of points to award for each step, adding comments, as appropriate. The scorecard provides the student not only with a final score, but also information on which steps need additional practice.

Both checklists and scorecards are valuable for helping learners understand the criteria on which their learning is being evaluated. However, they are limited in describing quality or details.

Self-Evaluation and Peer Evaluation

Teachers are not the only people who can assess learning. An important goal of education is to teach students how to evaluate their own work and determine what improvements are needed. As work situations in the adult world increasingly depend on group interaction and effort, the ability to evaluate peers has become more important. The abilities to give honest appraisals of others' efforts and to accept other people's assessment of one's own work are important job-related skills. Consequently, teachers often incorporate both **self-evaluation** and **peer evaluation** into alternative assessments.

Although self- and peer evaluation are valuable assessment tools, they can be challenging for students. It helps if students are introduced to these methods, in simplified form, in the early grades. Using checklists, scorecards, and rubrics can help focus and structure students' analysis and feedback.

Teachers need to stress the importance of honesty. With peer evaluation, students need to learn how to phrase their comments in positive and helpful ways. Older students often worry that negative ratings or feedback of others will affect how they themselves are evaluated. Peer evaluations can be confidential, or they can be shared with peers personally or as a general summary. It is valuable in checking their own understanding of a project.

Learning assessment does not always tie to grades. Teachers may need to practice using self- and peer evaluations with students until they become a natural and expected part of learning.

Choosing Assessment Strategies

There are a number of factors that play into selecting an assessment tool. First, choose an assessment that will actually measure your learning objectives. This is called **validity**. If an assessment tool is valid, it measures what it is supposed to measure. **Reliability** is a characteristic of an assessment that will measure the same over time. The results will be similar with different learners and under different circumstances.

The assessment tool you choose should be developmentally appropriate for the learners. They should be able to understand and perform what is being requested of them. For example, an essay test would not be appropriate for a young child. The assessment should be at the appropriate difficulty level. It should measure the type of learning required for the developmental stage of the learner.

The assessment tool should not become the focal point, taking away from the learning process. For example, if a teacher focuses only on the test to be taken at the end of the learning unit, creativity and flexibility can be lost. Students may be less likely to internalize what is learned.

Time and other resources are always a reality for teachers. Teachers should consider what is available and how much time an assessment tool will require.

Determining Grades and Providing Feedback

The learning process depends not just on acquiring new knowledge, but also on learning how to learn. Grades are one way teachers provide feedback to students about their learning, but they are not the only way. Direct feedback can play a major role in helping students improve their learning skills.

Grading Students

There are few aspects of education that cause as much anxiety, confusion, and concern as grades. This is true for teachers, as well as students and parents.

The main purpose of grading is to communicate students' performance and progress. However, there is little consistency in the way students' grades are determined. Although some schools have written policies regarding grading, it is usually up to individual teachers to decide what counts toward grades and how they are calculated, 14-6.

Keeping basic principles in mind can help teachers set up a fair and workable grading system. These include the following:

- Every teacher needs to establish a grading plan before classes begin and communicate the plan to students.

- Grades should reflect students' learning, not behavior, attendance, or other factors.

14-6

Effective teachers develop a fair and workable grading system.

- Report card grades should be based on a variety of individual assignments, tests, and other work. However, not every activity and assignment should be scored, especially those that are part of the learning process.

- While report card grades are often given in letter form, student work should be recorded as a number.

- In determining report card grades, the scores for some types of work may be weighted more than others. For example, the average of test scores might count for 50 percent of students' grades, while other types of work might count for smaller percentages.

Giving Effective Feedback

Providing students with personalized feedback about their learning is more effective at improving learning than assigning grades. The goal of feedback is to help individuals know what they are doing well and what specific improvements are needed.

Feedback can occur throughout the learning cycle. A teacher might emphasize particular parts of instructions for specific students. It might be verbal reinforcement during class activities or a written response to work completed.

From your own experience as a student, you know it feels great to get an "A" on a test or a "94" on a paper. However, that only tells you that you did well overall. If you get a "C" on a paper, how do you know what you need to improve? Thoughtful comments, particularly written ones, can help you do better. Your teacher might write such comments as, "You raised an interesting point. Good thinking! Next time do more research to provide additional evidence to support your point of view." An elementary teacher might write on a student's test, "Jody, you often miss questions that you know the answers to because you don't understand the directions. Try reading the directions carefully before you begin and again as you check your work before turning it in. I think your grades will improve." In both these cases, the teacher provided the students with real guidance. "Good job!" or "Try harder!" are too vague to be helpful.

Course Evaluation

Good teachers never stop learning. They want to be better teachers. They want to gain additional knowledge and find more effective ways to help students learn. As a teacher, you may sometimes leave the classroom thinking, "That really worked!" while other times thinking, "I need to use a different activity next time."

Earlier in the chapter, you learned that assessment can be used to measure how well students meet objectives, their learning progress over time, and the effectiveness of teaching. All provide helpful information for **course evaluation**—making judgments about how well a course meets its goals and how it might be improved.

Course evaluation is important for several reasons. It helps teachers improve their teaching. They can identify what worked and what did not work in the classroom. They can evaluate their motivational methods, classroom management skills, classroom arrangement, schedule, or other factors that might improve teaching and learning. Change does not take place without taking time to reflect, 14-7.

14-7
Taking time to reflect on how well a course meets its goals can lead to improvement.

Course evaluation is often based on a combination of the daily notes teachers often keep, feedback from others, and considering important questions about a course. Questions such as "Are most students meeting the learning objectives for the course?" and "Are students motivated and interested in learning?" can trigger insight.

Teachers may work individually on course evaluation, analyzing a unit of study or an entire course. Often, teachers teaching the same course will collaborate on course evaluation. Some schools have a formal process for doing so. Regardless of the form it takes, course evaluation can be a powerful tool for enhancing students' learning.

Summary

Assessment is the evaluation of learning and teaching. Formative assessment is used during the teaching process to check students' understanding so that teaching can be modified as needed. Summative assessment occurs after learning and is designed to check students' achievement of the learning objectives.

Assessment can evaluate different aspects of learning and teaching. Those include whether students have achieved the objectives, whether they are making appropriate progress in learning, and whether teaching methods are effective.

Various strategies can be used for assessment. Standardized tests evaluate students' achievement in comparison with that of other students and schools. Teacher-developed tests check whether students meet course learning objectives. Alternative assessments utilize methods other than tests. They allow students to show what they know in more creative ways.

Teachers consider various factors when choosing the type of assessment strategy to use. Their choice must fit the learning objectives, the abilities of students, and the time available.

Providing feedback to students is a key to helping them learn more effectively. Grades convey information about achievement to students and parents. Teachers must develop and communicate their grading policy. Giving students specific feedback about their learning strengths and identifying strategies for improvement can help them improve their learning skills.

Effective teachers evaluate their courses in order to make them better. This process involves looking at student achievement and progress, feedback from others, incorporating technology, and personal analysis of what works well and what needs improvement.

Review

1. Imagine that you are a fourth-grade teacher presenting a lesson on mountains. Describe one specific example of formative assessment that you might use with this lesson and one summative assessment strategy.

2. Why are formative assessments not recorded as grades?

3. Assessment often measures whether students are meeting learning objectives. Where do those objectives originate?

4. Standardized tests are evaluated for validity and reliability before they are used. Which of these characteristics is most difficult for a teacher to guarantee when developing a test? Why?

5. Why is it important to match test items to the level of the learning objective they assess?

6. Give an example of one assignment that could be used as a learning activity or as an alternative assessment. What would be the difference, depending on its intended use?

7. Which is the most detailed tool for evaluating alternative assessments— a scorecard, checklist, or rubric?

8. Why do many students have difficulty giving a realistic assessment of their peers' work?

9. Give two examples of types of alternative assessments that would be time-consuming to complete. Why might teachers choose to use these types of assessments, in spite of the time involved?

10. Why do teachers need to clearly communicate their grading policy at the beginning of a course?

11. Identify at least three questions, in addition to those listed in the chapter, that teachers might ask themselves as part of a course evaluation.

Reflect

1. Imagine that you have just graduated from college and accepted your first teaching job. In your new school district, you will have a mentor teacher. Identify at least eight characteristics you hope your mentor teacher will have and explain why each would be important to you.

2. Think about a standardized test you have taken. What was its purpose? What type of preparation, if any, occurred before the test? What types of questions did the test include? How difficult did you find it? How were scores reported?

3. Think about your experiences with teacher-developed tests. What types of questions are generally easiest for you to answer? Which were most difficult? Did the tests usually include just low-level questions (knowledge, comprehension, application) or higher-level questions as well?

4. Give several examples of how technology can be integrated into alternative assessment strategies.

Act

1. Keep track of the types of assessment used in your classes for three days. Make a list. Which were formative and which were summative? Which types of assessment helped you learn best?

2. Write at least three examples of four of the types of test questions described in this chapter. Base your questions on a chapter from this book. Pay attention to format and the other guidelines identified in this chapter.

3. Write clear, step-by-step directions for a learning activity. You may use an activity from a lesson plan you developed or another of your choice.

4. Look online to find the grading policy for an elementary or secondary school or school district. Print a copy. Write an analysis of the policy. How detailed is the policy? Does it suggest using formative, as well as summative, assessment in determining grades? As a teacher, do you think that you would find the policy helpful or limiting?

Add to Your Portfolio

Design a rubric for a common type of alternative assessment, such as a written report, presentation, or group project. Decide the approximate grade level that will use the rubric. Determine criteria that would be important and levels of performance. Then describe quality at each level for every criterion. Ask your teacher to review your rubric and give you specific feedback. Revise the rubric and add it to your portfolio.

15 CLASSROOM MANAGEMENT

Objectives

After studying this chapter, you will be able to

- **analyze** and evaluate the classroom management strategies.

- **plan** a way to minimize behavioral problems.

- **develop** a set of class rules to enhance the learning environment.

- **apply** behavior management strategies by suggesting appropriate responses to common behavioral problems.

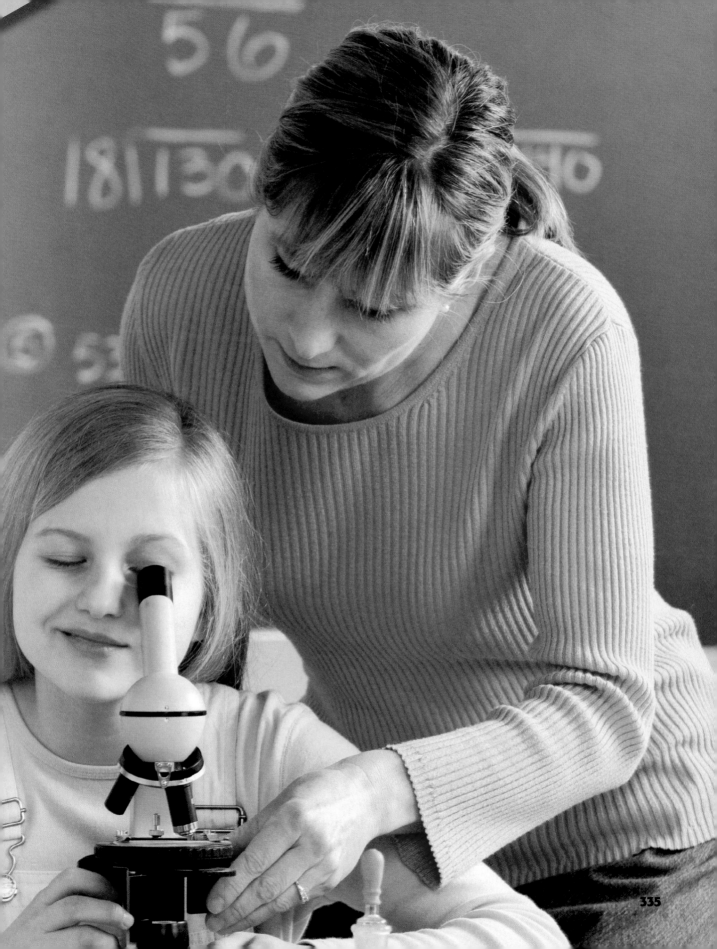

Today was the first day that Jordan was to observe Mrs. Lee's second grade classroom. He was excited to be working with Mrs. Lee, the same teacher he had as a second grader. He had happy memories of the year spent with her and was looking forward to learning from her again. She was one of the reasons he was considering a career as a teacher.

When Jordan walked into the classroom, the students became very quiet. They were aware that a stranger had entered the room and seemed curious to see how Mrs. Lee would respond. When she greeted Jordan warmly, they all settled in and watched and listened to their conversation. Mrs. Lee introduced Jordan to the students. She told them that he would be acting as her assistant teacher and they should treat him as a teacher.

Before long, Mrs. Lee went into action. Jordan tried to get a feel for the individual students' personalities and learn their names. The students were studying marine life and were getting ready for a trip to the local aquarium later that week. As Mrs. Lee led the students in a learning activity, she walked among the students. When a couple of girls began whispering, Jordan noticed Mrs. Lee move toward them. They quickly quieted down. Another student started taking things off another classmate's desk. Mrs. Lee called the boy up front to help her set up a display of seashells. When the boy went back to his seat, he was no longer distracted by his neighbor's things.

The class atmosphere was lively, and students had much to say. He noticed that Mrs. Lee only called on students who raised their hands to speak. She made positive comments about their contributions. When one student was handling a dry sea star, the point of the leg accidentally broke off. Mrs. Lee assured the student that it was an accident and then brainstormed with the class the proper way of handling a live sea star during the aquarium visit. The incident created a lively discussion.

When Jordan left at the end of his visit, he was amazed at Mrs. Lee's skill in meeting the learning needs of all her students. Mrs. Lee knew what was going on around the classroom. Even an unexpected incident became a valuable part of the lesson. Jordan knew that he was learning from a master teacher.

Every class is really a group of individuals with different needs, desires, interests, and abilities. Some students concentrate intently on the learning activity. Others daydream. A few squirm and fidget. There are nonstop talkers and quiet reserved ones. There may be some students who show off, talk back, or tell exaggerated stories. Others only want to please you.

The goal of all teachers is to provide a classroom environment that promotes learning for all of these diverse students. To accomplish that, teachers need excellent management skills. **Classroom management** refers to the steps teachers take to organize their classroom for optimal learning, engage students in that learning, and minimize behaviors that disrupt it. New teachers find classroom management one of their greatest challenges.

Fortunately, there is helpful information available about classroom management, and skills can be learned. Successful teachers develop the ability to observe, comprehend, and respond to quickly changing classroom behaviors. They know their students. As teachers become confident in their role as the classroom leader, classroom management becomes second nature. It also becomes more of an art rather than just a collection of skills. This chapter will give you a closer look at what is involved.

Creating the Classroom Environment

Even before the first student walks through the door, teachers set up their classroom environment. Like the set designed to stage a play, the arrangement and look of a classroom sets the atmosphere for learning. It can either support or undermine a teacher's attempts to maximize learning.

Where learning takes place does make a difference. As a teacher, you may find yourself teaching in a new state-of-the-art classroom or one that is 75 years old. Effective teachers find ways to make the best of what they have.

Once students arrive, a new challenge starts. Each new group of individual students must be brought together to form a class that feels and functions as a whole. Each of these elements contributes to making the classroom not just a functional learning environment, but an inspiring one.

Arranging the Space

Figuring out how to best arrange a classroom begins with the teacher's analysis of the ways in which the room will be used. A kindergarten teacher may need learning centers, such as for blocks, art, and reading, 15-1. Each has equipment and materials for specific types of activities. An elementary classroom must be versatile to adapt to the variety of classes taught each day. A middle school or high school science classroom must accommodate learning new information, performing experiments, and secure storage of equipment and supplies. Regardless of specific use, some general guidelines for arranging space apply.

- *Ease of student use.* The arrangement of students' desks and other elements must be practical. Does it allow students to enter, exit, and move around the classroom easily? Can everyone view the board and other areas critical for instruction? Is storage suitable for collecting students' work with minimum disruption? Signs and labels can help students find what they need within the classroom.

15-1

Kindergarten classrooms are often arranged according to learning centers.

- **Ease of teaching.** Each teacher has a unique style of teaching. Classroom space should be organized to best accommodate this. Depending on a teacher's preferences, student desks might be arranged in a circle, U-shape, groups of four, or traditional rows. One teacher may use the computer often for presentations, so its placement and students' ability to see the screen may be key. Another may have students work at the board on a daily basis. That requires space in front of it for ease of use. Some teachers use their desk as their work center, while others use it mainly for storage and place it out of the way. Such considerations shape decisions about classroom layout.

- **Ease of supervision.** The arrangement of a room can make it easier or more difficult for teachers to monitor students and critical areas. For example, some teachers prefer an arrangement that allows them to see every student's face during instruction to more easily gauge students' understanding. The ability to see what students are doing can minimize problem behaviors. Areas such as computer stations may need special supervision, so they should be placed accordingly.

Developing a Stimulating Learning Environment

You have experienced enough classrooms to know that some energize you for learning, while other environments are boring. The difference is teacher ingenuity and effort, along with an understanding of the impact that environment can make.

What makes a classroom inviting? That depends somewhat on the educational level. At all levels, the addition of objects and materials related to the subject area can spark students' interest and prompt additional learning. A teacher might post a "Did you know...?" poster for each learning unit, giving students interesting related facts. Books and other reference materials are easily accessible. Elementary teachers often provide a reading corner with a soft chair, rug, or pillows where students can choose and read books. Displaying students' work adds interest. Many classrooms are painted in bland colors, so teachers try to add bright colors in other ways. They might put colored paper over a bulletin board or fabric over a table. Maps, pictures, and colorful charts can add color while reinforcing learning. The possibilities are endless. The goal is to have a rich environment that supports learning, not just a disorganized collection of things, which may be distracting.

Teachers periodically change elements to match the topics being studied. This generates new interest. Where do these items originate? Most teachers make the best possible use of what is available through their school. They may have a small budget for supplies, but this must cover all learning needs. Teachers often supplement that with things they find or buy on their own. They may repurpose pizza boxes to organize supplies, use bricks and boards to make additional shelves, or turn garage-sale finds into objects to organize classroom space. They rely on imagination and creativity to provide a better environment for their students.

Building a Sense of Community

How would you describe the ideal environment for learning? Perhaps you would like students to be relaxed, but focused on learning. They move from one activity to the next and quickly get started. They are able to work together effectively in groups, drawing on each other's strengths and respecting others' opinions. Students handle routine tasks automatically. Behavioral issues are minimal and dealt with quickly and fairly.

While no classroom is ideal all of the time, successful teachers find that building a positive atmosphere helps greatly. When students feel a sense of belonging within the class, they participate more, put forth greater effort, and are less likely to misbehave, 15-2.

15-2
Students who are engaged in a lesson often feel a sense of community within a class.

There is no single formula for developing a feeling of community, but most teachers focus on a number of key areas.

- *Positive relationships.* Teachers set the tone by modeling acceptance of, and interest in, their students. It begins with learning students' names as quickly as possible. Getting to know students as individuals helps them feel they are valued. Most teachers balance authority with an attitude of friendliness. Teachers also help students develop positive relationships. Depending on the grade level, teachers can use various techniques. In elementary school, this might include lessons on topics such as friendship. In middle or high school, a teacher might focus on teamwork skills or handling differences of opinion as part of group activities.

- *Respect.* Respect is one of the most essential elements in classrooms that work. Teachers must not only expect respect from students, but show them respect, as well. Disrespect among students should not be tolerated. Respect often begins with getting to know others, particularly those with whom students do not normally interact. Group activities and opportunities to share can help students learn about each other as individuals and break down barriers. Teachers may use various grouping strategies so that students have opportunities to work with all of their classmates. A sense of respect within the classroom is crucial to students' feeling that they can offer ideas and opinions without fear of ridicule or rejection.

- *Student involvement.* When teachers ask for students' feedback and ideas about classroom issues, students feel their opinions are important. It also helps them develop a sense of responsibility for the class. Student feedback can be valuable. Students may come up with workable solutions for class problems. They can identify which activities were most helpful and which were most enjoyable. They can share ideas on how to improve class routines. By asking and following through on useful suggestions, teachers build class bonds.

- *Class identity.* A sense of community depends on students seeing themselves as a group. It is much like the feeling of cohesiveness that members of a baseball or debate team develop. Such connections grow over time with the encouragement of a teacher. Classroom routines, traditions, and whole-class experiences help strengthen these bonds. One seventh grader, on seeing his third grade teacher, said, "I always remember that we started each day saying together, 'I *can* do my best. I *will* do my best. *We* will all succeed together.' It sounds kind of strange now, but in your class, we all worked hard and tried to help each other."

Keeping Students Involved in Learning

One of the biggest challenges for teachers is keeping everyone involved in the learning process. Whether a student is daydreaming, whispering, poking someone nearby, or texting during class, the result is the same. That student is not learning. Others are usually distracted, as well.

No teacher manages to have every student paying attention and on task every moment of every day. Students' lives outside the classroom come with them to school. You know, for example, that if you did not get enough sleep or argued with your best friend, it affects your concentration. Still, there is much that teachers can do to keep students' attention so they can learn effectively.

Presenting Engaging Lessons

Skillful teachers know that their efforts to make learning interesting pay off. Students learn and remember more. In addition, students involved in learning are less likely to engage in problem behaviors.

Making lessons relevant to students' lives increases their appeal. Math concepts might be linked to their actual uses in business, industry, or everyday life. History can come alive when first-person accounts are included or students put themselves in a different time and place. In every subject area, there are many ways to add relevance and to engage students, 15-3. Teachers know that a constantly quiet classroom is not necessarily an effective one.

15-3
When a history lesson becomes relevant to students, they are more likely to participate in the class.

In earlier chapters, you learned about the importance of using a variety of techniques for teaching and learning. This helps accommodate students' personal learning preferences and strengths. It also keeps learning fresh and interesting. Mixing lecture, demonstration, and discussion varies instruction. Using both individual and group activities and alternating desk work with activities that involve movement helps keep students alert and interested. When students are given options for completing some assignments, they often learn more and show greater enthusiasm.

Managing Transitions

Effective teachers make a real effort to keep downtime to a minimum. Most problems occur during *transitions* when students are changing from one class or activity to another. Here are some examples of how experienced teachers handle transitions.

- *Greeting students.* When her middle school students are changing classes, you will find Mrs. Daniels in the hall by her door. She greets her students by name, asking questions of some and encouraging others. At the same time, she is on the alert for student conversations or body language that might be clues that certain students are having problems. Her presence in the hallway also helps keep overall behavior in check.

- *Class start-up assignment.* Mr. Menendez' high school math classes know that there will be a problem to solve on the board as soon as they get to class. The math problems usually involve challenging real-life situations. Students can work in small groups to solve the problem and there is friendly competition among them. Having the students engaged gives Mr. Menendez time to quickly take attendance and complete any other administrative tasks. It helps get the class off to a smooth start.

- *Students who finish early.* When Mrs. Chin began teaching third grade, she struggled with how to handle students who finished activities before their classmates. They often resorted to talking, disturbing those still at work. Now, she gives students two alternatives. Since she encourages reading for enjoyment, every student keeps a library book in his or her desk and can choose to read silently. Students may also go to a table in the back of the room and pick a puzzle or activity sheet from the table to complete at their seat. Students know that their work must be completed first, and they cannot disturb others.

- *Transition to small groups.* Mr. Poplau uses many different learning formats with his fifth-grade class, even though his classroom space is limited. Often, this necessitates moving the furniture in the room to accommodate various learning activities. For group activities, he usually divides students into groups of four or five. Early in the semester, he showed students how he wanted desks and chairs placed for small group work and put tape on the floor to show proper placement. Now, if he says, "Let's move into groups," students automatically rearrange the furniture and find their group. It has taken practice and perseverance, but now students try to better their previous time in getting everything in place. The payoff is less confusion, more time learning, and little disruptive behavior.

- *Lesson ends early.* Ms. Simpson has been teaching middle school health for six years. She knows it is not always possible to time lessons exactly. Occasionally, a lesson is completed before the period is over. She has developed techniques to help fill that time with learning. For most lessons, she plans an extra optional activity that can be used in such situations. She also has a set of short activities on topics she would like to add to the curriculum. She keeps these in her desk for use when the opportunity arises. Students get a chance to tackle thought-provoking topics, and it eliminates a free time when unwanted behaviors can occur.

Noting Success

When a teacher commends a student for special effort, it reinforces that desired behavior. Most teachers praise top students. Not all go beyond that group, but doing so can yield real results. Students who feel they can be successful in school are less likely to have serious behavioral problems. Those who feel their efforts are unlikely to have positive results—that they fail to measure up—often eventually stop trying. If they are required to attend school anyway, being disruptive may seem like a reasonable alternative.

Teachers who take the attitude that all students can experience success can help break the cycle of failure. That does not mean giving good grades for inferior work. Helping students overcome a negative self-image and learning deficits requires a caring attitude, encouragement, and practical help in catching up, 15-4. It takes long-term effort. Outside resources are often needed. Changing attitudes can change lives.

It is easy for busy teachers to simply respond to behavior problems in a sharp or harsh way. This may stop the behavior in the short term, but it creates a negative learning environment. Many teachers have found that changing their focus can significantly reduce behavioral problems over time. They try to notice and comment on achievement and good behavior more than bad. Perhaps a student who often plays the class clown puts real effort into a group activity. Another student who has trouble "remembering" to complete homework turns it in on time every day for a week. Giving positive feedback for real effort and following the rules helps encourage students to repeat such actions.

Managing Behavior

How well teachers manage behavior in their classroom has a direct impact on how much learning can take place. Even with a stimulating classroom environment and well-prepared and interesting lessons, behavioral problems inevitably occur. It is the teacher's role to keep them to a minimum and deal with them effectively when they do occur.

Understanding Teachers' Management Styles

Each teacher approaches classroom management somewhat differently. These differences are based on personal beliefs, experiences, the unique group dynamics of the class, and the teacher's personality.

15-4
When a teacher commends a student for successes, the student can develop a positive self-image.

These differences are particularly evident in how teachers deal with student behavior. Educational researchers identify the three following general management styles:

- *Authoritarian style.* Teachers with an **authoritarian style** have regulations for everything and consequences for every infraction. It is a management style that seeks to control students' behavior through many rules, procedures, and consequences. Teachers who use this style try to control students' behavior by exerting power. Authoritarian management may result in lower student self-esteem and creativity and can provoke hostility.

- *Permissive style.* Teachers who have a **permissive style** may have some rules and expectations, but they rarely follow through with consequences when students fail to meet them. This is a management style that sets few expectations and rules for students and enforces them inconsistently. Basically, anything goes. Students often lack respect for permissive teachers.

- *Authoritative style.* Teachers who use an **authoritative style** have high expectations for students' behavior and clearly explain why some behaviors are acceptable and others are not. This management style seeks to shape students' behavior through setting high expectations, explanations, and consistent application of consequences. There are consequences for failure to meet expectations. Such teachers are firm, but friendly.

Many of the ideas in this chapter are based on implementing the authoritative style. Research shows this to be the most successful approach. Experienced teachers support the authoritative approach. The combination of high expectations, holding students accountable, and warm teacher-student relationships provides the best atmosphere for learning. Within that framework, individual teachers still must determine the most effective ways to implement this approach on a day-to-day basis in their own classrooms.

Developing a Personal Behavior Management Plan

It is important for teachers to have a carefully considered plan for behavior management before classes begin. Some schools require them to submit a written version of their plan. Even when this is not the case, effective teachers determine up front how they will manage and respond to behavioral issues. This helps them deal with problems in a consistent way and create a classroom atmosphere that is conducive to learning.

Developing such a plan requires real thought. It begins with asking yourself key questions. Some examples of key questions include the following:

- What realistic expectations for student behavior should you set?

- How will you reward students for appropriate behavior?

- What steps will you take when inappropriate behavior occurs?

Some of the answers to these questions are based on your personal beliefs. Some will be based on your knowledge of education and child development. Some are linked to common sense.

Although the same general principles for student behavior may apply to all ages, your expectations for first graders would be different from those for sixth graders or high school juniors. Older students should be held to higher levels of behavior. They are capable of understanding the reasoning behind the need for standards of behavior.

Similarly, rewards for appropriate behavior may also vary by age. Verbal or written praise works with all ages. For example, a teacher might write a note to a student's parent or guardian complimenting good or improving behavior. However, teachers of younger students are more likely to use small prizes, such as stickers or stars, to reward students who show desired behaviors. Sometimes, in elementary or middle school, a point system is used, with points given for appropriate behavior. When used with a whole class, points can add up and be redeemed for class prizes such as an extra recess or a party. However, high school teachers are much less likely to use tangible rewards such as these. Some authorities caution against using tangible rewards because it conditions students to expect them. Instead, praising specific behavior helps the students learn to reward or praise themselves. This helps the students develop self-discipline—an important goal of a good behavior management plan.

Consequences of misbehavior are generally based on both age and the severity of the problem. To a second grader, having a shorter recess period may be an appropriate consequence for some offenses, 15-5. In general, the consequences also should be related to the inappropriate behavior. If a middle school student will not work to finish an assignment in class, a teacher might have the student stay after school to do so. If a student says something unkind about a classmate, the consequences may include apologizing and giving the classmate a compliment. Consequences should always be reasonable, respectful, and, ideally, related.

With younger students, teachers often devise a system to keep behavior in check. For example, some teachers use a green, yellow, and red card for each student. Each day, every student starts on green. The first time the student engages in misconduct, the yellow card is substituted. The second time, the red card is used, and the associated consequence is more severe. For example, the teacher may send a note to the child's parent. What works with one class or one child does not necessarily work with others.

15-5
A time-out from a reading group could be a consequence of misbehavior.

In developing a personal behavior management plan, a teacher commits to its overall goals and methods. Details can be adjusted, as needed. Every teacher learns by doing.

Establishing Classroom Rules and Procedures

Appropriate student behavior is identified in several ways. **School policies** (in some districts called *rules, regulations,* or *procedures*) set overall guidelines and generally address major issues such as attendance and dress code. These are the same for all students. **Class rules** are guidelines for student behavior specific to a class or teacher. They identify expected classroom behaviors and attitudes necessary for an appropriate atmosphere for learning. Teachers identify a set of general rules as part of their behavior management plan. **Classroom procedures** are more specific. They translate the class rules into concrete actions expected of students.

You have been on the receiving end of classroom rules for years, so developing them as a teacher may seem difficult. Educational experts and experienced teachers have some suggestions:

- *Establish class rules during the first few days of class.* Knowing a teacher's expectations and limits can give students a sense of security. It also builds a positive classroom environment. Some teachers ask the students for input.

- *Involve students in setting rules and procedures.* Being part of the process helps students take ownership of the rules. Students can suggest ideas. Through guiding the discussion, teachers can help students formulate statements that incorporate the teacher's own priorities. Even young students can take part.

- *Keep the rule list short.* Many experts suggest about four to six rules. That is a short enough list for students to remember, but long enough to include key concepts.

- *State rules and procedures in positive terms.* Instead of saying, "Never interrupt," you might say, "Only one person talks at a time." Stating things positively tells students what they should do.

- *Define the terms.* If a procedure is to "Turn in homework on time," what does that mean? "All homework must be in the assigned box when the bell rings to be considered in on time," clarifies the procedure.

- *Adjust rules and procedures if they are not working well.* A teacher may need to add or modify guidelines if the need arises. This is part of good management.

Minimizing Problem Behaviors

In addition to the measures discussed so far in this chapter, teachers use various techniques to avoid problems with behavior. They help students develop the skills needed to make good decisions that avoid unwanted behaviors. They identify common causes of problems and develop routines and procedures to help keep them at the lowest possible level.

Developing Personal Responsibility

The goals of education go beyond teaching students to read and write and compute. Schools are partners with parents in teaching students the skills they need to function effectively in society. Among these is developing the ability to make appropriate choices. When students take responsibility for their own behavior, they make choices based on an inner code of acceptable conduct. School and classroom rules are part of this effort. In other words, the goal of discipline is to help students develop self-discipline.

Young children behave primarily to gain adult approval. Even so, they need frequent reminders about what is acceptable and what is not. Over the years, brain development, experience, and explanations help students understand the reasoning behind expectations. They begin to think through the possible consequences of their actions for themselves and others. This helps them keep their behavior within acceptable bounds by choice. This ability to monitor personal behavior and accept the consequences of misbehavior can be fostered by the way teachers handle classroom management.

Utilizing Routines

Having class routines helps students know what to expect and what is expected of them. An elementary teacher can set up the order in which particular classes are taught. Each day might start with spelling, and students would know to expect a particular type of spelling activity each day of the week. New words are introduced on Monday, specific activities occur Tuesday through Thursday, and students take their spelling test on Friday. Similarly, students in other grades and subjects know the routine for the beginning and end of class. What are they to do when they come in? How are papers collected? Where are homework assignments posted?

Establishing and adhering to routines can reduce problem behaviors. In fact, students often remind those who are not following routines that they should do so.

Assigning Seats

Many teachers use assigned seating as a classroom management tool. In assigned seating, students do not choose their desks. Instead, teachers designate the seating arrangement. A seating chart will help substitutes as well as teacher aides in the classroom. Some teachers have "photo seating charts" to avoid any confusion.

Assigned seats have a number of benefits. With a seating chart, teachers learn students' names and behaviors more quickly. They may rearrange seating periodically to place students in the location where they learn best. A student who is easily distracted might be seated away from the door and windows. Students prone to chatting with one another during class can be spaced farther apart. If students are seated in groups, assigning different combinations helps them interact with new people.

Monitoring the Classroom

New teachers quickly understand the importance of keeping track of what is happening throughout the classroom, even when they are involved in an activity. Over the generations, students have described teachers who do this well as having "eyes in the back of their head." In other words, they seem to see everything that is going on in the classroom.

By scanning the classroom regularly, minor misbehaviors can be stopped quickly before they continue. Fewer people are distracted. When students believe that their teacher always knows what is going on, they think twice before misbehaving. Many teachers move around the room as they teach. This, too, is a deterrent to inappropriate behavior.

Using Nonverbal Cues

Teachers often use **nonverbal cues** to stop minor misbehavior. These include techniques such as eye contact, body language, gestures, and physical closeness. Sometimes, nonverbal cues are reminders to the whole class. For example, a teacher might momentarily dim the lights to get the attention of the class. The advantage of these methods is that they can occur without interrupting the flow of a lesson. They remind students to monitor their behavior.

Eye contact is a powerful way of communicating expectations. For example, if students are whispering when it is not appropriate, sometimes just a look from the teacher can stop the behavior, 15-6. Adding gestures such as shaking the head or pointing to material being covered can add emphasis.

When a teacher moves closer to the misbehavior, it usually stops. For example, if the teacher moves close to the whispering students, it communicates to the students that their behavior is being observed and that it is not acceptable.

In the past, teachers were taught to use touch to reinforce their message. A hand on a student's shoulder would get the student's attention. Today, teachers must be very careful about using touch, since it may be misinterpreted. Placing a hand on the shoulder may work with younger students to draw their attention back to the subject. In general, touch should not be used with older children or teens.

15-6
How might this teacher handle the problem of students not paying attention during class?

Handling Problem Behavior

Inappropriate behavior includes a wide spectrum. On one end, a second grader may be tapping a pencil on his desk disturbing those around him. On the other, serious situations can sometimes erupt in classrooms. Fortunately, most problem behaviors are on the lower end of the scale. Regardless, the teacher is in charge and must make appropriate decisions about how best to handle situations.

A teacher's behavior management plan, along with school rules, district policies, and class rules and procedures, forms the basis for determining how to respond to problem behaviors. There are many possible approaches. Sometimes school procedures take precedence, but most often the teacher decides how to handle each situation.

Using Effective Strategies

Actually, how a teacher reacts when a behavior issue occurs is as important as the specific actions taken. Whether they seem to be paying attention or not, students are keenly attuned to how their teacher handles such situations. It affects their attitude toward the teacher and often shapes their own future behavior.

When teaching, it is essential to stay calm and project confidence. This sends the signal that you are in control and expect compliance. No matter what you are feeling on the inside, this is what must show on the outside.

It is easier to maintain this attitude when you see problem behavior such as a student having difficulty making an appropriate choice. The purpose of discipline is to help the student make a better choice in the future. Problems can be opportunities for learning better behavior.

Anger, humiliation, putdowns, and similar responses are inappropriate. They attack the student, not the behavior. They yield negative consequences, not positive. They also create a poor model for students on how to handle conflict. When a teacher goes up to a student to handle the problem behavior privately, rather than saying something in front of the whole class, the student's dignity is not as threatened, and compliance is more likely. Another reason for correcting a student in private is to keep the rest of the class from becoming the rallying section for the misbehaving student.

It is best to always use the least forceful method possible to deal with a problem. Keeping your response low-key and matter-of-fact can help prevent the situation from mushrooming. It also minimizes disruption to learning.

Applying Rules Consistently

Consistency in dealing with inappropriate behavior is essential to good classroom management. A teacher must respond in the same way each time a particular situation is encountered. That way, students know the teacher will follow through with consequences. They also know that consequences will be applied fairly, the same way for every student. Students gain respect for teachers who exhibit fairness. They are also more likely to accept consequences the teacher imposes if everyone is treated the same way.

Some teachers, like some parents, threaten consequences when misbehavior occurs but rarely follow through. Others only enforce rules some of the time. In both cases, students are willing to take the chance that they will avoid any repercussions and continue to do what they please.

Dealing with Common Behavioral Problems

In a typical school day, most teachers deal with multiple behavioral problems. Most of these are fairly common and fall into the category of minor misbehavior. Forgotten homework, talking to classmates while the teacher or another student has the floor, failure to participate in a discussion or activity, and similar situations seem small individually. However, left unchecked, they derail lessons and learning.

When teachers respond to such problems quickly and consistently, their impact on learning is kept to a minimum. Specific measures depend on a teacher's philosophy and practice, 15-7. However, most use simple techniques that are usually effective. The goal is to draw the misbehaving student back into the learning process, not to embarrass him or her.

What are some of these methods? Often, the nonverbal cues, such as moving toward the student, are all that are needed. Asking the student a question related to the lesson is another technique. For example, you might say, "Adrienne, what do you think the elephant should do?" By asking what she thinks, rather than asking for one right answer, the student does not need to be embarrassed by providing a wrong answer. Sometimes, the teacher just inserts the student's name in the lesson, "As we learned yesterday, Seth, bears hibernate in the winter months," lets the student know the teacher is watching. A bit of humor may be all that is needed to make a point and regain attention. These sorts of interventions, if complied with, do not merit further disciplinary consequences.

A next step might be to simply state directly and clearly what the student should do, and then walk away. "Tomas, sit down in your seat and finish your math problem." This method has several advantages. It reinforces the expectation that the student will follow class rules or procedures. The student has the choice to obey, still saving face because, with the teacher gone, the focus is off the situation. If the student is just seeking attention,

15-7

Each teacher must develop his or her own philosophy and practice in dealing with common classroom behavior problems.

this does not feed that desire. (Saying, "Tomas, why are you not sitting down?" would do so.) In addition, there is no debate, so the situation is less likely to escalate to a higher level. Disruption of the class is limited.

If that does not stop the behavior, there is a pattern of repeated offenses, or the problem is more serious in nature, the teacher might simply say, "We will talk after class." Sometimes the teacher begins on a positive note, praising another aspect of the student's behavior that is appropriate. The discussion might include asking the student what happened and discussing the consequences and impact of the inappropriate behavior. If the teacher has set a specific consequence for such behavior, the student must accept this. Otherwise, the teacher and student might discuss how to appropriately make up for the misbehavior. In this case, the consequences should be linked as closely as possible to the offense. Keeping the focus on learning self-discipline, the teacher might ask, "How can I help you act appropriately the next time?" or "What can you do next time?"

When a situation is not completely clear, the teacher must gather additional information. For example, two students may blame each other for something that happens. The teacher might ask each to explain the situation. The real facts usually come out. It is always a good idea to restate expectations, especially honesty. The teacher often acts as a mediator, helping the students reach a settlement or an agreement.

Dealing with Serious Behavioral Issues

From time to time, teachers may have to deal with behavioral problems that are serious in nature. These include situations such as attempts to undermine a teacher's authority, physical violence, bullying, serious threats, harassment, and issues such as drug and alcohol use. Common behavioral problems, if they continue for a long period and become worse, may also fall into this category.

One of the most difficult repetitive misbehaviors to handle is defiance or insubordination. Defiant students often show hostility, talk back, or refuse to do what they are asked to do. Many teachers, particularly new teachers, find this behavior threatening, even frightening. It can easily become a power struggle between the teacher and the student. The best way to deal with defiance is to pause and react calmly. Reacting angrily tends to escalate the problem. Your actions should be quietly decisive. It is best to listen to the student before responding, and this is best done outside the classroom. A teacher should never respond with threats, but the defiant behavior should be treated seriously.

Although teachers should feel confident in their ability to respond to disruptive or serious misbehavior, it is often appropriate to involve other school personnel. In a nonemergency situation, it is best to first analyze the problem behavior. Try to find out why students are misbehaving. This will help you find a solution. Sometimes finding a solution is best achieved when school resources are used. If not in a self-contained classroom, the student's other teachers may help to provide insight.

Keeping Records

As teachers deal with serious or repetitive behavior, it is important to keep accurate records. Each time a problem occurs, the teacher records the date and time, what happened, and any other useful information, 15-8. This can be helpful in several ways.

- It establishes that a pattern of misconduct exists and shows its frequency. This can be helpful in communicating with students, parents, or administrators about the problem.

- It helps the teacher remain objective about the situation or student. Dealing with disruptive behavior can be mentally and emotionally wearing. By keeping records, the teacher can see what circumstances trigger emotional responses for both the teacher and the student.

- It helps in analyzing the problem and the effectiveness of the teacher's responses. The teacher may better understand underlying causes. A colleague might suggest a different way of handling the problem.

15-8
By keeping detailed records, a teacher can document patterns of misbehavior and devise ways to solve them.

- It provides a basis for gauging improvement when new strategies or responses are put in place. If the student's behavioral problems become less frequent or less severe, the notes will document the positive changes.

Involving Parents or Guardians

The need to involve parents or guardians in behavioral issues depends on the severity of the problem and the success (or lack of success) in dealing with them in the classroom. Most problems can, and should, be resolved directly with the student. Some teachers, especially in the elementary grades, do communicate with parents or guardians on a regular basis about their child's behavior.

When teachers establish regular communication with parents, contacting them about behavioral issues is easier. It is always best when the first contact is not a negative one. By cooperating, parents or guardians and teachers often can work together to help students get back on track.

Utilizing School Resources

As a teacher, you do not have to handle severe disruptive misbehavior alone. Schools have people and support systems to help you. Sometimes several teachers find they are having similar problems with the same student. They may coordinate efforts to improve the student's behavior. Administrators can reinforce with students the need to follow class rules and the consequences for not doing so.

In many schools, problems such as fights between students, drug or alcohol use, and safety issues violate school rules, and they are dealt with at the school administration level. The principal, dean, or other designated person will follow up according to school rules and/or district policies. As a teacher, it is important to be familiar with school district policies so classroom rules and teacher practices are in alignment.

School counselors can be a valuable resource when emotional and social issues are involved. Sometimes a student is not misbehaving, but seems to be depressed or shows a marked change in attitude. A counselor may help directly or recommend the student receive outside counseling.

Effective teachers assume responsibility for classroom management issues. They try to solve most problems themselves before taking them to a school administrator or parent. However, they also know when to ask for help, rather than let a serious situation grow worse. That is in everyone's best interests. If a teacher even suspects that a student is contemplating suicide or that a student may be in an abusive situation, the teacher should not hesitate reporting these suppositions to the appropriate authorities. This is the law in most states.

Summary

Teachers want students to learn as much as possible. To accomplish this, they need effective classroom management skills. This includes creating an appropriate environment, keeping students involved in learning, and managing behavior.

Teachers shape the environment of their classroom in a variety of ways. They arrange desks and other elements to meet students' needs and their own. Displays and materials are used to add interest and stimulate learning. In addition, they help students form bonds as a class.

Students who are involved in a lesson learn more and misbehave less. Successful teachers work to present lessons that are challenging and interesting. They find ways to smooth transitions from one class or subject to another. They also acknowledge effort and appropriate behavior as a way of encouraging students to maintain those.

Teachers deal with behavioral issues on a daily basis. With up-front planning, clear rules and procedures, and consistent follow-through, problems can be kept to a minimum.

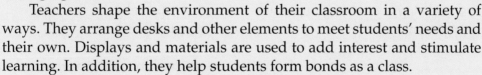

Review

1. Explain how classroom management is linked to learning.

2. How does creating a sense of community among class members help increase learning?

3. Why do behavioral problems occur more frequently during transitions?

4. How might teachers with each of the three management styles react to a middle school student who is tardy to class?

5. Identify at least three benefits of developing a personal behavior management plan.

6. How are class rules and procedures related? Give an example that shows their relationship.

7. How do students develop a sense of personal responsibility? How does having one impact behavior?

8. Nonverbal cues help get students back on track without interrupting the flow of the lesson. Why is this a benefit?

9. Explain why consistency is so important in handling behavioral problems.

10. Give an example of a clear, direct statement that a teacher might give to a fifth grader who is being disruptive, rather than participating in a small group geography assignment.

Reflect

1. Think of a class that you have taken in which students felt connected as a class. What was the grade level or subject area? What did the teacher do to foster this feeling? What was the impact on learning? What was the impact on behavior?

2. How does commenting on students' positive achievements and behavior influence effort and future behavior? Explain your reasoning.

3. How do you feel about using rewards, such as stickers and parties, to encourage achievement or good behavior? Is it always appropriate or inappropriate? Is it effective or ineffective?

4. As a new teacher, would you be more likely or less likely to ask for outside help with behavioral issues? Why?

Act

1. Spend a day observing an elementary school teacher. Focus on the types of classroom management strategies used. Which strategies were most effective in promoting an effective learning environment? Which strategies were least effective? Did the teacher use different strategies with different students? What did you learn?

2. Analyze the way the space is arranged in a classroom in your school or one you visit. Consider ease of student use, ease of teaching, and ease of supervision. Make at least one recommendation for improvement.

3. Devise a plan for handling the transition from science to lunch period for a second grade class. Your goal is to develop a routine that will minimize the time the transition takes and behavioral problems during the transition.

4. Come up with at least two nonverbal cues for communicating each of the following to first graders: "Quiet down," "Good job," "Sit still," "Line up," "Stop that behavior," and "You can do it!"

5. Develop a plan for how you would keep records about student behavior issues. Include at least two sample entries in the format you develop.

Add to Your Portfolio

Develop a set of class rules you think would create an atmosphere that enhances learning. Your list should include four to six general rules. Include a rationale for your choices. Place your list in your portfolio.

16

THE NEXT STEPS TOWARD BECOMING A TEACHER

Key Terms

advanced placement courses

dual credit courses

in-service training

Objectives

After studying this chapter, you will be able to

- **complete** a personal portfolio.
- **develop** a personal career plan.
- **use** effective techniques for comparing potential colleges and universities.
- **identify** the benefits of participation in professional associations for students and teachers.

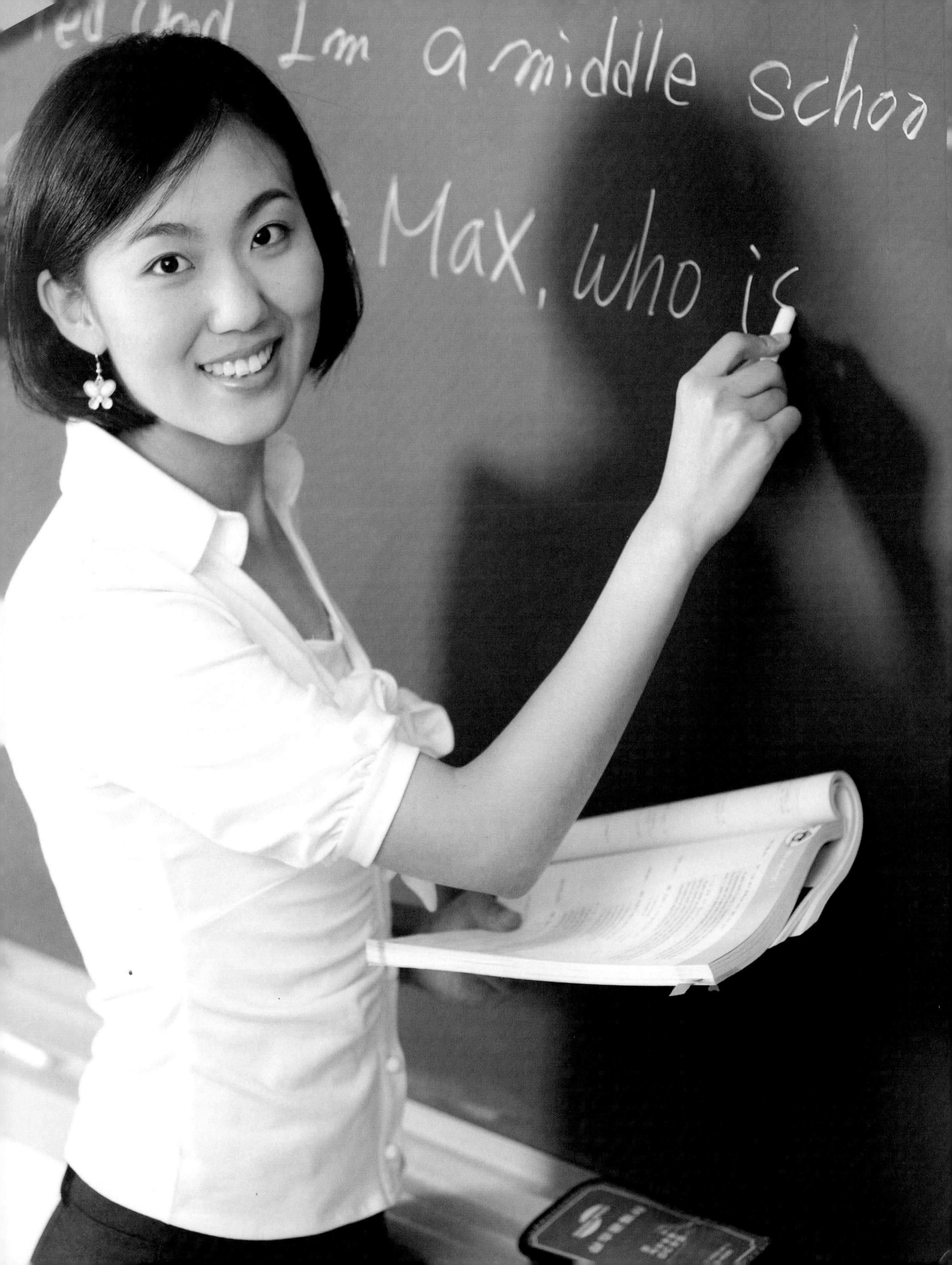
a middle
Max, who is

This course has given you insight into what being part of the teaching profession involves. Along the way, you have had opportunities to try out some of the roles, responsibilities, and activities of teachers. You have considered the challenges teachers face and the satisfaction that can come with helping students learn and grow. Most importantly, you have reflected on these experiences to help you decide whether a career in education is right for you.

There are many ways to continue this quest on your own. Take advantage of opportunities to observe what you see around you. Look for examples of effective teaching and learning. How do teachers form nurturing relationships with students? How do they meet the needs of individuals? Which classroom management strategies are most effective?

Look for opportunities to gain experience working with children and teens. Get to know different age groups. Observe how they interact, how they learn best, and what interests them, 16-1.

Talk to people who work in different capacities in the field of education. Although this course focuses primarily on the role of teachers, education relies on caring and qualified people in other roles as well. Find out more about what principals, early childhood educators, speech and

16-1

By observing teachers and students and interacting with children, you can learn about effective teaching and learning.

hearing pathologists, school librarians, guidance counselors, and others do. You will better understand the big picture and may find an alternative role for yourself, if you decide not to pursue teaching.

In this chapter, you will learn more about specific steps you can take to move forward. It will give you the confidence to make realistic plans and prepare yourself for success in college and your career. You have made a great start!

Polishing Your Portfolio

Throughout this course, you may have been developing a portfolio, either as a class requirement or to help document your progress. As explained in Chapter 2, a portfolio is a collection of materials that shows your learning, accomplishments, strengths, and best work. It also contains your reflections about these materials and their importance to you.

Beyond this class, your portfolio has a variety of practical uses. It helps you grow, as you think about what you have accomplished and learned. Reflecting on your experiences can give you a clearer perspective about teaching and your possible role as an educator. You may use material from your portfolio to gain admission to a teacher preparation program or to apply for a job. You may find other uses as well. For example, by keeping an accurate record of all work and volunteer activities, you will have the details available whenever you need them.

The next step is to prepare your portfolio in a final format for this course. Your teacher may give you more specific guidelines, but these general steps will help you.

- *Select.* Remember that a portfolio is meant to showcase your best efforts. This means being selective about what you include. Choosing items to showcase will become increasingly important as you gain more experience and accumulate more material for your portfolio.

  Choose pieces that show the breadth of your experiences related to teaching and the skills needed for that career. Include personal information about your education, volunteer and work experiences, and achievements. Select the papers, projects, and reflections that convey your best work. Your teacher can help you decide what you might include.

  What should you do with the materials you decide not to include in your final portfolio at this time? Unless you are sure that you will never want an item for another purpose, store it for possible later use. Just be sure to clearly identify each piece (what it is, how it was used, its significance, and the date). Keep your stored items organized. It can be a great help to prepare a master list of all your portfolio items, including a brief description of each piece and its location.

- *Prepare.* Once you have made your selections, you must prepare your portfolio for use. First, check to see if any items need updating. For example, you might revise your philosophy of teaching statement based on your experiences in this class. Be sure to keep the original version. You might include both to show how your thinking has evolved.

  Your portfolio must look professional. Begin by carefully proofreading all material, preferably several times. Pages must be neat and well organized. Clearly identify each item. If you are using a binder for your portfolio, bulky items might be placed in clear plastic sheet protectors or envelopes. You might include photos of larger items.

- *Organize.* If your teacher does not specify how to organize your portfolio, think about how to divide things into logical sections. For example, information on relevant volunteer and work activities could be placed together. You could group examples of teaching materials you have developed. Personal information would go up front.

  Once you have decided how to organize your items, prepare a table of contents. This will give those looking at your portfolio an overview of what is included and help them find materials of particular interest. Any time you revise your portfolio, update the table of contents, 16-2.

16-2
After you have prepared your portfolio, keep it updated and organized.

Developing a Personal Career Plan

A career plan helps you map your way to achieving the future you want. It identifies the concrete steps you need to take to reach your career goal. By taking the time to develop a plan, you can focus your efforts most effectively. You will know where you want to go and how to get there.

Step 1: Define Your Career Goal

Chapter 2 suggested writing your career goal as a concise statement. For example, Colin wrote, "To become a high school math teacher." If you wrote a career goal earlier in this course, take another look at it. In light of what you have learned about teaching and about yourself, you may decide to revise it. It is good to review the range of opportunities that fit your interests and strengths. Your goal should reflect your best assessment of what you think you want to do. You can change or refine it at any time.

Step 2: Identify Career Requirements

What education, skills, and characteristics does a person need to succeed in the career you have identified? If you are aiming for a career in teaching, the minimum educational requirements in most states is a bachelor's degree. (Some states require a master's degree, so check the state where you intend to teach.) Throughout this book and course, you have learned about skills and characteristics teachers need. For the purposes of your career plan, identify six to ten that seem to be most important. Consider management skills, interpersonal skills, and technical skills.

Step 3: Evaluate Your Accomplishments, Skills, and Interests

What are your accomplishments? What do you do well? What are your interests? Honestly assessing your strengths can help you consider how these can help you reach your career goal. For example, being selected for the National Honor Society shows you are known for your scholarship, service, leadership, character, and citizenship. That honor will be a plus in being accepted at a college or university, and those characteristics are important to success in many careers. Are you good at expressing yourself verbally or bringing a team together to achieve a goal? Those skills are valuable in school and the workplace, 16-3. Perhaps you are a top soccer player in your league. That might earn you a college scholarship. It would also be an advantage if your career goal includes coaching soccer, as well as teaching. When you identify your skills, interests, and accomplishments, you can turn them into assets.

16-3
As members of a debate team, these students are developing research, verbal, and leadership skills that will help them to reach career goals.

Step 4: Identify Possible Obstacles

Think carefully about what may impede you from reaching your career goal. Why is this important? When you are aware of potential problems, you can figure out ways around them. Obstacles may range from limited financial resources to lack of leadership experience, mediocre grades, or difficulty writing well. Regardless of what is on your list, there are things you can do now to help overcome obstacles. A guidance or career counselor can help you find out more about financial aid. You might join a club or organization at school that will help you use and improve your leadership skills. You can commit to studying harder and ask teachers for extra help. You might take an extra writing course or ask if you can become involved in the school newspaper. Try to come up with workable solutions and ask for help, when needed. Working to solve these problems now will make the road ahead much smoother.

Step 5: Determine Steps to Reach Your Career Goal

Although starting your career may seem years away, the path begins now. Identify six to ten steps or goals you need to achieve in the next three to five years in order to make your dreams happen. What concrete things do you need to do this year? Next year? As you start college? Do you want to graduate in the top 10 percent of your class? Do you need to improve your math skills in order to do well on college entrance tests? When do you need to apply for college admission? The next section of this chapter may give you some additional ideas about what to include. Put your steps in order, starting with those you need to act on first.

Preparing for College Success

A career in teaching requires additional education beyond a high school diploma. Now is the time to take action to make a successful college experience a reality. Much like training for competition, getting yourself ready can help make success in college a reality.

Choosing where you will go to school is a big decision to make, so you will want to allow plenty of time. There are deadlines for various aspects of the process. There are many other steps that you can take now that will increase your chances of success during college. It makes sense to use your remaining time in high school in ways that will make your transition to college easier.

Choosing a College or University

You may have already begun thinking about where you will continue your education after graduation. If not, begin to explore possible colleges and universities. The goal is to find schools that might best match your needs and wants. What are your expectations about academics and college life? Even if you are thinking about a particular college or university, take time to evaluate others. Here are some points to consider:

- *Size.* Would you prefer a large school environment or a smaller campus? Large schools offer more options. Smaller colleges and universities may have fewer students per class and more opportunities for involvement with faculty.

- *Reputation.* Look at a school's reputation in your area of study, not just its overall reputation. If you plan to teach, ask your guidance counselor and teachers which schools are noted for teacher education. Middle and high school teachers usually specialize in one or more subject areas. Check what schools offer in those areas, as well.

- *Location.* Do you want to attend school in another part of the country or closer to home? Would you prefer a school in an urban environment or a smaller city or town?

- *Admission requirements.* Some schools are highly selective and accept a small percentage of applicants. Others accept a broader range of students. Check information from schools that interest you to see if you are likely to meet admission criteria.

- *Cost.* A college education is a major expense. Tuition costs vary from school to school. (In general, state universities have lower tuition for in-state students than private colleges and universities.) Books and living expenses also must be considered. Students often rely on a combination of methods to meet those expenses. These include help from family, personal savings, scholarships, grants (which do not have to be repaid), loans, and part-time jobs. Some financial aid is available directly from colleges and universities. There are also scholarships and grants available that are not linked to a particular school. Your school guidance counselor can help you get started. There are also many Web sites and books to help guide your search, if you need financial aid.

Do not rule out schools immediately because of their tuition costs. Some may end up being more affordable than they appear. Scholarships from schools are usually not awarded until after you apply and are accepted. Apply to several schools that you are seriously considering and then compare your options. (Note that most schools have nonrefundable application fees, and these can add up quickly.)

Gathering information about colleges and universities can help you identify ones that seem to meet your needs and wants. Check schools' Web sites. In addition to the information posted for possible applicants, you can often delve deeper to find out more about degree requirements and campus life. Attend college fairs or similar events in your area. These give you an opportunity to talk to representatives of various colleges and universities. Contact the admissions offices of schools of interest and ask for informational packets. Talk to people about the schools they attended. Find out as much as you can, 16-4.

Some students start their college education at a community college and then transfer to a four-year college to complete their bachelor's degree. That can have advantages. Most community colleges work to coordinate coursework with four-year colleges and universities in their state to facilitate transferring. Tuition at community colleges is less expensive than at four-year schools. In addition, many students can live at home to save on housing costs. Class sizes tend to be smaller, and schedules more flexible. Students who have jobs can more easily schedule their classes around their work schedule. Studies show that students who complete their first two years at a community college and then transfer fare as well academically as students who spend all four years at a college or university. Community colleges are a way of getting your first 60 hours at a lower cost than at a major university. However, take care to make certain that your credits

16-4
You can gather information about various colleges and universities by asking your teachers about the schools they attended.

transfer to the university where you plan to receive your degree or you could lose the financial advantage of going to the community college.

Late in your junior year or by early fall of your senior year, you should narrow your choices. Continue your research on these schools. Try to visit your top choices. You can arrange for a guided tour through the school's admissions office. Plan to spend some time on your own, as well. Ask if you can sit in on a class and eat in a dining hall. Walk around the campus to get a feel for the school's learning and social environment. Talk to a professor. Talk to students. Watch people. Ask questions. Visiting a campus is one of the best ways to assess what a school is like.

College applications generally must be submitted in the fall of your senior year. When it comes time to make your final choice, discuss your options with those people whose judgment you value. If you have done your homework, there is an excellent chance that the college or university you choose will be a good match. Often, there is no one "right" choice. Every school has advantages and disadvantages.

Remember, too, that you can get an excellent education at almost any school. It depends mainly on choosing challenging courses, the effort you put into your classes, and taking advantage of the many opportunities a school offers. Commit to make the most of what is available.

Maximizing Your High School Experience

Even though you are looking ahead to college, it is vital to make the most of your remaining time in high school. Your choices and performance during your last semesters in high school can make a difference in whether or not you gain admission to the college or university of your choice.

Choosing Courses

Now is a good time to make an appointment with your guidance counselor to review your course of study. First, check what high school courses colleges and universities that interest you expect applicants to have completed. You will want to make sure you have enough credits in the right courses by the time you graduate. Common college expectations are listed in 16-5.

16-5

Many colleges expect applicants to have completed a course of study similar to this one. Your guidance counselor can advise you about what courses to take.

Common College Expectations	
Math	2–3 years
Laboratory science	2–3 years
English	4 years
Social studies	2–3 years
Foreign language	2–3 years
Visual/performing/practical arts	1 year

Also explore the possibility of taking advanced placement or dual credit courses, if these are available. **Advanced placement courses** are more difficult than regular high school courses. They include content comparable to beginning-level college classes. At the end of the course, students take a standardized advanced placement test. A passing score on this test may give a student credit at the college level for having completed that college requirement. With **dual credit courses**, a high school student actually enrolls in a college or university and takes one or more college classes while still attending high school. These may be taught in a high school or at a college or university. Successful completion gives college credits that may be transferred if the student attends another school after high school graduation. Both options require a high degree of dedication and maturity, but they give students a head start on college.

Joining Student Organizations

Participating in student organizations at the high school level can be an excellent way to broaden your experiences and polish your skills. Commit to being actively involved in any organization you join. This will give you opportunities to practice teamwork, leadership, planning, organization, service, and other key skills. Such skills are linked to success in college, on the job, and in other aspects of adult life. Their importance is underscored by the role they play in the college admittance process. Most colleges and universities evaluate applicants' involvement in activities and organizations, as well as their academic record and test scores. All of these help determine who will be accepted for enrollment.

Most school organizations provide opportunities to build key skills. Two are worth special consideration by students interested in teaching:

- *Future Educators Association (FEA).* Future Educators of America groups (formerly Future Teachers of America and Future Educators of America) are active in many high schools and colleges. They bring together students who are interested in pursuing teaching as a career. FEA seeks to attract students to the teaching profession, promote teaching as a career, and provide resources and programs related to the profession.

- *Family, Career and Community Leaders of America (FCCLA).* Family, Career, and Community Leaders of America (FCCLA) is an organization for high school and college students. Its aim is to promote personal growth and leadership development in students preparing to enter the adult world of work and family. In FCCLA, student groups complete projects that require them to apply knowledge, interact with others, adapt to new technology, and logically think through problems. The focus is on the many areas related to family and consumer sciences and education in general, including child development and teacher preparation. These have practical applications regardless of a person's specific career goals. For example, all adults must manage multiple roles, including family member, wage earner, and community member. FCCLA seeks to improve the quality of life for students and their families and to prepare students for the adult world.

Staying Focused

It is easy, as your time in high school winds down, to lose your focus. There is the distraction of choosing where to continue your education. It is natural to be excited about upcoming graduation and college life ahead. Spending time with friends may seem more important than classes and homework.

Sometimes called "senior slump," it begins even earlier for some students. The pattern is all too familiar and worrisome to veteran teachers. Along with lost learning, students' grades can drop significantly. This may leave some students unable to graduate and jeopardize others' class rank and even admission to college.

There is an added concern. It indicates that some students are unable to handle the shift to more independence. That is a point where self-discipline and good personal decision making need to replace that imposed by parents and others. Once out of high school and into college or the working world, those who cannot stay focused on their goals are unlikely to reach them. College professors do not issue constant reminders about homework and studying. Students having difficulty in a subject must seek out help. Failure to keep up means failure of a course. Employers do not tolerate unreliable workers. They simply replace them.

When you keep your focus, regardless of what others are doing, you show the maturity you will need for college, 16-6. There, you will face more choices, distractions, and independence. Remember that reaching your goals is worth the effort.

Managing Your Time

It may seem that the days are rarely long enough to accomplish all that you need and want to do. Actually, demands on your time will steadily increase in the years ahead. In college, you will be juggling challenging courses, significant amounts of homework, extracurricular and social activities, and other responsibilities. Many students also have jobs to help offset college expenses. Life as a teaching professional will be even busier.

16-6
Staying focused both in high school and college will help you to meet your career goals.

The best strategy for coping is to develop good time-management skills now. Doing so will pay real benefits—immediately and in the years to come. There are plenty of books and articles on time management, but these basic steps will put you on the path:

- *Write down what you need and want to accomplish.* This both keeps you from forgetting important tasks and serves as a reminder to tackle them. Find a system that works for you—low-tech or high-tech. You can use anything from a simple index card to an electronic version. When your list gets long, divide it into categories.

- *Prioritize your list.* Decide which items on your list are essential, which are important, and which you will do if you have time. (Some people use *A*, *B*, *C* or *1*, *2*, *3* to designate priorities.) Homework, team practice, and a part-time job schedule might be *A* priorities, for example.

- *Use a planner or calendar to schedule your time.* This will help keep you on track and accomplish more. That does not mean that every minute must be scheduled. However, without a schedule, important things slip through the cracks, and time can just melt away. When you have a big project, start early. Schedule segments of time to work on it over days or weeks. You really will do a better job and feel less stress than if you try to do it all at the last minute.

- *Get organized.* Not being able to find what you need is one of the biggest time wasters. At best, you spend time looking for things. At worst, you have to do work over because you cannot find what you already did. Start with simple techniques like putting things in specific places. Organize documents and information in files, paper or electronic form. Identify your own organizational trouble spots and devise solutions to improve them.

- *Establish routines.* When you do tasks automatically, things get done, and you do not have to worry about them. You might do your homework right after school or dinner. If you always pack up everything for school before you go to bed, you will be ready to go in the morning, even if you oversleep. You will never forget your homework again! How can you make routines work for you?

When you first try out steps such as these, they may seem awkward. Give them a fair trial. It takes at least several weeks for new habits to become comfortable and automatic. If you make the effort to find ways to use your time efficiently, you will be ahead of many of your classmates. These are habits that will serve you well over a lifetime.

Keeping Your Life in Balance

Like that challenging point of balance on a playground seesaw, it is often difficult to arrive at a balance in life. Just what is meant by a "balanced" life? It is one in which there are no extremes. All components of life have a place. A person's focus remains on his or her goals.

Why is this so important? It is all too easy to get off track in one direction or another. You may know people so obsessed by grades that they have no time for friends and activities. You may also know people whose primary concern is something like sports or partying. By neglecting their schoolwork, they jeopardize their futures.

Think about your own life by looking at the big picture. How much time do you typically spend on school, work, family, friends, and other priorities? Does this seem like a reasonable balance? If not, what changes can you make to be a well-rounded person?

Stress throws life out of balance and can be increased by being off balance. Everyone feels the effects from time to time—overwhelmed; anxious;

frazzled; trying to make deadlines, unexpected events, and relationship issues. A bit of stress is not all bad. It can prompt you to get things accomplished, even to think more creatively. However, with too much stress, the body reacts as if it is facing a physical threat. Constantly being in this state has many negative long-term effects. By learning strategies to cope in high school and college, these can be applied to the day-to-day challenges and stresses of finding balance in the life of a teacher.

As with demands on your time, you can expect stress to increase as you start college. It makes sense to improve your skills for coping with stress and maintaining your balance.

Eating Well and Staying Fit

One of the best ways to strengthen your ability to withstand stress is to stay in great physical shape, 16-7. When you feel well, you have more energy and are better able to cope with challenges.

Adequate nutrition and regular physical activity are the building blocks of good health. If your eating habits need improvement, start to make changes now. Beginning each day with a good breakfast can give you the fuel you need to revive your body. Making smart food choices for the rest of the day can help you feel your best. Also make sure you build physical activity into your daily routine. If you need to boost your activity level, consider joining a sports team. Even if you are not a star player, the conditioning will help you get in shape. Working out or a simple walking program are other options.

16-7
Adding physical activity to your daily routine is a great way to deal with stress.

Remember that you can start with small changes and build on them. The results in how you will feel are well worth the effort.

When you get to college, make a point to eat well and exercise right from the start. It is easy to let good habits fall by the wayside when you are in a new environment. Today, colleges and universities are making it easier for students to incorporate healthy habits into their life. Many offer on-site fitness centers and other programs to promote wellness. As you visit schools, check out this aspect of campus offerings.

Coping with Stress

Learn to recognize how you react to a buildup of stress. Some people develop headaches or neck pain. Others find themselves becoming short-tempered or eating more. When you are attuned to your own signals, you can take appropriate action.

The first step is to figure out the true source of your stress. Often the source of stress is misidentified. For example, you find yourself running to a college class. You have overslept. Worse yet, you planned to polish the presentation you are to give in class when you got up this morning. Now you are stressed because you overslept. It is probably not the oversleeping itself that is causing the stress but perhaps your concern over not having time to practice your presentation. If you back that up a step, the real issue is that you hate presentations because of your concern about how you will be perceived by others.

Often, stress levels rise when you feel pressure from a number of situations. Perhaps, in addition to the presentation, you are worried about your mom's health and you are not sure you will make the final team cuts.

Second, make what changes you can to reduce pressure. Stress develops when the demands in your life exceed your ability to cope with them easily. Often, perceived demands are self-established and may be unattainable. In this case, oversleeping may be a sign that you are not getting enough sleep on a regular basis. You can do something about that. You might also adjust your attitude about the team cuts. You have done your best, and you have no control at this point over whether you are cut.

Third, remember that you have some control over how you react. If you stay calm, your presentation will go better. If you do not make the team, you will be able to join another extracurricular activity, such as the on-campus Big Brothers Big Sisters group.

Fourth, consider long-term strategies for reducing stress. If you often leave assignments until the last minute, working ahead can help relieve many stressful situations. That way, when something unexpected happens, you are more likely to be able to cope. Find your own ways to manage stress. Some people find that regular physical activity helps. Others find a friend to talk to when things seem overwhelming. Try out several techniques and use the ones that work for you.

Succeeding as a Professional Educator

Look into your future. Imagine that you have graduated from college and are now a certified professional educator. What makes a teacher a professional? The term implies someone who is educated and takes on significant responsibility. Professionals are expected to show personal integrity, the ability to make complex decisions, decisiveness, commitment, and community awareness. Effective teachers exhibit all of these things.

These characteristics do not automatically come with a college degree or a teaching job. You develop them over time. As you move forward on your career path, pay particular attention to the ways educators act as professionals, 16-8. How do they handle difficult situations? How do they show commitment to becoming better teachers? How do they become involved in their profession and their community?

Professional Ethical Standards

Teaching involves more than helping students learn information. Teachers help to shape their students' lives. They model the roles of learner, professional, and citizen. Because of this influence, teachers are held to high ethical standards. Their behavior in the classroom and the community must live up to that responsibility.

16-8
Observe the professionalism of educators you encounter and work to develop those characteristics.

Many aspects of ethics are based on common sense. Teachers must obey laws. They must be honest. For example, it would be unethical to change a grade so that a student can qualify for sports. It would be dishonest to provide inaccurate information about one's educational background on a job application.

Other aspects of ethics deal with professionalism. A teacher should dress and act in a professional manner. A teacher may have a friendly rapport with students, but still must maintain a professional teacher-to-student relationship at all times. As a professional, a teacher keeps personal information about students confidential.

Unfortunately, not all situations present clear-cut ethical issues, thus, a teacher must use good judgment that keeps the best interests of students in mind. The teacher might consider, "How would I want a teacher to act if this were my child?" It is also a good idea to involve the principal or other school personnel to help clarify the best course of action.

A teacher's effectiveness—and even ability to find a teaching job—is linked to the teacher's personal reputation. Communities trust teachers with what is most precious—their children. A teacher who violates that trust through inappropriate behavior breaks that bond with the community.

Ongoing Professional Development

Today's world is characterized by constant change. To keep pace, employees must commit to being lifelong learners. This is especially true for teachers.

Professional development is learning linked to improving a person's professional expertise. For teachers, this can take various forms. The goal is to make them better educators.

Most teachers take additional college courses after obtaining their bachelor's degree. Many school districts give salary increases based on successful completion of graduate-level courses (those beyond the bachelor's level that can lead to a master's or doctoral degree). Sometimes districts also partially reimburse teachers for the cost of such courses.

As with a bachelor's degree, a master's degree requires a specific course of study. Some teachers just take courses they feel will help update them in their subject area or improve their teaching skills. Since many courses are now available online, it is easier for teachers to access graduate-level courses. There are also courses specific to other areas in education, such as those to become a counselor, a librarian, or an administrator.

Many school districts and other groups offer other opportunities for professional development. For example, a school district might arrange for an expert on curriculum development to speak to all the teachers in the district or conduct a training session. Education, such as this, that is organized by the school for its staff is called **in-service training**. Professional groups may offer workshops on topics of interest, such as using the newest technology to enhance learning. Conferences related to teaching may also be part of professional development.

State teaching licenses are usually valid for a limited number of years, and then they must be renewed. Most states require that teachers meet specific professional development requirements in order for their license to be renewed. This is meant to make sure that teachers continuously update their knowledge and skills.

As lifelong learners, teachers use every opportunity to increase their knowledge and skills. Such learning can come from many sources besides formal classes. Teachers also learn through work experiences, self-study, travel, and hobbies. Continual learning helps teachers keep their teaching fresh, interesting, and relevant.

Professional Associations

One of the best ways to stay updated on education issues and practices is to join one or more professional organizations. There are many available for teachers. Some are available to teacher education students, as well. If you have an opportunity to attend a professional meeting as a student, be sure to do so.

Professional associations vary in their purpose. Some focus broadly on education. Others concentrate on some aspect of it, such as teaching social studies. Figure 16-9 lists just some of the professional organizations for teachers. You can check the Web sites of associations to find out more

Examples of Associations of Professional Educators
The American Council on the Teaching of Foreign Language
American Association of Family and Consumer Sciences
American Federation of Teachers
Association of American Educators
Association of Childhood Education International
Association for Career and Technical Education
The Council for Exceptional Children
The International Reading Association
Music Teachers National Association
National Art Education Association
National Association for the Education of Young Children
National Council of Teachers of English
National Council of Teachers of Mathematics
National Council for the Social Sciences
National Science Teacher Association

16-9
Membership in a professional association can keep teachers up-to-date and create networking contacts.

about them. Look for information about the goals of the group. The site should give you a good overview of the activities, resources, and opportunities for members, as well as the costs of membership. Check whether the organization has affiliated state or local groups.

Membership in a professional association can offer real opportunities for teachers. Through newsletters, journals, online postings, and conferences, you can keep up with current events and future trends. Most associations hold conferences and meetings that offer sessions to keep professionals up-to-date in various aspects of their field. These conferences and meetings also provide opportunities for both formal and informal interactions, creating valuable networking contacts. Teachers can serve on committees or take on other leadership positions within organizations.

Community Involvement

Effective teachers are good citizens. Many become actively involved in making their communities better, in addition to what they contribute through teaching, 16-10. They put their knowledge and skills to work helping others and their communities. In the process, they often have opportunities to work with parents and other community members, strengthening those bonds.

As a college student, participate in community service opportunities. On-campus groups often work to be a positive force within the community. Such activities will help you gain experiences that can be helpful in your future. You will also have the satisfaction in knowing that you have made a positive difference in the lives of others.

16-10
This teacher is actively involved in her community's recycling efforts.

Summary

As you complete this course, it is time to organize the materials you have gathered and developed into a portfolio that you can share with others. Your personal portfolio serves as a visual résumé. It is designed to show others your accomplishments, strengths, and work related to a possible career in teaching.

Preparing a career plan is an excellent way to help you reach your career goal. It involves identifying where you are going and what you must achieve. Analyzing your own characteristics can help you identify specific steps to take toward your goal in the next few years.

It is smart to use your remaining time in high school to position yourself for success in college. Choosing a college or university to continue your education is one of the biggest decisions you face. Research and analysis can help you make an appropriate choice. Make sure your course schedule includes the classes you need, and commit to doing well in them. Also work to improve your time management skills and learn to keep your life in balance.

Success as a teacher requires demonstrating the qualities of a professional, as well as teaching skill. You can begin now to develop those qualities through observation and practice.

Review

1. Identify and briefly explain the three steps involved in finalizing a portfolio.

2. Choose four skills and characteristics needed for success in a teaching career. Explain the reasoning behind your choices.

3. Give an example of an obstacle a student might identify in developing a personal career plan. Identify a practical way the student might overcome that obstacle.

4. What are at least four good sources of information you can use when researching possible colleges and universities?

5. Explain the similarities and differences between advanced placement and dual credit courses.

6. Give a rationale for why colleges and universities consider high school students' involvement in organizations and activities as part of the admissions process.

7. Give an example of how stress might cause a college student's life to become unbalanced. How might that lack of balance cause more stress?

8. Identify another profession in which personal reputation and ethics are essential for success. Explain your selection.

9. Do you think that states should specify a professional development requirement for renewal of a teaching license? Explain your answer.

10. Identify at least three benefits of professional organizations for teachers.

Reflect

1. How has your philosophy of teaching changed since you began this course? What has influenced that change?

2. When students take dual credit courses while still in high school, they begin to build a college academic record. What are the potential benefits and drawbacks of this?

3. Analyze your personal time management skills. What are two areas that could use improvement? What are some specific techniques you might try?

4. A teacher's reputation is important for success as a professional. What types of actions of students in high school and college potentially affect their reputation into the future, positively or negatively?

Act

1. Follow the steps outlined in this chapter to develop a personal career plan.

2. Interview a college student about the college selection process. How many schools did the student seriously consider? How many campuses did the person visit before making a final choice? What was the student's first impression of the school he or she now attends? How did it compare to the reality of attending school there? Ask for advice about your own search.

3. Check online or use a college catalog to find the admission requirements for a college or university you are interested in considering. What are the requirements for being accepted into the teacher education program at the school?

4. Research two professional organizations for teachers or future teachers. Find out their goals, number of members, member benefits, cost of membership, publications, and professional development opportunities. Compare your findings with those of your classmates.

Add to Your Portfolio

Use the guidelines in this chapter and those from your teacher to prepare your portfolio for evaluation. Keep in mind that it should show a clear purpose, reflect your uniqueness, show your progress, and reflect professionalism.

GLOSSARY

A

abstract thinking. Thinking about ideas and concepts and connecting feelings with thoughts (for example justice or love). (1)

acceptable use policy. A set of school rules or "computer code of conduct" students must follow in order to use school computers or other technology. (13)

accommodations. In teaching, modifications to the environment, learning strategies, or materials that are made to help students with particular special needs succeed in the classroom. (9)

accountability. Providing proof that standards, such as educational goals, are being achieved. (7)

accredited. In education, describes a school that has passed quality assessment, and credits earned generally qualify for graduation at traditional schools. (13)

achievement gap. The differences in learning and graduation rates among schools, often linked to differences in school populations and funding. (8)

active listening. Asking questions and restating ideas to discover the true message of the sender by giving verbal feedback. (10)

advanced placement courses. Courses that are more difficult than regular high school courses. They include content comparable to beginning-level college classes. At the end of the course, students take a standardized advanced placement test. A passing score on this test may give a student credit at the college level for having completed that college requirement. (16)

aggressive communicator. One whose verbal or nonverbal communication aims to hurt or put other people down in a disrespectful way. (10)

alternative assessment. A method of assessing learning other than through testing. (14)

apprentice. Someone who learns a skilled trade by watching and helping someone in that trade. In early America, some apprentices worked without pay for an agreed-upon period in exchange for their learning. (6)

articulate. To express thoughts into words. (2)

artifacts. Physical items that are part of a portfolio, such as projects or papers, examples from a related volunteer activity, and academic and other awards. (2)

assertive communicator. One who expresses thoughts, ideas, and feelings in respectful ways. (10)

assessment. Determining how much a student or class has learned or is in the process of learning. (10)

asynchrony. When body parts grow at the different rates. (5)

at risk. Describes students or groups with characteristics that make them more likely to fail academically. (8)

auditory learners. People who learn best by hearing or listening to information. (9)

autonomy. Independence that includes personal responsibility and decision making. (5)

authoritarian style. A management style that seeks to control students' behavior through many rules, procedures, and consequences. (15)

authoritative style. A management style that seeks to shape students' behavior through setting high expectations, explanations, and consistent application of consequences. (15)

B

baby boom. The great increase in births after the end of World War II. (7)

back-to-basics movement. Move toward focusing teaching on the basics of reading, writing, and math. (7)

behaviorism. A theory based on the belief that individuals' behavior is determined by forces in the environment that are beyond their control. (3)

bilingual education. Education in two languages. (7)

Bloom's Taxonomy. An analysis developed by Benjamin Bloom, that is used as a basis for understanding and teaching various levels of thought by dividing thinking skills into six levels. (12)

C

career clusters. Sixteen general career areas, each having a wide range of related opportunities. (7)

career and technical education. Courses of study that prepare students for careers related to a specific trade or occupation. (6)

career goal. A concise statement of the specific career toward which a person is working. (2)

case studies. A teaching strategy in which students analyze a particular problem or story that requires a solution. (12)

certified teacher. A person who has met the state requirements for teacher preparation. (2)

chain of command. The official organizational structure that tells who reports to whom. (10)

charter school. A public school that operates under a charter with freedom from many of the regulations that apply to traditional public schools. (7)

checklist. A simple list of items to be noted, checked, or remembered when evaluating learning. (14)

classical conditioning. The theory that behaviors can be associated with responses. (3)

classification. The ability to sort items by one or more characteristics they have in common. (4)

classroom management. The steps teachers take to optimize learning by shaping their classroom environment, engaging students in learning, and minimizing inappropriate behavior. (15)

classroom procedures. Specific guidelines that translate the class rules into concrete actions expected of students. (15)

class rules. The guidelines for student behavior specific to a class or teacher. (15)

closure. A summarizing process that helps students draw conclusions based on what they have learned. (12)

cognition. All of the actions or processes involving thought and knowledge. (3)

cognitive development. The way people change and improve in their ability to think and learn throughout life. (3)

collaborative learning. Learning that takes place when students work in groups to discuss and solve problems together. (1)

common schools. Public schools available to children from all levels of society. (6)

competency-based education. Teaching methods that require students to demonstrate their abilities in subject areas. (7)

concrete thinking. Thinking about things that are actually experienced. (1)

conservation. The ability to understand that a simple change in the shape of an object does not change its amount. (4)

cooperating teacher. An experienced teacher who supervises and mentors a student teacher. (2)

cooperative learning. A form of small-group learning that involves students working together to achieve a common goal. (12)

corporate-education partnership. An arrangement in which a business or industry provides support for a school. This support may involve financial resources, sharing expertise, or a variety of other forms of help. (8)

corporate trainers. People who design, conduct, and supervise programs to improve the skills of a company's employees. (1)

course evaluation. Making judgments about how well a course meets its goals and identifying suggestions for improvement. (14)

course plan. A detailed outline of what a particular teacher will teach throughout a course or year based on curriculum but adapted to the characteristics of the teacher, students, and teaching circumstances. It typically includes a series of instructional units. (11)

curriculum. The courses taught in a school, what is taught in each course, and how the courses are sequenced. (1)

cyberbullying. Intimidation or bullying through e-mail, social networking sites, text messaging, or other electronic means. (8)

D

dame schools. In early America, schools run by women in their own homes. Parents paid a fee for their children to attend. (6)

development. The gradual increase in skills and abilities that occurs over a lifetime. (3)

developmental delay. A noticeable lag in a specific aspect of development that is beyond average variations. (4)

developmental theories. Comprehensive explanations, based on research, about why people act and behave the way they do and how they change over time. (3)

dexterity. The skillful use of the hands and fingers. (4)

differentiated instruction. Teaching that incorporates learning options to better meet the specific learning-related characteristics of individual students. (9)

disposable income. Income beyond that needed for basic necessities, allowing people to buy or do things that they want. (6)

distance education. A learning situation in which the teacher and student are not in the same location. (13)

dual credit courses. Courses in which a high school student actually enrolls at a college or university while still attending high school. These may be taught in a high school or at a college or university. Successful completion gives college credits that may be transferred if the student attends another school after high school graduation. (16)

E

educational standards. Statements of what students are expected to know and be able to do at certain points in their education. They are set by national organizations, states, and many school districts. Sometimes called *instructional goals.* (7) (11)

egocentrism. Focused primarily on one's own concerns. (5)

English language learners (ELL). Students whose native language is not English and who are not yet proficient in the English language. (9)

ethics. Conduct based on moral principles. (10)

ethnicity. A particular racial, national, or cultural group, including that group's customs, beliefs, values, and often language and religion. (9)

exceptional learners. Students who are gifted, talented, or have special needs, such as a disability, and need, or can benefit from, programs matched to their abilities and potential. (9)

executive strategies. Skills used to solve problems, including assessing problems, setting goals, developing a plan to meet goals, and implementing and evaluating solutions. (4)

experimental lab. A lab experience that uses formal processes to research problems. (12)

expulsion. When a student loses the right to attend school for a specified period of time. (8)

extracurricular activities. Activities that take place before or after school. (1)

F

facilitator. One who creates situations that help students learn by developing activities that actively involve students in learning, rather than just presenting information. (10)

fine-motor skills. Physical skills involving smaller muscles in the body, such as the hands and wrists. Examples include picking up objects, writing, and keyboarding. (3)

formative assessment. Assessment that is meant to provide feedback about students' learning and understanding while the learning is occurring, rather than after it is completed. It is designed to guide teaching decisions and is normally not graded. (14)

G

global economy. The interconnection of economies of nations around the world through finance, international companies, and trade. (7)

grants. Money that is given for a specific purpose, such as educational expenses, that does not have to be repaid. (2)

gross-motor skills. Physical skills involving larger muscles of the body, such as the legs, hips, back, and arms. Examples include jumping, hitting a baseball, balancing on a balance beam, and carrying a heavy object. (3)

growth. Refers to physical changes in size, such as gains in height and weight. (3)

growth spurts. Rapid increases in height and weight, such as those associated with puberty. (5)

guided practice. An activity designed to reinforce and apply learning that includes feedback from other students or the teacher. (11)

H

hand-eye coordination. The ability to move the hands precisely to coordinate with what the eyes see. (4)

hornbook. A flat wooden board with a handle. A sheet of paper—usually containing the alphabet, a prayer or two, and Roman numerals—was pasted on the board. A thin, flat piece of clear animal horn was attached to cover and protect the paper. Used during the Colonial Period. (6)

I

illiterate. Unable to read or write. (7)

inclusion. Placing students with special needs into a regular class, using modified class assignments, if they will benefit from the class experience. (9)

independent practice. An activity designed to apply and reinforce recent learning that students complete on their own. (11)

individual accountability. Holding each person in a group responsible for participating and contributing. (12)

Individualized Education Program (IEP). A written educational plan developed for a specific student with disabilities. (9)

in-service training. An opportunity for professional development, it is often a training session organized by the school for its staff. (16)

instructional methods. Basic teaching formats, such as lectures and discussions, used to develop specific learning activities. Also called *instructional strategies* and *teaching strategies*. (12)

instructional objectives. Clear statements of what students will achieve as a result of a lesson that will be shown in an observable way. (11)

instructional strategies. Basic teaching formats, such as lectures and discussions, used to develop specific learning activities. Also called *instructional methods* and *teaching strategies*. (12)

instructional technology. The application of technology for the enhancement of teaching, learning and assessment. (13)

instructional units. Related topics that are grouped and taught together over a period of time. A course plan is typically divided into instructional units. (11)

interactive whiteboard. A multifunction presentation device that can function as a dry-erase board but also, when connected to a computer and projector, functions as a large computer screen with many capabilities for teaching and learning. (13)

invincibility. Feeling incapable of being defeated or having anything bad happen to you. (5)

J

job shadowing. Following a person on the job for a few hours, a day, or even longer to experience what the person's career typically involves to gain valuable insight into the person's daily tasks, activities, and interactions with others. (2)

K

kinesthetic-tactile learners. People who learn best by performing hands-on or physical activities. (9)

L

learner-centered methods. Teaching strategies in which the teacher acts as a facilitator, or guide, but students are actively involved in directing and achieving their own learning. (12)

learning activities. The learning experiences used to help students learn the content and reach the instructional objectives. (11)

learning diversity. Differences in learning based on abilities, interests, or experiences. (9)

learning styles. Preferred methods of absorbing and processing information. (9)

lesson plans. Detailed outlines for teaching a specific topic or skill, including what will be taught, how it will be taught, why it is being taught, and how learning will be evaluated. Sometimes called *instructional plans* or *teaching plans.* (11)

lifelong learners. People committed to staying up to date in their knowledge and skills. (10)

limited English proficiency (LEP). Describes students who are not proficient in English. (9)

M

magnet schools. Schools designed to emphasize a particular subject area or area of talent and attract qualified students from throughout the school district. (9)

mainstreaming. Placing students with special needs who show the ability to keep up with the curriculum in a regular class. (9)

McGuffey readers. The first widely used textbooks published during the American Common School Period. They included moral lessons along with science, grammar, and other subjects. (6)

mediation. The process of bringing about agreement or reconciliation between opponents in a dispute. (10)

mediator. A neutral person who oversees conflict resolution in order to help others reach a peaceful settlement. (10)

mentor. An adult who commits to a long-term relationship with a student to provide support, guidance, and help. (8)

mentor teachers. Experienced, skilled teachers paired with new teachers to help them improve their skills, solve problems, and become comfortable in their new role. (14)

metacognition. The ability to think about thinking. (5)

mission statement. The official version of an organization's purpose and goals, along with policies and procedures. (10)

mixed message. When there is a discrepancy between verbal and nonverbal messages. (10)

model. In learning, an example of similar excellent work that students can use as they complete an assignment. (13)

moderator. In a panel discussion, the person responsible for the introduction, summary, and relaying questions to the panel. (12)

Montessori method. The teaching principles developed by Maria Montessori, an Italian doctor, emphasizing self-directed learning through sensory experiences. (6)

multiple intelligences. Howard Gardner's theory that individuals have a broad range of types of intelligence, each to a different degree. (9)

multitasking. Trying to do many things at the same time. (5)

N

national standards. Standards of knowledge and skills to be mastered in specific subject areas. (7)

neural connections. The links between brain cells that develop when actions are repeated. (5)

nonsectarian. Not based on, or affiliated with, any religion. (1)

normal schools. Schools that prepared men and women with the necessary skills to become teachers. (6)

nonverbal cues. Communication without words using techniques such as eye contact, body language, gestures, and physical closeness. (15)

O

online learning. Sometimes called virtual education, a common form of distance education in which teaching and learning take place via the Internet. (13)

open-ended questions. Questions designed to require more than a few words as an answer. (12)

operant conditioning. The theory that states that people tend to repeat behaviors that have a positive result or are reinforced. (3)

organizational culture. The "personality" of an organization based on the assumptions, values, standards, behaviors, and actions of people, as well as the tangible signs of an organization. (10)

P

pacing. The rate at which a teacher presents components of a lesson or the lessons throughout the day. (12)

panel discussion. A discussion format in which a group of people present and discuss a topic and answer questions. (12)

paraprofessional. A person who has less education or experience but works under the supervision of a more highly educated professional. (1)

passive communicator. One who is unwilling to say what he or she feels, thinks, or desires in order to avoid conflict. (10)

peer evaluation. Students' assessment of each other's learning. (14)

permissive style. A management style that sets few expectations and rules for students and enforces them inconsistently. (15)

personal portfolio. An organized collection of materials and information that shows how personal knowledge, skills, and attitudes have developed over time. (2)

philosophy of teaching. A personal statement about your thoughts, views, and values as they relate to teaching. (2)

physical development. Advances in physical abilities. (3)

plagiarism. The use of someone else's original words or ideas without giving that person credit. (13)

postsecondary education. Education that takes place after high school. (1)

prerequisite course. A course that must be completed before entering a program or prior to taking a higher-level course. (2)

productive lab. A lab experience that focuses on producing an end product. (12)

professional development. Taking part in professional organizations, attending seminars and conferences, pursuing an advanced degree, or other activities meant to improve one's professional knowledge and skills. (10)

proficiency test. A test that measures skill and knowledge in a subject area. (2)

Project Head Start. A federal government program designed to help preschool children from low-income families develop the skills they need for success in kindergarten and beyond. (7)

Progressives. Members of a reform movement that began in the late 1800s. They believed that education should be more individualized and teach students the skills that would improve the ills of society. (6)

puberty. The physical transformation from a child to an adult capable of reproduction. (5)

pull-out programs. Programs that allow students to leave the regular classroom for certain periods of the day for additional instruction to meet their particular needs. (9)

Q

quotas. Limits. Immigration laws set limits for people coming to the United States from other countries. (6)

R

reciprocal agreements. In teaching, agreements between states that allow teachers certified to teach in one state to teach in another state that is part of the agreement. (2)

reflective responses. A teaching strategy that asks students to think deeply about a situation and describe that thinking process. (12)

reliability. A characteristic of assessments that measures learning consistently and fairly, even with different groups or under different circumstances. (14)

resilience. Being able to bounce back after a defeat or setback. (5)

role playing. A type of unscripted skit in which people take on particular roles and interact to resolve an issue or problem. (12)

rubric. A scoring tool that lists the criteria for judging a particular type of work. It also describes levels of quality for each of the criteria and is often organized as a chart, with the *criteria* (characteristics that count for scoring) on the left, followed by columns that describe different levels of quality for each characteristic. (14)

S

school-based curriculum. A curriculum developed by the teachers and staff of a school or school district for use in their own classrooms. (1)

school funding gap. The problem that occurs when schools in districts with lower levels of income from property taxes have a higher proportion of students who are low-income and need a higher level of services. (8)

school policies. Overall guidelines that generally address major issues such as attendance and dress code. (In some districts these are called *rules, regulations,* or *procedures.*) (15)

scorecard. A tool for evaluating alternative assessments that lists the characteristics or factors to use when evaluating learning. They typically identify a maximum point value for each criterion but do not describe levels of quality. (14)

self-concept. A person's own assessment of himself or herself based on an evaluation of personal abilities, successes, failures, and comments from other people. (4)

self-contained classroom. Refers to an arrangement in which the same teacher and group of students remain in one classroom for most of the day, with one teacher teaching most or all subjects. (1)

self-evaluations. Students' assessment of their own learning. (14)

self-paced learning. A form of learning that allows students to move to the next learning task as soon as they master the previous one. Students progress at individual rates, rather than as a class. (9)

seriation. The ability to place objects in order by a characteristic, such as smallest to largest. (4)

service-learning. A type of volunteer effort that links classroom learning with hands-on experience in order to meet community needs. (2)

sequence. A consistent step-by-step pattern that consistently follows one after another, as in development. (3)

simulations. Learning activities that put students in a situation that feels real even though the situation is not. Students function within that environment. (12)

skits. Scripted stories that involve students in learning through acting out parts. (12)

social-emotional development. Development that includes the areas of relationships and feelings. (3)

special education. Educational settings that provide adapted programs, extra staff, and specialized equipment or learning environments or materials to help students with special needs to learn. (9)

special needs. A broad range of physical, mental, social, and behavioral challenges that impact learning. (9)

spending per pupil. The average amount of money a school spends to educate a student for one year. (8)

standardized tests. Tests that measure students' performance compared to that of thousands of other students. (7)

stereotype. Preconceived generalizations about certain groups of people. (9)

student portfolio. A collection of a student's work selected to show growth over time, highlight skills and achievements, or to show how well the student meets standards. (14)

student teaching. A period during which a teacher education student practices and acquires teaching skill under the supervision of an experienced teacher. (2)

summative assessment. Assessment designed to evaluate students' learning after instruction has taken place. It measures results, whether learning objectives have been met. (14)

T

teacher-centered methods. Teaching strategies in which the teacher's role is to present the information and to direct the learning process of students. (12)

teacher education programs. University or college programs that prepare students to become teachers. (2)

teaching academies. Specialized programs within high schools that help students to explore the teaching profession through classes, observations, and hands-on experiences. (2)

teaching license. A formal document, issued by a state, verifying that a teacher is qualified to teach at specific grade levels or particular subject areas. (2)

teaching strategies. Basic teaching formats, such as lectures and discussions, used to develop specific learning activities. Also called *instructional methods* and *instructional strategies*. (12)

technical schools. Postsecondary schools that are designed to teach the specific skills needed to begin working in a trade. (1)

transition. Smooth ways to move from one part of a lesson to the next. (11)

transitivity. The ability to understand that relationships between two objects can extend to a third object. (4)

V

validity. A characteristic of assessments that actually measures the learning objectives. (14)

visual learners. People who learn best if information is presented in a way that they can see. (9)

visual-motor coordination. The ability to match body movements to coordinate with what is seen. (4)

W

wait time. A pause between asking a question and accepting an answer, designed to allow students to mentally process the question and to formulate their replies. (12)

WebQuest. An inquiry-based learning project utilizing information from preselected Web sites. (13)

Z

zero tolerance policy. A policy that states that prohibited behaviors and actions will not be tolerated—no exceptions. (8)

INDEX